ACTING NATURALLY

ACTING NATURALLY

MARK TWAIN IN THE CULTURE OF PERFORMANCE

RANDALL KNOPER

University of California Press
Berkeley · Los Angeles · London

University of California Press
Berkeley and Los Angeles, California

University of California Press, Ltd.
London, England

Library of Congress Cataloging-in-Publication Data

Knoper, Randall K., 1953–
    Acting naturally: Mark Twain in the culture of perfor-
mance / Randall Knoper.
        p.   cm.
    Includes bibliographical references and index.
    ISBN 0-520-08619-8 (alk. paper)
    1. Twain, Mark, 1835–1910—Knowledge—Performing
arts.   2. Popular culture—United States—History—19th
century.   3. Performing arts—United States—History—
19th century.   4. Acting—United States—History—19th
century.   5. Performing arts in literature.   6. Acting in
literature.   I. Title.
PS1342.P45K57 1995
818'.409—dc20   94-14467
                                                                        CIP

Printed in the United States of America
9 8 7 6 5 4 3 2 1

For my parents

Contents

Acknowledgments

The research for this volume was helped along by summer stipends from the National Endowment for the Humanities and from Lafayette College. Some of the materials came to hand only through the help of the staff at the Mark Twain Papers at the Bancroft Library, University of California at Berkeley. My thanks to them, particularly to Victor Fischer.

At the beginning of this project, Christoph Lohmann and Patrick Brantlinger helped me shape my ideas and decide what was important. At later stages the following friends and colleagues read parts of the manuscript and generously offered their advice and encouragement: Richard Burt, Deborah Byrd, Margo Culley, Peter Elbow, Deborah Fairman, Amy Kaplan, Richard Millington, Michael Robertson, and Joseph T. Skerrett, Jr. Thanks, too, to Forrest G. Robinson, and to Howard Horwitz and the other, anonymous, reader for the University of California Press, who provided crucial advice, corrections, and information for additions. For making the transformation from manuscript to book such a smooth process, I am grateful to Doris Kretschmer and Dore Brown, of the University of California Press, and my copy editor, Ruth Veleta.

My special thanks go to four friends and colleagues who read the entire manuscript and whose support and critical comments made this book much better than it would have been: Nicholas Bromell, Deborah Carlin, Robin Roberts, and Bryan Washington. And for their friendship, and an intellectual vitality that has had more to do with this book than they may suspect, I thank Deborah Brandt, Patricia Donahue, and Janis Greve.

Introduction

Performance is a capacious term. Using it to mark out a territory, I started researching this study by looking at the relations between Mark Twain's writings and popular performances—the wide range of shows that dominated nineteenth-century entertainments, from Yankee monologuists and blackface minstrels to Shakespearian actors, from P. T. Barnum to lecturing mesmerists and mediums. I finish the book with a more abstract, and at first glance more disparate, set of concerns in Twain's fiction and in his culture: performance and representation, the relation of performance to masculinity and race, the ways in which psychologies of "acting" and "character" redefine each other, the expressiveness of the body, and the workings in public spectacles and street theater of impulses toward social order and disorder. Performance has remained the rubric, even as its meanings have proliferated, thanks largely to the richness of Mark Twain's "acts."

Although in this shift of concerns the book became less about Mark Twain and his "influences," and more about his culture, a fundamental aim remained of changing our understanding of Twain by teasing out and multiplying the meanings for him of "performance." Always obviously pertinent to his writing and his persona, performance has nonetheless been equated with Twain's theatricality and usually disparaged or discounted. In the most influential tradition—including the work of Bernard DeVoto, Edgar Branch, Henry Nash Smith, John C. Gerber, Warner Berthoff, Dwight Macdonald, and, most recently, Guy Cardwell—performance is persistently contrasted to literary realism, with Twain engaged in a drama between the two, either periodically (and all too often) surrendering his abilities at discovering and interrogating reality to the allure of showmanship and rendition, or ultimately outgrowing comically theatrical caricatures.[1] My first impulse was, instead, to treat Twain's theatricality seriously, following, in a way, James M. Cox, for whom this theatricality was equivalent to Twain's genius for imaginative play, or Constance Rourke, who saw in that theatricality an exemplification of American humor.[2] I concluded, eventually, that Mark

1

Twain had already done this, not only repeatedly and seriously investigating his own theatricality, but also shrewdly exploring, even destabilizing, the meanings of theatricality and realism.

As in many of the doublings that gave provisional order to Twain's world, the oppositions between staging and realization, posing and expression, broke down; the terms intermingled. Like Chang and Eng, the freakshow Siamese twins who kept surfacing in Twain's writing, mimicry and mimesis, the performative and the informative, were joined at the hip. The questions of whether "acting naturally" is an oxymoron and whether "realism" and "performance" define each other through their opposition, or might have some other relation, are rehearsed in different guises throughout Twain's writing. Performance as artifice turns into performance as machinelike production; acting blends into automatism; unconscious obtuseness reveals itself as mask. William Dean Howells's admiring declaration that Twain was both "dramatic and unconscious" (while too comfortable with the paradox) identified the conundrum whose ever-receding answer Twain pursued.[3]

One effect of such intermingling on the course of my investigation was a refocusing of Twain's pursuit of fidelity in representation through the lens of performance. For, to Twain, performance meant much more than theatricality, posing, mimicry, and "effect." It also meant unconscious slips of the body and tongue, reflexes of gesture and thought, mediumship, identification—all of which became the test cases, the very criteria for judging what he called the "authentic" and the "genuine" in expression and representation. Or, at least, such dimensions of performance existed as the goals of Twain's realism until he scrutinized them as symptoms and unraveled their mechanisms, discovering unreliability in them that rivaled the displacements of theatricality, or watching the dynamics of identification swallow up both medium and ghost. Now, when narrower definitions of realism are used to cast doubts on whether Mark Twain's writings in fact belong in that category, I want to affirm that Twain was indeed a realist, partly in his grasping for the "genuine," partly in his persistent sense that it was out of reach. To group Twain's concerns with performance and representation, "sincerity" and "authenticity," under the term *realism* may be inappropriate to the extent that they do not exactly coincide with the more specific meanings the term *realism* had for Howells, its main promoter.[4] But Mark Twain did question and try out theories of representation, both enacting and doubting ideas about resemblance and reference in ways, I would suggest, that must make us revise any notions of him as unsophisticated about these matters.

Twain always managed admirably to get himself into trouble, and because his troubles were so interwoven with the troubles of his culture, he can remind us why questions of performance and representation—in whose difficulties his thinking was entangled from the start—matter so much beyond the aesthetic sphere. My concern to rethink Twain as a realist looks consistently to the ways his culture and society conditioned his writing; his aims and terms of representation drew their existence and urgency from cultural contradictions. In his writing, as in his (dominant) culture, sentimentality could be the extreme of inauthenticity, while "femininely" private pathos could be the extreme of sincerity. Racial blackness could quite obviously be reduced to a set of performed markers—dialect, mumbo jumbo, boasting—but could also be a basis for undoing, and seemingly redeeming, the artifices and inhibitions of middle-class gentility. The vernacular of artisans, apprentices, and raftsmen could signify unglamorized and unmediated reality as well as embody working-class, insolent braggadocio and posing. Mark Twain undertakes his investigation of performance through such terms, and therefore what was at stake was not simply the distinction between a tear-jerk and catharsis or a mimic's turn and an emotional outpour. Enacted in categories that mattered to Twain, performance and its analysis shaped white, male, middle-class identity, and thereby worked at defining the identities of others. To a great extent for Twain, I will argue, the ease and variability with which the ordering and hierarchizing terms of theatricality and authenticity could be filled with meanings of gender, race, and class posed both a threat and a freedom, an imperative to reconceive social reality and an opportunity to do so.

Twain's explorations and confusions of masks and faces, posturings and unveilings, therefore always had social and cultural resonances. Seeing these confusions, as I have seen them, has been made possible, clearly enough, by the contemporary currents in literary studies that have invited the performative and rhetorical powers of language to overrun reference and mimesis—at the same time that they have tried to unfix any stability in the divisions between act and essence, rhetoric and realism. Part of my aim has been to let these critical developments help us see performance and its effects in Twain and his writing in new ways, but to prevent them from obscuring his investments in reference and essence. Also necessary for my version of Mark Twain, however, have been new social histories, especially of popular culture, and newly historicizing literary studies, some of which, like the work of Forrest G. Robinson and Susan Gillman, have focused on Twain.[5] The course of this book is to some degree a symptom of the kind of questions raised by this turn to history, culture, and society: To what extent is Mark Twain America's fool because America made him thus, providing the conditions of celebrity and entertainment, spectacle and spectatorship, of which he is both epiphenomenon and epitome? To what extent is he the genius of nineteenth-century popular performance? But the overarching aim is to bring together Twain as a literary writer and Twain as a public performer, and to explore at the same time the ways in which he was a theorist of representation and a careful critic and analyst of cultural performance.

My situating Mark Twain's writing, particularly his earlier writing, among such intensely popular entertainments as minstrelsy, music hall, and the burgeoning middle-class theater has much to do with making him a part, again, of a complex culture—by reasserting his *popularity* against a tradition of critical effort that has tried to distinguish his work from "low" culture, save him for literature, and, ultimately, place him in a pantheon of canonized texts. Franklin Rogers's study of Twain's "burlesque patterns," though indispensable, exemplifies this tendency of a certain period in Twain criticism in its focus on belletristic burlesques of novels and its minimizing of the vast supply of popular theatrical burlesques that Twain clearly enough drew upon.[6] To find, instead, interest and urgency in Twain's popularity, in his kinship to the popular theater, is to think of him as a catalyst and tool of social meaning—if a genius, then one of "cultural work," whose ambitions were realized because they meshed with those of his culture(s). The first chapters of this study concentrate on meanings of Twain's performances enabled by and intertwined with an understanding of their milieux.

Twain's earlier writings—the pieces Edgar Branch characterized as the slapstick turns of a "literary acrobat," and even James Cox dismissed as "*acts* by a comedian intent on fulfilling expectations he imagines his audience to have" (24)—perhaps paradoxically gain in interest and respect when they are considered not as intrinsically interesting but as inextricable from their performative contexts and occasions. Chapter 1, "Acting Like a Man," treats them as complicated performances of white masculinity, multileveled because they were driven by heterogeneous needs and audiences. Within the male subcultures they emerged from, these writings served generally to define white masculinity and particularly to rehearse rituals of aggression, mockery, exclusion, and status. Parodic performances of femininity and race had concrete and local purposes among men. But Mark Twain also performed these acts between classes and between local and mass audiences, and, to a great extent, he displayed the strutting and theatricality within the male subculture as a spectacle for middle-class America. A bourgeois bohemian on the boundaries of his parent culture, Twain opened the proscenium of his performances to a mass audience that could watch his experiments with masculinity and watch him perform male versions of both class and race that spoke to the fracturing Victorian constellation of domesticity, manly "character," Anglo-Saxonism, and gentility.

Twain's performances, like the general landscape of theatrical entertainment, made graphically visible the divisions between local and mass cultures, lowbrow and highbrow tastes, and "homosocial" and heterosocial groupings. Coinciding with Twain's rise to fame were the divisions Lawrence Levine has reminded us of in *Highbrow/Lowbrow: The Emergence of Cultural Hierarchy in America*.[7] The distinctions within a theater—between the pit, where Clemens's 1856 persona, Thomas Jefferson Snodgrass, ate peanuts and hollered and cursed, and the boxes, from which, eleven years later, an exaggeratedly genteel Twain looked down on the "interesting" and rowdy Bowery boys—became, at least in larger cities, distinctions between theaters.[8] Portions of the respectable middle classes became reconciled to the theater as a respectable theater emerged, divorcing itself from the mainly male amusements of low variety, minstrelsy, and burlesque, and doing its best to attract a new audience, including bourgeois women, that supposedly wanted unoffending shows and disciplined spectatorship.[9] Always so public, theater helped clarify social and cultural divides—lending itself to categorical simplicity—so that distinctions in class, neighborhood, theaters, gender, taste, and kinds of performance came into conceptual alignment. Performance styles, as a result, connoted a range of conflicts, and became media in which to articulate and act out these conflicts. Twain's adoption of styles from minstrelsy, burlesque, melodeons (music halls), and saloon entertainments carried for middle-class America a high-voltage charge of subversion, threat, and fascination.

The "deadpan style" that was so much a part of Twain's initial popularity provides a special case, I argue in chapter 2, because it served as both battleground and mediator for the social and cultural conflicts that performance styles had come to signify. At the same time that Twain's deadpan brought him national recognition—in the 1860s and 1870s—a similar deadpan style of seemingly unconscious humor came to dominate the middle-class stage in the performances of such comedians as Joseph Jefferson III, E. A. Sothern, and John T. Raymond. Derived from Yankee and minstrel caricatures, the deadpan style in these performances was transformed from a familiar role on burlesque and variety stages to a vehicle in the middle-class theater of an unconscious humor that exuded pathos and expression. Poised between working-class, masculine entertainment and the increasingly legitimate middle-class stage, retaining some of the mask and bluff of performances in the male subculture at the same time that it became a medium for the middle-class theater's spectacle of interiority, the deadpan style during these years engaged and negotiated socially resonant chasms of taste. The ways in which Twain's deadpan illuminates and is illuminated by the social and cultural operations of deadpan stage performances—as they both crystallized and mediated conflicts—situate his work as an act among others in a very large, national theater.

The middle of this book, chapters 3, 4, and 5, takes a different approach, joining Twain's fictions of the 1870s through the 1890s with contemporaneous theories of acting, gestural expression, and mediumship in order to spotlight Twain as an astute interrogator of representation in performance—though, as always, with cultural and social, never narrowly aesthetic, interests in view. Influenced by new developments in psychology and physiology, Twain's conceptions of performance led him directly to the effects on representation of gender, race, and class. Issues of "character" and cross-identification are played out repeatedly in his novels, as a clustering of these rehearsals shows: Twain's most famous character, Huck Finn, cannot identify with or successfully play the role of a girl, although he can lose his identity to any number of white-boy roles; King Arthur cannot be drilled into a peasant role, cannot empathize with his subjects' suffering—and then, suddenly, momentarily he can; the character given a white identity in *Pudd'nhead Wilson* can nonetheless immediately and unexpectedly adopt a black one, and his mother can gradually work herself into the role of his unrelated slave. From these cases emerge theories about representing others, the kinds of selves best suited to represent other selves, the conscious and unconscious processes that might enable identification with and representation of another, and the ways these matters are inflected by one's color, status, and sex.

Mark Twain's thinking and the theories of acting and emotional expression he drew upon were infused with late-nineteenth-century psychology. Especially crucial were reconceptions of "character" as fluid rather than stable, multileveled rather than unitary, subject to alterations from the unconscious and "autosuggestion." Also important was the materialist impulse to root psychology in the body, to characterize certain mental operations and most emotional expressions as physiological, electrical, or reflexive. The tendency in acting theory to identify involuntary and unconscious bodily expressions of emotion as markers of credibility, and therefore to privilege identification with a role over disciplined and controlled performance, had insistent echoes in Twain's writing. Identification, unconscious expression, and automatisms of both thought and gesture became badges of immediacy and authenticity in representation. Even more extremely, gestural expression as a reflexive response caused by an electrical nervous-system circuit became a kind of model for all expression and representation. The physical nature of involuntary self-betrayal by the body paralleled the Twainian version of mediumship as "mental telegraphy," an unconscious electrical transmission. And such mediumship paralleled the workings of his own psychic system when he served as an unconscious "amanuensis" for the stories of his characters.

But these conceptions complicated Twain's investigation of representation in performance and produced a constellation of larger, unavoidable concerns. The recommendation of identification and mediumship in actorly representation raised the specter of the too-malleable artistic self, which led Twain repeatedly to stage a conflict between effective actors and stable identities (a central issue in chapter 3, on acting and representation). The privileging of physical transmission in emotional expression and intrapsychic processes led to disillusionment due to noise in the circuit, the very density of physical material that enabled "direct" transmission ultimately derailing its reliability (a focus of chapter 4, on the expressive body). And investing unconsciousness and the body as guarantors of expressive immediacy also privileged passivity and forced Twain to grapple with gendered dimensions of representation, especially a femininity ascribed to both mediumship and novel writing (a problem investigated most fully in chapter 5, on masculinity and mediumship). Twain's various efforts, in other words, to grasp stability in meaning—to allay the social anxiety about how reliably others represented themselves, and the existential doubt about the trustworthiness of one's own self-definitions—got pushed to their points of breakdown and failure. And the failures in representation became the symptoms of an irremediable worry about identifying and understanding others.

Although these chapters make forays into nineteenth-century psychology, physics, and physiology, it is my contention that Twain's interests in performance and expression are consistently associated in his thinking and writing with the theater. The centrality of theater for Twain is obvious enough in his early interests and journalism; newspaper writing invariably involved reporting on the "manly" pursuits of the theater and the "sporting life," and much of Twain's work, especially for the San Francisco *Call* and the *Dramatic Chronicle,* consisted of theater reviewing. It is his later claim, in the autobiography, that has to be countered—that, after his days as a reporter in San Francisco, when he had to go to six theaters a night, seven nights a week, every day of the year, the mere sight of a theater gave him the "dry gripes."[10] His continued playgoing after the 1860s (Alan Gribben lists over fifty plays Twain saw—or probably saw, judging by notebook references or ticket purchases),[11] his history of playwriting, and his tendency to write roles for actors he knew belie the memory. He joked in 1899 that he had written 415 plays and had not been able to get even one accepted;[12] in reality, he left behind well over a dozen dramatic pieces, if one counts fragments and aborted efforts, one of which—*The Gilded Age,* or *Colonel Sellers* (1874), as the play came to be known—was very popular and lucrative, and repeatedly led Twain to value playwriting over novel writing.[13]

As Peter Brooks, Nina Auerbach, Martin Meisel, and a host of Dickens scholars have amply demonstrated, nineteenth-century theater and novels were imbued with each other, novelists in particular writing for an audience in tune with stage conventions, echoing theatrical values of melodrama, burlesque, variety, spectacle, "situation," and "effect," and rehearsing a preoccupation with performance and role-playing.[14] For Mark Twain this is especially true, though curiously unexplored. He worked on plays while he worked on novels; conceived of *The Prince and the Pauper* and, possibly, *Tom Sawyer* first as plays and eventually turned them back into plays; and permitted a host of other authors, who saw theater in his writing, to dramatize his novels.[15] Widely perceived as a medium for actors rather than playwrights, nineteenth-century theater reinforced Twain's attention to performance—his own writerly performance and the performances of his characters. Unlike the company of still-canonized nineteenth-century literati who wrote unsuccessfully for the theater and then disparaged it, Twain was not predisposed to think of theater as a necessarily demeaning realization of an author's conception, as an unfortunate materialization of the ideal, or as inevitably involving the solicitation of a concrete audience that turned creation into marketing. An actor's "living, breathing, feeling pictures," he wrote, could convey reality—and teach morality.[16] And the immediacy possible in theatrical performance could stand as a model for his own literary performances.

When the mature Twain does evaluate and diagnose the derailments of representation in performance, as I argue in chapter 6, he can do so in a way sharply attuned to the dissimulative effects of power. As he became himself a cultural icon whose performances benefited from a new, media-created sphere of magnified performance and spectacle, and whose acts exercised powerful cultural force, he also became a self-reflective analyst of national theater and mass-cultural sensation. He directed his attention partly to the ways in which cultural pedagogies involved subterfuges, and the ways in which collective meanings and theatrical representations of social order might involve dramatizations of power specializing in reemphases, displacements, refocalizations, and communal amnesias. Twain understood that power, be it that of an imperial state or of an entertainer, could masquerade in the guise of realistic fidelity. Part of his critique and disillusionment, however, belonged specifically to a

late-nineteenth-century moment that looked more and more pessimistically on the possibilities of realistic representation and increasingly felt a modern dissociation. Drawing on earlier distinctions
between imagination and sense, "symbol" and "show," but also tied
to emerging, and now familiar, discourses about "mass culture" as
degenerative and "commodification" as an evacuation of significance, his grim view of modern spectacle traced a continuum from
alibis and ruses to meaninglessness. If theatricality in *A Connecticut
Yankee* could involve fetishism and Hank Morgan's spectacles could
involve disavowal, their products could also be radically unmoored,
available for sale but not for representation.

The middle of this book, then, focuses on Twain's efforts to secure
fidelity of representation in performance, whereas chapter 6 stresses
Twain's doubts. I argue in my last chapter that the later fictions rehearse, and search for resolutions to, the tensions Twain had elaborated within performance. In *Joan of Arc* he posits and tests the possibilities of sincerity in public; of pure and unequivocal signification
in a spectacle; of femininely mediumistic representation in a national,
public theater; and of divine ideas performed in female flesh. The figure of the transvestite crystallizes this dynamic, pushing Joan of Arc
beyond such gendered oppositions at the same time that they are
preserved. *The Mysterious Stranger Manuscripts,* in a related way,
overlay the opposition between spirit and matter, or between mind
and body—an opposition that organized and bedeviled thinking at
various cultural levels, from popular science to psychological esoterica—with distinctions between genders and conceptions of "materialization" in performative "effects." The very final gestures in these
writings toward a monism of mind attempt to finesse problems of
both gender identity and theatrical representation, although to Mark
Twain's credit the route to this end is convoluted and unsure.

Sir Henry Irving, the English tragedian, reportedly told Twain,
"You made a mistake by not adopting the stage as a profession. You
would have made even a greater actor than a writer."[17] But Twain's
friend William Dean Howells knew better—that Twain already was
a "great and finished actor" in his platform performances and more
generally was "realistic," yet "essentially histrionic."[18] If acting and
theater could serve as means to comprehend Twain's performances,
however, their public topography could also serve as terms for mea-
suring. Howells's likening one "sort of fiction" to "the circus and the

variety theatre in show-business," a fiction for "the masses" rather than for "the most cultivated classes," could rebound in Twain's famous declaration that he "never cared what became of the cultured classes; they could go to the theatre and the opera; they had no use for me and the melodeon."[19] But the inscription on the literary act of cultural distinction could also be confounded in that performative moment when the line between theatrical flourish and expressive gesture is impossible to trace. Twain traced and retraced that line, defining and redefining theatricality and realism, conceiving and reconceiving the cultural and social distinctions arrayed for him along that divide.

One of the earliest pieces the young Samuel Clemens wrote described a performance that interwove distinctions between theatricality and realism, the ideal and the material, and the pedagogical and the grotesque with concerns of brow level, masculinity, and show business. It exemplified from an early moment, that is, the way that Twain's concern for representation through performance intersected with larger cultural questions. I offer a reading and a contextualization of it here, along with some thoughts on method and historicization, in order to provide a touchstone for the ensemble of concerns in this book and a pattern for what is to follow.

In "Historical Exhibition—A No. 1 Ruse" (1852), the narrator, W. Epaminondas Adrastus Blab, recounts the following tale, supposedly relayed from a friend.[20] Not long ago, one of the town's business firms exhibited a show titled "Bonaparte crossing the Rhine." Somewhat mysterious—none of its customers would talk about it afterwards—it attracted one of the town's adolescents, Jim C——, who, surrounded by a crowd of other boys, plunked down five cents for the show. Abram Curts, the exhibitor, then solemnly pulled out "the *bony part* of a hog's leg" and "a piece of meat skin"—"properly speaking, the hog's rind"—and began "slowly passing the piece of bone back and forth across the skin," in a lewd joke that he nonetheless gravely maintained was "a *very* apt illustration of that noted event in history, 'Napoleon crossing the Rhine.' " The crowd laughed and laughed—at the joking replacement of Bonaparte and Rhine with bony part and rind, and undoubtedly at the simulation of sexual intercourse, the old back-and-forth—but also at the swindled Jim, who, far from joining in the fun, set his face in "the most woe-begone look," and in a far from jovial state of "mental abstraction," strode out of the house, spitting out the words "Sold!—cheap—as—dirt!"

Crystallized in this short sketch are several interlocking tensions: between high cultural history and low cultural joke, fidelity in representation and the very different order of puns and homophones, an idealized distant reality and a present grotesque one, the ordered propriety of pedagogy and the profanity of meat and genitals, naïveté and an initiated masculine sexuality, the depiction of a performance and the enactment of one. The sketch invites us to see how Clemens managed in his performance to implicate concerns of status, culture, and gender; the lowness here, for example, of culture and caste is related to a certain kind of masculinity and sexuality. But it also, as we shall see, emphasizes contests—not only between kinds of masculinity and kinds of culture, or between texts of history and trickery, but also between serious and parodic ways of reading—in ways that address and question assumptions of realistic representation.

I would like, in fact, to use young Clemens's sketch as an instructive example for reading Mark Twain—an example that invites us to believe in realistic representation, but not to do so unwarily; that gives both reference and material reality their due, but that is attuned to the performative turns—on stage, in writing, in discourse, in social interactions—that subvert aims and claims to faithful representation. Part of the lure of the showman Curts's Napoleonic history, the narrator Blab's story, and Clemens's sketch is access to an actual reality, historical or social. (The editors of these *Early Tales* cite the sketch as evidence of Clemens's "impulse to write realistic fiction" and declare it "based four-square on a local event and real people" [78].) But the overbearing consciousness of the story is that of the potential for trickery, misrepresentation, and displacement, of the likelihood that the very means of representation will decisively bar access to its object. If, as readers and scholars, we are uncomfortably situated between believing enough in reference to posit historical contexts for the texts we study and disbelieving in the reliability of such contexts as they prove themselves to be tricky constructions, then this mediation in Clemens's sketch between history and ruse is an aid. Constructing and looking for understanding in historical contexts, in social relations, in enactments of domination and subordination are now critical imperatives—and so are a wiliness and misgiving about such contextualization as a rhetorical strategy.[21]

As if to underscore the paradox that writing and performance include both history and ruse, the ruse itself in Clemens's sketch is historically specific, and resonated, in Hannibal in 1852, with larger cultural developments. The ruse refers. This may not at first seem obvious, since the sketch can indeed be seen as a limning of rather ahistorical vicissitudes of representation; that is, writing and performance here are slippery, presenting (at least to Jim) the "fact" as lure and the trick as the final truth. Implicit in the title is the ambiguity of whether "Historical Exhibition—A No. 1 Ruse" voices a protest about history wrongly turned into a ruse or presents an equation suggesting that any "exhibition," any such holding forth or theatrical display, might involve a swindle. The latter imputation may be strengthened by the implication that, in the opposition here between denotation and joke, it is the joke—which does not exist without the laugh—that prevails, because it openly acknowledges the reality of stratagem and exchange. And as denotation is overborne by joke, so an imagined signified of the past (Bonaparte and the Rhine) is overborne by the immediate signifiers in the present (bony part and the rind). The expectation of iconic similarity (which, presumably, is what such exhibitions provide) and of a re-creation of history gives way to the phonetic level of the pun. And whether Jim and the boys want the signified of Napoleon and the Rhine or of penis and orifice, the bone and the meat skin impose, and interpose, themselves. Instead of transports of the imagination or desire, they get a ruse, a joke, a dead hog.

Far from being the eternal uncertainties of representation, however, these vicissitudes of realism and joke, imagination and meat, are inextricable from Mark Twain's historical circumstances. They allude, of course, to shows like those of P. T. Barnum (to whom Clemens referred in print a couple of times in the year before "Ruse" appeared, once by suggesting an edge of hoax to Barnum's paragon of sincerity and transparency, Jenny Lind).[22] The connection exists not only because Clemens's sketch is similarly occupied with hoaxing, but also because Barnum's museum (very famous by 1852) most prominently epitomized the cultural form that joined apparently moral or informative lectures with swindles, and that brought together what passed for high culture in the eyes of many bourgeois with vulgar theatrical amusement.[23] "Historical Exhibition—A No. 1 Ruse" and Barnum's museum existed as both symptoms and enactments of that larger cultural struggle, focused in popular theatrical entertainment, that established an antagonism between high and low culture—and exacerbated the previous cultural manifestations of class factionalism. "Historical Exhibition," that is, appears to some extent to rest on the separation in entertainment of tragedy and farce, seriousness and vulgar comedy, Shakespeare and minstrelsy, "respectable" middle-class theaters and "low" halls for minstrelsy and seminaked "artistes." For a sharp opposition exists here between the genre of the serious exhibition and that of the rowdy, men-only sex show.

A question of representation, of serious fidelity to another scene, hinges on this cultural divide. For the cultural antagonism appears in this sketch at the expense of the serious lecture, whose various features—gravity, the transmission of information and lesson, the authority of the lecturer, the passivity and receptivity of the auditor— are all pilloried: the show, with "the attractive title of 'Bonaparte crossing the Rhine,' " is supposed to include "a lecture, explaining its points, and giving the history of the piece." This enticement appeals to a desire not only for information, but also for comprehension, for the full grasp that assumes transparency of representation. Curts, "the learned lecturer," pedagogically says to the youths that he hopes "by this show to impress upon your young minds, this valuable piece of history, and illustrate the same in so plain a manner that the silliest lad amongst you will readily comprehend it." His lecture, delivered "deliberately" and "lucidly," caricaturedly combines plainly transmitted history, a clarity of content insured by illustration, and invisibility of form with the passivity of the audience—minds ready to receive a direct impression, and, in the case of Jim, ready "with mouth, eyes and ears wide open."

Then, feature by feature, the lecture and its supposed directness of representation are cancelled. The hog parts obstruct the representational transparency. The lucidity of the lecture turns out to be a mimicry. The pedagogical stance of Curts is replaced by the communal hilarity of the boys, as the respectfulness and obedience of Jim ("Yes, sir," he says at the start to acknowledge his submission) become ridiculous in the new frame supplied by the disrespect of the horny joke and the guffaws of the gang. Jim's silent, spectatorly role of "seeker after knowledge under difficulties" is rendered completely inappropriate when the situation is recast as one of "general merriment." The conditions of emerging middle-class theatrical entertainment—the newly disciplined and respectful audience, and a realist discounting of performance and the present in favor of supposedly unimpeded expression and representation of the past—are pointedly juxtaposed with the older theatrical conventions of manly rowdiness, irreverent inversion, and performer-audience exchange.[24]

In other words, the discounting of reference itself in Curts's exhibition relies on reference to a cultural contest—a contest in which the dismantling of supposedly edifying and therefore sanctioned representations apparently operates as a tactic of insubordination. The antirepresentational performance, male ritual, punning, and sexual joking serve to weaken any faith in reference; as we shall see, the sketch further undermines such faith by finally presenting its own reportage as a possible joke. Yet the sketch resonates with—and refers to—not only a larger, culturally shaped understanding of tensions between highbrows and lowbrows, but also the social and demographic changes precipitating (and molded by) this cultural understanding.

If this securely grounded "context" is not assuredly available to us, the difficulty ought not to prevent us from discerning in Clemens's sketch glimmers of social structure and strands of the cultural activity that made society intelligible. But to help mediate the divide between the generality of national transformations and the specificity of Clemens's little piece in the *Hannibal Journal*, consider the more local hierarchies of society and culture in Clemens's home town. Hannibal at the time may have had a population of only around three thousand,[25] but, Twain later asserted, distinct classes were apparent, "grades of society—people of good family, people of unclassified family, and people of no family. Everybody knew everybody, and was affable to everybody, and nobody put on any visible airs; yet the class lines were quite clearly drawn and the familiar social life of each class was restricted to that class."[26] These divisions effected similar cultural divides. On one side, men such as Sam Clemens's father promoted lectures and debates through the Hannibal Literary Institute,[27] and the respectable young men of Hannibal's Murdoch Histrionic Association acted out entertainments presented as "rational amusement and pleasing instruction," entertainments devoted to "the improvement of themselves in literary taste and elocutionary practice."[28] While Baptists and Methodists might shun this theater ("Church members did not attend shows out there in those days," Twain recalled),[29] the thespians' training in taste aimed to distinguish their productions from the more fully profane: such low-culture shows as the river-traveling circuses, blackface minstrels, medicine shows, and showboat variety troupes. It would be important, too, to shun the audiences and hangers-on of these shows, the groups perceived as toughs, drinkers, knife fighters, gamblers, and "mountebanks."[30]

The cultural contest smoldered hotly enough to bring the Hannibal city government in 1845 to institute penalties for any showman who chose to "exhibit any indecent or lewd book, picture, statute [*sic*] or other things, or who shall exhibit or perform any immoral or lewd play or other representation."[31] "Napoleon crossing the Rhine" would thus fit into a class of entertainments that had to tangle with the law. However, while there was a chasm between these regulating lawmakers and the local youths who periodically terrorized Hannibal by riding up and down the streets firing their revolvers,[32] it would be wrong to overemphasize the clarity of the divide or the purity of proper middle-class revulsion. For Sam Clemens attended and was profoundly fascinated by circuses and minstrel shows,[33] and he, like other middle-class boys and men, had some license to be "a person of low-down tastes from the start, notwithstanding my high birth, and ever ready to forsake the communion of high souls if I could strike anything nearer my grade."[34] Nor would it be right to stress the novelty of this cultural antagonism, since it obviously partook of more old-fashioned, religion-based hostilities to theater and idleness. Converging in Clemens's sketch, in other words, were live, local tensions fueled by uncertain borders between higher tastes and low-down ones, respectable persons and persons with no respect, past prejudices and new conditions. A preoccupation with these terms, the social order their clarification promised, and the disorder their permeable borders posed, surfaces in "Historical Exhibition."

It is important, obviously, to give the complexities of what we can grasp of Clemens's milieu their due, and in particular to acknowledge the malleabilities of constructions of class, culture, and gender. Clemens could partake of a rough masculinity and a respectable one; he could, as a middle-class male, attend and help define what was deemed entertainment for "low-down tastes"; he could claim membership in the class repelled by and pledged to control lewd and indecent "representations" as well as in the subculture that fascinatedly consumed them. Among the "contexts" for "Historical Exhibition," that is to say, were interlocking *contests*, cultural conflicts both internalized and projected, which were complicated in themselves—a matter I illustrate by considering Clemens's sketch, finally, in relation to another text: the report of and response to a burlesque of Shakespeare, performed in Hannibal in 1848 by Dan Rice, probably the most famous circus clown to travel the Mississippi.

"Shakespeare actually *was* popular entertainment in nineteenth-century America," Lawrence Levine asserts (4); the readiness, for instance, of the duke and the king in *Huckleberry Finn* to perform both the scene from *Romeo and Juliet* and the nonsense burlesque of "To be or not to be" rests on common practices and common knowledge of these plays (13). It also rests, Levine argues, on a typical freedom with Shakespearian texts that characterized both serious theater and burlesque in antebellum America—a freedom, however, that was interdicted by America's intellectual elite during the second half of the nineteenth century as Shakespeare was sacralized and annexed as the property of people with "cultivated" taste (90). If, from about midcentury on, middle-class representatives intensified their efforts to distinguish their respectable entertainments from the low shows they sought to regulate (while irreverent male subcultures like that in Clemens's sketch fought back), then the occasion of Dan Rice's performance in Hannibal effectively reproduces the conflict. Billed in Hannibal as "the modern Shakespearian jester," Rice undoubtedly performed one of his usual travesties of Shakespeare, turning the language into nonsensical soliloquies (like the duke's in *Huckleberry Finn*) and quoting Shakespeare for incongruous purposes in a free and supposedly "indecent" banter with his audience.[35] This time his performance was followed by a letter from "A Looker On" to the *Hannibal Journal* (the paper edited by Sam Clemens's brother Orion). "As to Rice, the 'great Sheakspearian [*sic*] clown,' " the writer declared, "we think that the title Sheakspearian *blackguard* would suit him much better." Rice's low wit and lack of decency, his "dramshop slang" and "sacrilegious tongue" had defiled the beautiful language and sublime ideas of the "immortal 'Bard' " with "moral filth and uncleanliness."[36] We have here quite obviously a public contest over the ownership of Shakespeare, one in which "A Looker On" has indeed sacralized the bard and has pitted high culture against the language and tastes of the dramshop.

But also present is the assumption about representation that lies behind this sacralization—that performance of Shakespeare should "realize" his language and ideas with a minimum of interference; the verbal rearrangements typical of the widespread nineteenth-century Shakespeare burlesques, in this view, shamefully cloud the bard. Fidelity in representation appears here as a marker of taste, pitted against the opaque filth of Rice's act. This overlay of a question of representation on a division of taste and class matches a similar alignment in "Historical Exhibition," in which the expectation of mimesis, of the re-creation of the historical event, belongs with the aspiration to a higher level of taste and knowledge, while the defilement of this historically sublime representation with pig body parts and "moral filth and uncleanliness" belongs with lowbrow horseplay and raillery.

Finally, in both instances—the Rice episode and Clemens's story—these issues of representation, brow level, and class intersect with contesting forms of masculinity. Most obviously, there is a contrast here between a more official and respectable manhood and a rowdy one. The first is represented by "A Looker On" and Jim, the isolated individuals here, and it enshrines self-improvement, self-education, quietness, privatism, detachment, and deference. The second is represented by the showmen and their audiences, and it exalts boisterous and disorderly hooliganism, camaraderie, obscenity, tall tales, impudent performance, and rites of male sexuality.[37] The respectable manhood, which spanned classes but of course had its class associations, is bound to a passive, silent spectatorship that is bound, in turn, to an expectation of immanent meaning. And "A Looker On" (whose alias says much) uses his schema of truth-revelation as a weapon in a contest of manhoods. Though, he writes, he gullibly went to see Dan Rice and his "motley gang of Bacchanalian mountebanks," their effort to dupe and swindle him backfired, because Rice and his troupe "exhibited, or rather *exposed* themselves" for the low hucksters they were. "Looker," in other words, *has* gotten revelatory truth out of a performance designed to impede it, and in so doing he has bested the players. In his account, re-

spectable manhood, highbrow and higher-class culture, and exposure of underlying reality prevail.

In Jim C——'s case, a serious absorption and interiority that preclude low-masculine horseplay are stressed throughout, from his beginning state of wide-eyed and passive receptivity to his ending
states of "mental abstraction" and "profound reverie, seemingly entirely unconscious of the jeers cast at him by the company." The contrast to the vulgar performance of Curts is so great that one might like
to put Jim on the side not only of privatism and interiority, but also
of chaste domesticity. The story takes the shape of an initiation into
a kind of masculine sexuality that Jim fails, or refuses. One of "the
uninitiated," he arrives quite aroused—"gasping and out of breath,"
ready to throw down his money "in as great a hurry as if life and
death depended upon the speed of his movements," and declaring,
"I want to see it the worst kind." He is, indeed, in a state of excitement, "so anxious to see the show that he could scarcely stand still."
But at the crucial juncture, the climax—when Curts tells his "juvenile
audience" to "draw near and give me your attention a moment, for
this is the most interesting part of the exhibition," and then proceeds
to pass the bone across the rind—the results are laughter from the
surrounding boys and humiliation for Jim. Seemingly, Jim sought an
initiation only into a sexuality fully sublimated into the pursuit of
truth. When confronted with this scene of quite another sexuality
and masculinity, he withdraws inside himself, ultimately into
"reverie" and "meditations."

It is significant, certainly, that Jim's one moment of retaliation—
after the situation of truth seeking has been demolished, clearly replaced only by that of manipulation and conflict—involves angrily
calling Curts "nothing but an old swindler." Separating himself from
rowdy sexuality, Jim also separates himself from the masculine
world of marketplace chicanery, as if his pursuit of realism and truth
is foiled just as much by their commercialization as by the hoax itself.
The "exhibition," after all, has all the marks of a marketable commodity. Mounted at the store of "the enterprising firm of Curts &
Lockwood," it is well publicized (news about it "had been pretty ex-
tensively circulated"), and one of its most prominent features is that
it costs " 'one dime per head, children half price.' " The transformation of the exhibition into pig parts and a ruse may even serve as an

allegory for the transformation of realism into commodity, and the placement of representation in a world of objects and hustling, where exchange replaces transparency. In recoil, the beaten Jim flees this territory of masculine sexuality and masculine marketplace, of the material present and of exchange. His final comment, "Sold!—cheap—as—dirt!" makes *him* the object of both exchange and defilement, though "opening his lips" he "ejaculated" these "significant words," as if by expelling the taint of selling and dirt he could preserve an unsullied (domestic? feminine?) interior.

In his well-known "Notes on the Balinese Cockfight," Clifford Geertz takes an event that mixes masculine status rivalry and masculine bonding and, laying out its multiple layers of meaning, argues that the event, like a kind of show or theater, provides a "simulation of the social matrix" and "a dramatization of status concerns" (436–37)—representing, interpreting, ordering, and rendering comprehensible the conflicts and hierarchies of everyday life.[38] "Historical Exhibition" does the same, I would argue, but it also does more than provide the kind of "metacommentary" Geertz thinks symbolic forms articulate about social structure. In addition to dramatizing conflicts between levels of culture, between classes, and between a bourgeois subjectivity and a "low" masculinity, the story offers a further commentary on representation itself, calling its capacities into question. By aligning oppositions between highbrow and lowbrow, the proper middle-class subject of knowledge and vulgar masculine irreverence, the historical sublime and the materiality of the lower bodily stratum, and the transparency of representation and its dismantling, it clarifies relations among levels of culture and society at the same time that it profoundly confuses their ontology—inviting us to think of class and gender as effects of uncertain representation, and to think of representation itself as an uncertain effect of class and gender. If this sketch, as Geertz claims for any cultural text, enables social tensions to be "more exactly perceived," it also, at a level of "metacommentary," undermines the security of our perceptions.

Moreover, while "Historical Exhibition—A No. 1 Ruse" may work to order and explain the conflicts of its context, and to some extent can claim the distance such tasks presume, it also is an instance of conflict. If performances, in Geertz's view, can be read as texts, as interpretive stories a culture tells about itself, this text can also be read as a performance, an act within—rather than merely a reflection of—

contending versions of brow level, class, and gender. "Historical Exhibition" displays a heightened, though perhaps tricky, consciousness of itself as a writerly act and of itself as an exchange between a performer and his audience. When W. Epaminondas Adrastus Blab begins by saying, "A young friend gives me the following yarn as fact, and if it should turn out to be a double joke, (that is, that he imagined the story to fool me with,) on his own head be the blame," we immediately have to recognize that, as Curts's historical exhibition was a ruse, so is this yarn. The duplication is underscored by the parallel alibis of Curts, that he is "merely an agent" for a "wholesale firm" and not responsible for Jim's dissatisfaction, and Blab, that he is merely a conduit for the story of his young friend. The implication, of course, is that far from being transparent mediums, relayers who take seriously their office of faithful representation, Curts and Blab—and Clemens—are tricksters, each presenting a joke in fact's clothing.

There exists a possibility that the story's readers could be doubles for Jim the dupe. This would require the predisposition to take this "yarn as fact." Given the particular situation of publication—the mischievous Clemens was editing a single issue of the *Journal* while the serious Orion was in Tennessee—readerly expectations may have run more toward report than joke and hoax. But the place more plausibly carved out for the reader doubles that of the "crowd of eager boys" that follows Jim into the show, an audience that does not have to put down a token of its gullibility and that is saved humiliation by framing Jim, making him bear all the embarrassment, and laughing at him heartily. That a reader could conceivably occupy either place further turns the sketch into a dramatization of opposing subjectivities and their opposing cultures. It also suggests the cultural force of readings themselves: Jim as a reader of realism actively resists the joke, just as the joke can be taken as a subversive "reading" of realistic exhibition; and a reader of Clemens's sketch could take it as truth, though the piece also works as a mocking reading of straight reportage. Because the drift of the sketch, however, is to humiliate Jim, cancel the representation with bone and rind, undermine propriety with raucous masculinity, mock education with gross sexuality, and displace fact with joke, the sketch takes on the character of an act within a cultural struggle. When a performance mimics what it designates, when it enacts what it denotes, the act of representation changes from the invisible to the palpable, and the depiction of society transforms into a social act. The performative moves of the "mere" representers—Curts, Blab, and newspaper editor Clemens— prevail, and the sum of the sketch's effects tally on the side of irreverence, burlesque, and communal hilarity, at the cost of serious representation, self-improvement, and privatized subjectivity.

But this was just a beginning skirmish, a moment of competitive performance whose enactments and embodiments set a stage for Twain's repeated rehearsals of the stakes in representation. In a multitude of ways over the course of his career, the fundamental difficulties of representation in performance meshed with concerns over social order, disorder, and change; his concerns as a "realist" in search of reliable expressions of meaning and identity intersected with the uncertainties of situating people by sex, class, and race. And this dynamic connected his double identities as performing artist and cultural critic.

1

Acting Like a Man

Mark Twain's work, Warner Berthoff wrote in *The Ferment of Realism* (1965), emerged from "a special sort of performing tradition: essentially a popular tradition, journalistic and theatrical," which developed "in newspapers and sporting magazines and on the popular stage." This tradition, in Berthoff's account, shaped Twain's work into an "art of the performer," a writing of exhibitionism, impersonation, manipulation, and flourish, redeemed only by moments of "visionary truth and beauty."[1] Although its cultural meanings have altered, this critical convention of dispraising Mark Twain's "theatricality," usually by contrasting it to some version of "realism," trails back to the nineteenth century; as I have suggested, there is reason now to stop using this opposition as a simple means of evaluation, and instead to place it historically—to show what performance and realistic representation meant in the popular tradition Twain's work emerged from, and to join the terms and practices of performance in the theatrical tradition Berthoff identifies to Twain's writing in a way that will show what was happening culturally and socially in these acts of entertainment.

Mark Twain's early writing emerged out of bachelor subcultures of artisans and bohemians and was closely related to male entertainments in music halls, burlesque houses, and minstrel shows, and to male performances on the street—in holiday festivals, parades, and general hooliganism. My concern in this chapter will be partly to trace the importance to his art not only of the male camaraderie he knew in the eastern artisan subcultures and the western river and mining areas, but also of the conventions in these subcultures of competitive and theatrical male performance. Appraising the impact on his writing of this performative tradition involves attention to Twain's fascination with people on the margins, including actors, popular musicians, music-hall dancers, and exemplars of the working-class performative masculinity that the official culture of his upbringing tried to suppress. My argument will be that in mimicking performance practices from minstrel shows, melodeons, theatrical burlesques, amateur tavern performances, and street theater, Twain's writerly "acts" also mimicked the effects of these performances by trying to reassert social distinctions between white men (mainly workers or disaffected bourgeois) and other people, including the genteel middle classes, women, and racial minorities. These performances of identity became especially complex to the degree that they aimed to occupy margins *and* marginalize others—claiming one margin among many while trying nonetheless to sustain white male prerogatives, dismantling mainstream cultural orders yet insisting on their own hierarchies.

As a middle-class bohemian, Twain also embedded in his mimicries a self-conscious sense of transgression that yet clung to mainstream values, thus making his performances serve, on another level, as a negotiation of ambivalences about, and within, his parent culture. As these introductory remarks suggest, rather than trying to save Twain's bohemianism and burlesquing for high culture, I aim to situate them in the conflicts between categories of class and culture and connect them to the "low" entertainments they drew on. And rather than characterizing Twain's embrace of the "vernacular"— often a rather uncontextualized category romantically referring to a language rooted in the common folk—as a product of the familiar biographical self-division between the roughneck Mark Twain (supposedly drawn to the vulgar and the marginal) and the genteel Mr. Clemens, I will consider it as a testing of various middle-class self-definitions by a bohemian busily crossing conventional boundaries into marginalized territories of the working classes, racial cultures, and lumpen communities.

Mark Twain's writerly performances took place within tensions between classes, cultures, genders, masculinities, and races. They were acts in the definition of these categories and embodiments of tensions and relations among them. Most especially, however, they were rehearsals of white masculine identities, and dramatizations and negotiations of the uncertainties that fractured these identities in the later decades of the nineteenth century. The subcultures of bachelors and bohemians in which Twain developed his craft forged experimental cultural spaces where masculinity was in flux. Twain's writings for these subcultures—his performances in print,

his comments about and reviews of theater, and his theatrical burlesques—juxtapose masculinities divided by race and class. They
shape white manhood in relation to African Americans, Chinese,
and women, as we shall see in Twain's relationship to performances
of race and in his role as a spectator before female performance (a
role that becomes a performance itself), and they register upheavals
in bourgeois stability.

CONTESTING MASCULINITIES
AND PERFORMANCE

A concern about the ways in which "masculinity" and "performance"
define each other—in larger cultural terms and in instances of Mark
Twain's writing—may seem an obvious enough choice, since in our
cultural lexicon *masculinity* still evokes notions of performance. In
the middle of the nineteenth century, however, the performative
masculinity that came to fascinate Mark Twain—the performance
of pugnacious self-display and boasting, or the successful performance of a trick or joke—had an uneasy place in a middle-class culture that had seemed much more ready to sanction quieter and
soberer masculine virtues of self-control and self-improvement, dili-
gence, thrift, and sincerity, and that seemed to find its securest identity in the supposed source of these virtues, the domestic interiors it
walled off from the streets.[2] The values important for consolidating
the self-awareness of the mid-nineteenth-century middle class, that
is, may have prized masculine performance in the senses of providing and accumulating, but official ideas of self and respectability
stressed control, integrity, containment, and privacy, recoiling from
the theatricality of male braggadocio. Yet Mark Twain took masculinities associated with territories outside the middle-class ideological enclosure—the cultures of working-class urban youths, river-
boatmen, and miners—and reenacted them as a route to success,
notoriety, and fame.

The question, then, partly concerns the attraction and cultural
meaning of this other masculinity, one of public display and swag-
ger. And for one explanation, we must look to the historical generalization that masculinity was in "crisis" in the later nineteenth century. Middle-class manhood suffered during this period, according
to a number of historians, because a bureaucratized workplace pre-

cluded classic individualism and heroic effort; patriarchal authority at home diminished, usurped by motherly power, critiqued by domestic ideology, and ignored by mobile children; and women's influence in public increased, with female workers and reformers raising male worries about a "feminization" of culture. In this context, a "new virility" looked attractive.[3] Add to this another familiar explanation, that the allure of new masculinities arose for middle-class males in accord with an emerging culture of consumption and imperialism, a culture that no longer meshed with the conservative and producerly "character" of older Victorian manliness.[4] Helpful as these generalizations are, when lifted out of the particulars of the historical studies that generate them they threaten to discount, for example, the investment bourgeois males had in the domestic, or their recoil from pugnacious manliness. Elaine Showalter's attunement, in *Sexual Anarchy: Gender and Culture at the Fin de Siècle,* to the forces of both disorder and reordering that circulated around this general "crisis in gender" is instructive.[5] Beginning to grasp Mark Twain's performances will require heightened sensitivity to middle-class ambivalences about home and market, the genteel and the vulgar, production and consumption, masculinities and femininities.

Understanding Twain's performances will require, too, sensitivity to the flexible meanings these ordering oppositions made, for they refused to hold still, changing a contest into an alignment, and then changing it back again—with the effect of making Mark Twain's poses into complicated dances within Victorian ideology of challenge and affirmation. Twain's ostentatiously lowbrow performances could seemingly affront bourgeois notions of proper character, for example, at the same time that they helpfully expanded them. His embracing of music-hall burlesque could attack the subjectivity associated with middle-class femininity seemingly from a working-class perspective, but it could also serve to celebrate traditional, middle-class male prerogatives. Brandishing a local culture of down-and-outers in the face of an emerging mass culture could show an affinity with a male bohemian elitism devoted to resecuring belles lettres for itself—and to repudiating a "feminized" literary culture. And racial and ethnic caricatures could serve to exclude social subordinates and affirm dominant stereotypes, but they also could be the vehicles for attacks on Twain's parent culture. Ambivalent stances toward a changing dominant culture, toward a changing femininity, and toward racial and social subordinates all combined and recombined in disorderly ways.

To grasp the ambivalences and contradictions that surface in Mark Twain's written acts—and in his writing about performances and theater—it will help to outline the culture of male performance, the theatrical subculture, and the relatively new social conditions the eighteen-year-old Samuel Clemens encountered when he first left home in 1853. His move from rural Hannibal to the cities—St. Louis, New York, Philadelphia, and Washington, D.C.—followed a typical pattern; like so many others, Clemens left home after apprenticeship in a trade and got work in the city as a "jour printer," a semiskilled journeyman. As historians note, however, the position of journeyman in the cities was becoming one of a wage laborer, an employee of an entrepreneur, with little hope of rising within the craft system. Shop masters tended no longer to take on the role of caretaker or mentor, and apprentices and journeymen no longer lived and dined with the master. Clemens worked with as many as two hundred other employees in a single shop, made enough money only to scrape by, lived in boardinghouses and hotels, and spent time with peers rather than family.[6] He was part of a new, marginal population, quite transient: during 1853 and 1854 Clemens spent no more than a few months in any one place. He joined the ranks of a mass of youths just liberated from the moral supervision traditionally exercised over their conduct in the home, family, and village. As a group, Carroll Smith-Rosenberg argues, they came to symbolize widespread worries over urbanization and the decaying village order and craft system.[7]

Members of a bachelor subculture, Clemens and his friends replaced the controlling hands of parents, guardians, and masters with peer relationships. Outside the workplace, they attended the taverns, theaters, music halls, gambling saloons, and billiard parlors of the city. Although Clemens dutifully sent word home that he spent evenings reading in mechanics' libraries and had not touched a drop of liquor (he had pledged his mother that he would not drink or gamble, and may have kept the promise), we know that he also pursued less respectable amusements far from the quietness and privacy of a reading nook. In New York, for example, he apparently went to a "model artist" show, in which women in flesh-colored tights and draped with transparent gauze posed in attitudes of Greek sculpture.[8] He wrote from Philadelphia that he took part in "what is called a free-and-easy at the saloons on Saturday nights," at which "a chair-man is appointed, who calls any of the assembled company for a song or recitation, and as there are plenty of singers and spouters, one may laugh himself to fits at very small expense."[9] The contrast be-tween quiet reading, the activity most fully invested with bourgeois values of privacy and self-improvement, and raucous "spouting" in a tavern, which negated such sanctified privacy and interiority, crys-tallizes in its most simple terms the specter posed by Clemens and his peers.

Both the model artist show and free-and-easies were relatively new entertainments, initiated for this emerging audience of single men—and for husbands fleeing family morality. Attended in groups, both existed as public rites of masculinity.[10] The free-and-easy, which had begun to appear in Philadelphia only in the late 1840s, especially exemplifies the performative masculinity of the bachelor subcul-ture.[11] It took place in a tavern, established by midcentury as the so-cial center for workers and the single men of boardinghouses,[12] and as individuals performed—getting cheers or hoots for their skill—the entertainment enacted the camaraderie that built group identity while working also as an occasion for competition, self-display, and the rituals of affirmation and humiliation that determined status. The dynamics of such self-consciously public performances, enacted for and within groups of men, powerfully shaped the performative di-mension of Clemens's earlier writings.

These performances, then, had somewhat different emphases at different cultural levels, locally embodying a dynamic of male ritual, of group and status, but in the more general territory of dominant cultural meanings serving to symbolize an emergent threat. For much of the northern, urban middle class around midcentury, these young men and their entertainments became an obsession, repre-senting a variety of fears and fantasies of unleashed masculinity. The situation of Clemens and his companions was grasped by the pre-vailing culture, and usually disparaged, in terms of the pervasive, or-dering oppositions between public and private, street and home, the-ater and hearth. Henry Ward Beecher, in his *Lectures to Young Men* (1844), asserted a guardianship in the home and shop over "our sons, our brothers, our wards, clerks, or apprentices" that was endangered by a "whole race of men whose camp is the theater, the circus, the turf, or the gaming-table."[13] William K. Northall, writing in 1851 about the theaters of New York, observed that "our boarding-house system of living" underwrites the health of New York playhouses; because there is "no domestic purpose" and "very little to make the fireside attractive," "the boarders are entirely thrown upon their own resources for amusement." Instead of "fireside enjoyments," "public places of entertainment offer the readiest means to these poor undomesticated animals."[14] In this specific mid-nineteenth-century version of antitheatricality, theater itself came to epitomize a changing public world of working-class male anarchy whose excitements, one writer feared, would create a distaste for "the quiet and pure enjoyments of the home."[15] Both alarmist and reformist, this arrangement of the cultural topography so starkly contrasts the order, comfort, and sense of classless togetherness promised by the hearth to the image of unsupervised bachelor life outside the parlor doors, that the emotionally barren boardinghouses, the streets, and the theaters become places fearfully alien to the idealized interior.

Young men at leisure surely provoked more worries than did young wage-earners in manufactories and shops. And in the years following the 1849 Astor Place riot, in which the working-class, nationalist supporters of the actor Edwin Forrest mobbed the performance of the Englishman Charles Macready at the highbrow Astor Place Opera House, this entertainment subculture of bachelors especially evoked fear in the middle classes.[16] Significantly, Clemens in 1853 (and for a couple of decades thereafter) was an intense admirer of Edwin Forrest; after seeing the actor play the title role in *The Gladiator* in October in New York, he (perhaps not coincidentally) traveled to Philadelphia, where Forrest was performing, and then to Washington, D.C., where he saw Forrest in *Othello*.[17] Like the other "boys in the pit," the artisans and laborers who occupied the cheap seats and set the tone for Forrest's appearances at the Bowery Theater, Clemens reveled in Forrest's unleashing of violent, "manly" emotions; he commented on the actor's seemingly uncontrolled absorption in "the fierce pleasure of gratified revenge." Since one middle-class strategy of distinguishing itself from social and economic inferiors was to stress decorum, self-control, propriety, hearthbound pastimes, and privatized leisure, it is telling that Clemens chose to idolize Forrest, whose romantic style and most famous roles—Spartacus battling his Roman oppressors, or Metamora defying the English conquerors—symbolized uncontrolled rage and worked to crystallize working-class resentment and male hooliganism. Clemens indeed seems to have felt an affiliation with the "Bowery boy" sub-culture of apprentices and journeymen. A youth culture of styles and tastes—a preference for Forrest, outfits of red flannel shirts, stovepipe hats, and high boots, a leisure milieu of theaters and tav-erns and fire companies, and an identification with the stage charac-ters of Sikesey and Mose—its "rowdies" positioned themselves against bourgeois propriety.[18]

In Victorian symbolic topography, Forrest's manly bellowing on stage existed on the same continuum with the Bowery boys' hooting in the pit or rioting in the streets, in somewhat the same way that au-dience shouting and performers' spouting at free-and-easies had a kinship. They existed in relationship all the more strongly because of their contrast to the image of proper middle-class pastimes: particu-larly the quiet pursuit of reading at home, but more generally a pas-sivity and receptiveness in consuming entertainment that stressed privacy, the spectacle of feeling, the transport of the imagination. As the middle class began to sanction the theater after midcentury and transported its model of consumption—darkening the theaters, de-manding audience silence and decorum, turning the collective ritual into a private experience—the conflict between styles of being enter-tained became sharp.

Samuel Clemens's 1856 sketch about Thomas Jefferson Snod-grass's trip to the theater embodies the tension. Usually dismissed as a simple and derivative story of a rube who cannot meet the imagi-native demands of the theater (like, say, Jonathan in Royall Tyler's *The Contrast*), the piece actually resonates with the specific midcen-tury frame that contrasted the more passive spectatorship of the mid-dle classes to the competitiveness and aggression of certain strains of working-class masculine performance. Failing to grasp *Julius Caesar* and *Don Cesar de Bazan* as fictions or representations, Snodgrass sees them as present-time events and through the similes of his male sub-culture. The murder of Caesar looks to him like an actual streetfight. And in a telling moment, Snodgrass tries to compete with the or-chestra by rendering "Auld Lang Syne" on his comb in an effort to "bring the house down, too."[19] For him, spectatorship is not divided from performance, and consumption is not divided from production, because the space of illusion is not divided from the present, and he does not have a privatized, passive subjectivity marked off from the publicly recognized self. His displacing the appropriate and private sensitivity to pathos with his ritual of competitive "showing off" corresponds, as we shall see, to the typical tactics of burlesque, which make consumption as aggressive an activity as performance. In this, the Snodgrass sketch reverberates not only with the tensions between low entertainments and the psychological spectacle of bourgeois theater, but also more generally with conflicting notions of the self that symbolized a social division—the raucous public self of male camaraderie, and the private, quiescent self of the genteel.

If the territory of public entertainment became a location for both symbolic and literal conflicts, these contests nonetheless cannot generally be grasped simply as reflections of class tensions, and such a simplification of course fails to account for Mark Twain's specific enactments of them. Although in middle-class paranoia ruffian masculinity was largely a signifier of class, there were of course among workingmen cultures of temperance and industry as strong as the "traditionalist" subculture that embraced drinking, gambling, brawling, and whoring. And if the latter, extroverted masculinity did indeed have an actual tradition, mainly a preindustrial, rural one to which punctuality and niceties were alien, it rapidly became mythicized for bourgeois delectation.[20] The Davy Crockett almanacs of the 1830s to 1850s, as Smith-Rosenberg has shown, made this tradition into an urban, bourgeois fantasy about a wild and violent backwoodsman who symbolized everything reform-minded people feared (and were fascinated by): ungoverned adolescence, uncontrolled sexuality, dirt, disorder, intemperance, illiteracy, poverty, insubordination, drunkenness, profanity, and so on.[21] Images of urban workingmen and frontier louts had a kinship based on the middle class's widely disseminated projections of otherness—projections of the preindustrial and the lower class, of vulgar and ungoverned masculinity.

To some extent Mark Twain certainly exploited both the experience and the romanticization of this masculinity, sending a reporter's dispatches from worrisome cultural territory and playing to that worry, a divided stance that his social position would seem to require. Although he joined the wage-earning subculture when he left home and seemed to revel in working-class entertainments, his sturdily middle-class background and the status he was able to hold onto, despite his downward mobility, as an artisan rather than a laborer undoubtedly imbued his perspective on the lower reaches of culture with profound ambivalences. And when he moved to the decidedly male riverboat world, then to the mining communities of

Nevada and California, his immersion in the rough masculinity of these subcultures was tinctured nonetheless with bourgeois values; the dramatized tensions between the "innocence" of the tenderfoot in *Roughing It* or the cub in *Life on the Mississippi* and the "experience" of the groups they are initiated into engage conflicts between these marginal male cultures and the dominant middle-class culture. Mark Twain's popularity lay partly in his ability to poise his writing in the divide between the middle class and its others.

His roughneck persona and self-conscious bohemianism in Nevada and California during the 1860s—poses so sharply fraught with contradictions—self-consciously engaged the tensions between accepted middle-class values and the lure of male and working-class subcultures and entertainments. Whether or not we agree that nineteenth-century bohemias functioned mainly to serve their middle-class parent cultures by exploring specifically bourgeois contradictions and dilemmas, as Jerrold Seigel has argued, Mark Twain, as a public poser, dandy, and ne'er-do-well, pursued the netherworlds of male leisure with a combination of pleasure and recoil which, even if both were poses, spoke to a dualistic response of bourgeois fascination and revulsion.[22] His writings of the 1860s are riddled with multiple and jostling voices accented by contentions between classes, masculinities, and genders.

For example, his report in 1863, for the Virginia City *Territorial Enterprise*, of a visit to San Francisco's Bella Union Melodeon—the best-known music hall for disreputable variety shows and minstrelsy—presents his persona of Mark Twain as ingenuously interested only in going to "a chaste and high-toned establishment." His companion, the Unreliable (modeled on Clement T. Rice, of the Virginia City *Union*), assures him that the show is properly "moral," but the spectacle of "half a dozen lovely and blooming damsels, with the largest ankles you ever saw"—with dresses, indeed, that "looked like so many parasols"—clashes quickly with the guarantee.[23] Mark Twain's additional remark, that forty-two single men and twenty-six married ones were in town from Nevada, and that all were at the music hall except two ("both unmarried"—a homoerotic/homophobic joke?), spells out the nature of the audience (men out on the town) and the appeal of the show (the spectacle of women's bodies). The performance in print mimics the male ritual of collective watching, and the collective rites of male readers and spectators together overshadow the actual sight of the performing female body. From the point of view of this subcultural male rite, the propriety of Twain's persona might signify an excluded bourgeois respectability, except that the persona is not sufficiently denied to preclude strains of identification with its sense of scandal.

The account, more elaborate but similarly structured, of his visit in 1867 to Harry Hill's saloon in New York—again, a notorious institution—also combines a foray into the demimonde of illegitimate male pleasure with a caricature of proper decorum. This time the "innocent" Mark Twain follows his companions into "a little sawdusted den of a tenth-rate rum hole" under the assumption that it is a men's club for "*savants*" and philosophers, a "retired spot" suitable for a "reflective mood." From the assorted toughs he picks out men who "must be" Louis Agassiz, John Ericsson, and Samuel F. B. Morse, and he expresses some surprise when these men "take each a lady" and variously dance with them, kiss them, seat them on their laps, or buy them drinks. He is further surprised by a floor show of music, minstrelsy, mimics, and a male dancer in a kilt whose highland flings serve to expose himself to the house, especially to a row of "young ladies" gathered by the footlights. After Mark Twain buys drinks for a friendly woman, then righteously refuses her request to see her home, he leaves, declaring to his friends his amazement about this philosophers' club; whereupon they inform him that the place is one of "the worst dens in all New York," and "the young girls were streetwalkers, and the most abandoned in the city." His response to this news condenses the contradictory attitudes that shape the episode; Twain declares that "my indignation knew no bounds, and I said we would go and hunt up another one."[24] This eager pursuit of wild, illegitimate leisure and pleasure is bound to a caricature of middleclass quietness, reflective contemplation, and decorum that, despite the caricature, outlines Twain's point of view and invokes a guilty sense of transgression. And the commitment of this experience of consumption and spectatorship to print, especially because it emphasizes these contradictory attitudes as poses, outlines the cruising at Harry Hill's and the reportage in his newspaper (the *Alta California*) as performances themselves in male ritual.

Such pieces plainly resonated at different pitches in different configurations of reception. Within a broad middle-class ideological dynamic, Twain's forays into cheap dives and music halls in pursuit of marginalized cultures and masculine styles held allure, plausibly enough, for a culture beginning to place consumerist hedonism over frugality and searching for a vitality and virility seemingly lost to breadwinners stuck as clerks and oppressed by wage-earning, rationalized labor. The echo of Twain's contrast between sissies and roughnecks in the desires and anxieties of the larger middle-class culture, however, would have had an emphasis different from that in the mainly male societies of urban leisure, the river, and the mining town, where they served more explicitly as acts in a homosocial dynamic, as exchanges between men—located on a continuum with the types of public performance that Twain sometimes wrote about: parades, fire company displays, political meetings and orations, sporting contests, informal street theater, impromptu acts and storytelling in taverns, and music-hall and minstrel performances.[25]

At this local level, the varieties of male public performance were interwoven. As John Dizikes has observed in *Sportsmen and Gamesmen,* by the 1860s there was a well-established "sporting theatrical world" in America that brought together performers and fans of the turf, the prizefight ring, and the stage.[26] Twain's newspaperman's culture was inextricable from this context. Virginia City, Nevada, had four theaters (along with at least six music halls or taverns that provided entertainment); it also became a center for pugilism and other sports.[27] Twain and his cohort from the Virginia City *Enterprise* had free passes to the theaters, went to the music halls to hear monologuists and minstrels, attended the prizefights, and wrote about these performances;[28] thanks to the sexual diary of his friend Alf Doten of the Virginia City *Union,* we can guess that Twain may have accompanied his companions also to dance halls, brothels, and prostitutes' balls.[29] Mark Twain also belonged to a drinking club that entertained visiting actors, and at which both writers and actors engaged in informal performances of poetry, tales, and jokes.[30] The circumstances of male performance and the rites of masculinity, in other words, shaped the conditions of entertainment. While there were moments when writing or onstage performance were separated from and mimed acts in the social dynamic, there also were moments when representations and social acts collapsed into a continuum. Mark Twain's writings were entertainments themselves, often *about* entertainments, but also themselves among the symbolic acts that reproduced and defined their culture.

As prizefighters in this culture used newspapers to convey "cards"—challenges and boasts—to each other, Twain and other newspapermen used newspapers to feud, often teetering on the line between kidding or mimicry of a fight and serious fighting. (One of these feuds prompted his flight from Virginia City to San Francisco.)[31] As monologuists and minstrels pattered and joked on stage, so Clemens did in print, following quite closely the conventions of popular performance. This writing was explicitly, and often self-consciously, preoccupied with public self-display, competition, braggadocio, and status—features of a masculinity that respectable society had chosen to suppress or ignore, and performances that helped constitute the milieux they arose from.

Acts in the definition of a male group, performances in this sub-culture tended to oppose themselves not only to the propriety of the dominant bourgeois manhood, but also to femininity and sentimentality, to the middle-class subjectivity associated with the feminine, and to a developing mass culture—also associated with the feminine. This pattern of symbolic exclusion is telling, partly because of the affinities it sets up. The writings by Mark Twain that emerge from this context are attuned to the connection between conceptions of middle-class masculine "character" and, to use Mary Ryan's characterization, the "cradle" of domestic femininity that nurtured them.[32] Twain and his comrades, ostensibly at least, pitted themselves against a perceived alliance in Victorian individualism between industrious masculinity and domestically based identity. Twain's burlesques of sentimentality look more complicated than the dismissive characterizations of his "antiromanticism" suggest when we grasp them as attacks on a particular subjectivity associated with both femininity and the northern middle class. If, as several historians—particularly Nancy Armstrong—have argued, consolidation of middle-class dominance involved the construction and exaltation of a domestic femininity of psychological depth, emotional resonance, and moral value that struggled to replace or suppress status and class as measures of personal worth, then in midcentury America there emerged counterstrains.[33] What appears to occur in many of Mark Twain's early writings is a clash between masculine systems of status and the sincerity and emotional expression of supposedly classless bourgeois domesticity. Invoking a working-class masculinity of aggression, mockery, posing, and braggadocio, Twain assaults affiliations among self-improvement, equilibrium and strength of character, tenderness, emotional expressiveness, and sincerity.

Opera's emotional spectacle served most especially as a signifier of the psychological interior and of the transparency of expression (though not of the equilibrium of character), and Twain's 1866 burlesque of *Il Trovatore*, therefore, exemplifies the contrast between a subjectivity of depth and the dynamics of masculine status competition. Written as a kind of summary of the opera, and characterized throughout by a profound misreading through uncultivated and masculinist eyes, the piece simply obliterates the existence of the emotional interior and its expression. When Count di Luna first appeared on stage, Twain reports, he began "to yell," until Manrico, offstage ("in the kitchen"), "crowded him down." In the passionate and well-known trio during the first act, sung by the count, Manrico, and Leonora, the two lovers finally "beat" the count "at his own tune"; in an equally well-known scene, when Azucena sings of her mother's death and her gypsy chorus departs, their voices dying prettily away in the distance, Twain again characterizes the singing as a contest, with gypsies who "blasted away and tried to beat her" but "made a fizzle of it and knew enough to curl their tails and leave." Misreading the signs of emotional expression as competitive performance, Mark Twain's persona violates the vulnerability of love and grief and erases the subjective interior. In so doing, the regime of masculine status displaces that of feminine feeling.[34]

Opera, for Mark Twain, epitomized not only a territory of emotional expression but also the power of publicity over what he considered a middle-class mass mind; to him it was ludicrous for Americans to sit in awe before a spectacle in an incomprehensible language, and this was possible only through a weak-minded surrender. Likewise, his sense of an emerging mass culture—the best term, given his frequent condescension toward sentimentalism, sensationalism, and melodrama—was interwoven with notions of femininity, emotional surrender, and "inauthenticity." On the one hand, in his reviews of popular theater Twain consistently attacks such plays as *East Lynne*, the "sickest of all sentimental dramas"; he scorns those San Franciscans who watch it and "whine and snuffle and slobber all over themselves."[35] He mocks Tom Taylor's temperance drama, *The Bottle; or, The Drunkard's Doom*, as "rather overwrought in the misery line" and in general rejects what he called "sensational, snuffling dramatic bosh, and tragedy bosh."[36] Consistently paired, then denounced, is behavior associated with the domestic interior (the expression and transparency of a limited range of emotions—the tender, quiet emotions appropriate to the home) and a submissive passivity. Ann Douglas, in *The Feminization of American Culture*, rightly identifies (though, as some critics have insisted, she may too readily accept and adopt) this nineteenth-century equation of the sentimentalism of the private sphere with a new, emotionally manipulating mass culture. Mark Twain surely perceives this alignment—to the detriment of both femininity and mass culture. And the concomitant contest Douglas sees between mass cultural sentimentalism and an "authentic" and tough-minded masculine opposition also clearly surfaces in Twain's writings.[37]

For example, what Twain contrasted to "sentimental bosh," with its connotations of inauthenticity and femininely passive consumption, was the banjo music of the minstrels Tommy Bree and Charley Rhoades and the black (not just blackfaced) minstrel Sam Pride, which he called "*genuine music*—music that will come right home to you like a bad quarter, suffuse your system like strychnine whisky, go right through you like Brandreth's Pills, ramify your whole constitution like measles, and break out on your hide like the pinfeathered pimples on a picked goose."[38] To be sure, there is passivity and victimization here as well, really an impregnation that echoes the contiguity of the homosocial and homosexual, and that more specifically invokes the white desire in minstrelsy to turn the threateningly wild black body into pleasure; but it is combined with a sense of overt and "manly" assault that is to be distinguished from emotional seduction and surrender and that may partly vitiate its eroticism. The similes here, of swindling, whisky, and disease, are violent rather than languid, bodily rather than emotional, and come pointedly from the low-masculine territories of the marketplace, the tavern, and the grotesque material body—far from an etherealized feminine sphere. The man-to-man assault, as Twain describes it, has a "genuineness" that the emotionally manipulative lacks. The direct physical effect escapes the dynamic of depth on which an uncovering of the emotional interior relied. The embrace of "black music," played in a music hall for a predominantly male audience, further separates Twain's tastes from the genteel and effeminate. (I will turn to the meanings of race and performance in relation to these distinctions of gender in a moment.)

Mark Twain upholds—against the ostensibly mass cultural and feminizing features of midcentury national culture—the qualities of

the *local* and the masculine, the aggressive and performative ethos of
the mining camp. This is perhaps best exemplified in his most famous pieces from this period, the two hoaxes entitled "Petrified
Man" and "A Bloody Massacre near Carson."[39] Twain claimed that
each of these was a burlesque—the first, of news articles in the popular press about supposed cases of petrifaction, which Twain called
a "wonder-business," the second, of sensation items in general, murder stories in particular. In other words, they were mockeries, as he
saw them, of mass-media-induced readerly wonder and gullibility.
The description of the petrified man—the details of which, when
carefully read, revealed the subject frozen in the act of thumbing his
nose—and certain details of the massacre piece supposedly disclosed
them as derision and sport. But each of them, the "Massacre" in particular, relied on local reference to mark them as burlesques. They
were jokes for insiders, and means for victimizing outsiders, vehicles
for contrasting serious truth and jokes and for making the ethos of
male joshing prevail over news. The pieces set up an opposition (a
mocking one) between the male subcultures and the mass press, between the knowledgeable locals and the gullible masses, and between manly raillery and passive consumption. Twain later criticized the "hurried" and "heedless" readers who mistook the pieces
for the truth because, he said, they went for the "marvellously excit-
ing" and "blood-curdling particulars," ignoring the elements of burlesque, travesty, and satire.[40] The scorn for this imagined audience of
witless readers relies on a conception of mass culture as eliciting
wonder and horror from the pliant and careless; it relies on a conception of a feminized and victimized mass audience.

The "Bloody Massacre near Carson," moreover, seems figuratively to match what Twain thought the burlesque-hoax did to the
unguarded portion of its audience. Pete Hopkins, whom local readers would know as a saloon keeper and a bachelor, kills and scalps
his wife and then his children. The echo of the masculinely aggressive bachelor and saloon culture scalping masses conceived as senti-
mentalized and feminized—and who, from the point of view of this
culture, might indeed deserve such scalping because of their passivity, gullibility, and vulnerability—is quite strong. The characters in
the story and the projected audiences are divided into masculine and
feminine, active and passive; it is the bachelors and saloon goers of
Virginia City who would be best able to spot the hoax as a fiction,
avoid getting figuratively scalped themselves, and take some plea-

sure in ridiculing the credulity of the distant and victimized masses. The locals would also take "Massacre" as a mockery of Hopkins himself, and "Petrified Man" as an insult to G. T. Sewall, the local judge who, the piece reports, gravely conducts an inquest into the petrifaction. Each piece, in other words, works as mockery and insult in the guise of seriousness and truth, and enacts a ritual that excludes the gullible and feminine and resecures the bond of laughing males. In addition to this subcultural enactment, each tale projects two different audiences, a vulnerable and victimized one and a wary and scoffing one, in a way that activates the distinctions between the feminine and the masculine, the serious and the rollicking, the atomized mass and the reveling locals.

As a final example of the attack on the conjoined values of femininity, tender feeling, and the serious representation or expression of emotion, consider Twain's 1863 burlesque of *Ingomar the Barbarian,* a play that directly embodied the middle-class myth of feminine "influence" and the power of the domestic over unbridled masculinity. In contrast to Edwin Forrest's unreconstructed barbarians, the hero of Friedrich Halm's play—the wild, warriorly, and sexually aggressive Ingomar—is transformed by his tender love for the Greek maiden Parthenia, which leads finally to their marriage and establishment as rulers in a new Greek city. It is a story of the taming of uncivilized masculinity and desire, the awakening of the tender emotions of middle-class subjectivity, and the repudiation of roving male bands for the closure of marital domesticity. Mark Twain takes these matters explicitly as the targets of his burlesque. In his version of the play, Ingomar's "rebellious spirit rises" at the requirement that he must "dress like a Christian; he must shave; he must work; he must give up his sword!" But Parthenia "tames it with the mightier spirit of love. Ingomar weakens—he lets down—he is utterly demoralized." The love of "Two Hearts that Beat as One" is mocked, as is grief (Parthenia's father, kidnapped from home, "weeps—he sighs—he slobbers. Grief lays her heavy hand upon him"). At the same time that Twain's piece discounts historical representation in typical burlesque fashion—by turning Greece into Nevada, Ingomar into a Comanche, and so on—it attacks marriage, love, family, and emotion in a generalized assault on the image of the feminine.[41]

The environment of theatrical burlesque out of which so much of Twain's writing emerged supports the contention that male "homosociality," including both friendship and rivalry, cements its bonds by taking "woman" as object of exchange, control, exclusion, and scorn.[42] Romantic narrative, sentimentalism, sobs, embraces, tears, "soul butter," and "flapdoodle" are the markers of femininity and mass culture that function as items of abjection whose mockery consolidates the opposed system of the masculine and the local. In addition to this masculine dimension, because the burlesque tradition that Mark Twain and his peers looked to was primarily a working-class, male entertainment—associated by the 1850s and 1860s with burlesque houses and minstrel shows that travestied the legitimate theater and played predominantly to audiences of mechanics, miners, and urban bachelors—burlesquing was accented by the insubordination of male groups who stood outside both the prosperity and the domesticity of the American middle classes.[43]

The terms conventionally (and ingenuously) used in formalist criticism to describe burlesque tactics—"puncturing" illusion or "deflating" pretension—encode penetration and aggression that not only connote a general gendering of artistic practices, but also resonate specifically with the sense of nineteenth-century burlesque as an attack on a subjectivity conceived as enclosed, feminine, and bourgeois. The enclosure of the space of illusion is violated, as is the private communion of the spectator/reader with the spectacle in this enclosure. Much like his friend Charles Henry Webb (whose *Arrah-no-Poke*, a burlesque of Dion Boucicault's *Arrah-na-Pogue,* began with the "grand effect of changing the flats"),[44] Twain travestied performances by foregrounding the background, focusing on real-time behavior rather than imaginative representation, or stressing "discrepancies" or errant details that ruined the "unity of effect"—all tactics of willful misreading that resisted enthrallment, emotional contagion, effects of feeling, the losing of the self through union/identification with the spectatorial space carved out by the representation. In his burlesque review of Daniel François Auber's *The Crown Diamonds,* for example, Twain directs all his attention and praise to a "furniture-scout and sofa-shifter," who "performed his part" of moving the stage properties in such a "sublime" way that "there was not a dry eye in the house." Partly an attack on drama reviewers, the piece nonetheless follows the burlesque practices of resisting the instructions for response in the play, refusing the emphases offered, and parodying the intended effect designed by the dramatic structure of pathos and sublimity.[45] Travesties of the popular theater—

that was finally, in the 1860s, becoming legitimate for the middle class and respectable women—enact tactics of symbolic violation, predation, and seizure that underscore their masculine gendering at the same time that they follow the practices of perverse readings that enabled men in working-class subcultures to evade bourgeois propriety and domesticity.

BOHEMIANS, BURLESQUE, AND THE
PERFORMANCE OF RACE

It would be wrong, however, to overstress Mark Twain's early alignment with outright challenges to the interlocked regime of interiorized subjectivity and serious representation, to the domestic versions of men and women and the privatized consumption of "realistic" images. Although Twain so clearly embraced a style of rowdy, performative masculinity—which the prevailing bourgeois ethos had taken pains to exclude from its identity—and then used it against the domestic enclosure of tender and sincere emotion, it is more apt to say that he forged ahead into emergent, middle-class *ambivalences* about the emotional and the physical, domesticity and bachelorhood, the building of "character" and hedonism, self-control and self-indulgence. His self-professed bohemianism in San Francisco in the 1860s aptly situates him: as a middle-class male seemingly disaffected from his origins, as an explorer of the boundaries of bourgeois life, as a person radically ambivalent about bourgeois culture and its contradictions as well as about that culture's excluded others.

In typical bohemian fashion, Mark Twain in San Francisco sought out, and represented himself as familiar with, people on the fringe of society. He wrote about street people (for example, the homeless, apparently schizophrenic, and notorious Emperor Norton, who considered himself ruler of San Francisco), prostitutes, and Chinese opium addicts. He circulated in a subculture that included a host of actors, notably such acquaintances as Junius Brutus Booth, Agnes Perry (who later married Booth), John McCullough (a protégé of Edwin Forrest), Frank Mayo (who later became nationally famous in the roles of Davy Crockett and Pudd'nhead Wilson), Charles Pope (whom Twain would later introduce to Howells to help launch Howells's playwriting career), the music-hall performers Lotta Crabtree and the Worrell sisters, and the minstrel Ralph Keeler. Although he worked hard at the *Morning Call,* instead of early morning industry, his job as drama reporter included "visit[ing] the six theatres, one after the other; seven nights a week three hundred sixty-five nights in the year."[46] The easier work writing theater news and reviews for the *Dramatic Chronicle* and, later, writing for the self-consciously literary and bohemian *Californian* and the *Golden Era* enabled him to maintain irregular work patterns, an addiction to night life and drinking, and a pose that combined ostentatious laziness, artistic pretense, and wild woolliness. Although the pose was more that of an unkempt bohemian with populist impulses than a true dandy, he also indulged in extravagances of dress and appearance that combined with the other features of his lifestyle to affront the canons of utility, industry, thrift, and self-control.

Mark Twain's fascination with a theatrical subculture that pressed against the boundaries of middle-class values meshed with that subculture's fascination with outsiders—including caricatured ethnic and racial outsiders, especially African Americans and Chinese. Twain reviewed and befriended tavern monologuists and music-hall performers in Nevada and San Francisco who enacted ethnic caricatures, from "John Chinaman" to various mocking impersonations of Yankees, Germans, and the Irish. Minstrelsy, which in the decades of midcentury had grown nationally into a culture industry, suited well the concentrations of males in Virginia City and San Francisco.[47] Ethnic and racial parodies circulated between the stages of music halls or tavern free-and-easies and street theater—parades, Fourth of July celebrations, and so on—all of these occasions serving the complex purposes of both ridiculing and excluding others and registering fascination, desire, and anxiety.[48] Intertwined with this broad range of acting and display, but inflected through his bohemianism, Mark Twain's representations of race are crossed by a cluster of contradictions related to his uncertain place in the West—as a white male fascinated by racial otherness, and as a middle-class bohemian enticed by working-class entertainments. The meanings of whiteness, his class status, and his masculinity, all of them in flux, intersect in his performances of race. He constructs race in a way peculiar to his vexed combination of identities.

His responses to minstrelsy and to actual African-American performances are, accordingly, very complex, exceeding a simplistic conception of white racism as something concerned only to fix and subordinate African-American identity. For example, in reporting on African Americans dancing the quadrille during an 1864 celebration in San Francisco of emancipation in the English West Indies, Twain writes that, for "pretentious, impressive, solemn, and excessively high-toned and aristocratic dancing, commend us to the disenthralled North American negro," who can far surpass whites "of the upper stratum" in "the slow-movement evidence of high gentility."[49] In this description of what appears to have been black cakewalk imitations of highfalutin white manners, Twain relays some of the caricature of the dominant by the subjugated. Coexisting in his remarks about the dancers' "natural propensity to put on airs" and to " 'let on' magnificently" is a condescending objectification of free African Americans, written by a white for the mainly working- and lower-middle-class white audience of the San Francisco *Call*, as well as an acknowledgment in African-American culture of mimicry and mockery trained against white elites, an upper stratum that the newspaper's audience would probably also be ready to ridicule. There was, I would suggest, a doubleness in Mark Twain's perception of his audience—as interested in deploying this image against both African Americans and the white elite, much in the same way that the black dandy in minstrelsy seems to have worked. There was also an interest on Twain's part in the *excess* of this mimicry, partly condescended to and partly admired as an antidote to certain pretensions of white middle-class culture. A fascination for this African-American dancing, along with an adoption of a working-class white view of it that mixed identification and disdain, worked to distance him from his parent culture as well as resecure his whiteness. Mark Twain's reproduction of "race," as well as his fondness for minstrelsy, insistently involves such doubleness. He embraces a mockery of blacks at the same time that he values black burlesques of whites in black culture, and white imitations in minstrelsy of black attempts to mimic whites.[50]

He was attuned, that is, to the resistant tactics of African-American language and masking within the racist image.[51] The contest of parody, the black burlesque of whites within the white burlesque of blacks, constituted for him part of the allure of minstrelsy. The argument from such historians of blackface minstrelsy as Eric Lott, Nathan Huggins, Berndt Ostendorf, David R. Roediger, and Michael Rogin that white audiences felt a range of identifications with and recoils from the black stage image—from primitivist identifications based on fantasies of sexuality and freedom, to both longing and disdain for antibourgeois blackface laziness and hedonism, to the always-present race hatred—points the direction for understanding Mark Twain's fascination.[52] If race had been important for forging respectable middle-class and working-class identities, by making African Americans the opposite of sobriety, discipline, thrift, and self-restraint, then the extruded and racially marked qualities returned as desirable for the bohemian Twain; representations of both the disreputable working class and African Americans held allure partly because of the affront to bourgeois respectability in their volatility, sexuality, indiscipline, intemperance, laziness, and corporeality. Also enticing were their symbolic skirmishes with and forays into the territory of the haute bourgeois, their attacks on genteel authority, regularity, and moralism. Minstrelsy combined working-class burlesque of pretension and glimmers, at least, of African-American mimicries of whites. The signifying, parodying, and performative features of such mockeries served as assaults on the middle class, its subjectivity of interiority, and its system of serious representation.

From his admiration of blackface minstrelsy in the early 1840s in Hannibal—when, he remembered, minstrelsy "was a new institution" that "burst upon us as a glad and stunning surprise"[53]—through his stay in California, when the editors of the *Dramatic Chronicle* announced of Twain that "as a general thing he prefers negro minstrelsy to Italian opera,"[54] to his fond memories of the form late in life,[55] minstrelsy functioned for him as the epitome of affront to bourgeois culture. The contrast, as he put it, "between Emerson and a nigger show" exemplified for him the polarization of taste in the United States.[56] Of course, his admiration of the endmen's "extravagant burlesque of the clothing worn by the plantation slave" and their "very broad negro dialect," which he found "delightfully and satisfyingly funny," evinces an obviously racist disdain, though it is quite aware of the counterfeiting at work in the minstrel image. But also discernible is a desire to emulate practices of burlesquing mimicry that are hostile, I would argue, to modes and registers of representation associated with genteel culture. Inasmuch as "serious" representation was increasingly associated with an emerging bourgeois "high" culture, and inasmuch as sincere "expression" was associated with pathos and sentiment, and ultimately with the middle-class fabrication of the "feminine," Twain's delight in minstrel endmen's typical conflict—a "jangle of assertion and contradiction," a mimicry of "signifying" argument, boasts, and oaths—was partly a delight in the dismantling of meaning. That is, Twain is arrested not only by mockeries of white pretensions in minstrel middlemen and interlocutors, and not only by the way in which the "courtly middle-man" is driven to distraction as he implores the endmen "to preserve the peace and observe the proprieties." Twinned with the mockery of bourgeois African Americans and plantation slaves is both a par-ody of high-toned whites and a reproduction of African-American "signifying." Within white working-class minstrel burlesque, that is, appear maskings and language games related to those in African-American culture.[57]

Henry Louis Gates, Jr.'s, characterization of "Signifyin(g)" as a ma-nipulation of language among African Americans that emphasizes and "turns on the sheer play of the signifier"—done in such a way that it "wreaks havoc upon the Signified" and amounts to a guerilla attack on "the nature of (white) meaning itself"—provides us with one way of grasping the pertinence of minstrelsy to Mark Twain.[58] The practice of avoiding "the game of information-giving," indeed, of acting in opposition to "the apparent transparency of speech" (52–53) and focusing instead on rhetorical structures and strategies, sounds, and the scrambling of sense that puns and homonyms entail, characterized minstrelsy as well. "Signifyin(g)," Gates acknowl-edges, "is a principle of language use and is not in any way the ex-clusive province of black people, although blacks named the term and invented its rituals." Gates's examples of white reproductions of African-American language that make signifying both "the object and the mechanism of parody" could easily have come from the min-strel stage. In sum, if the language of minstrelsy incorporated much of what we now know to be African-American dialect and vernacu-lar, and if the blacked face worked as a mask for satirizing the culti-vated language and behavior of socially superior whites as much as it served to perpetuate racist stereotypes,[59] then it is certainly plausi-ble to think that some of the language practices of "signifying" found their way into minstrel parody.

Mark Twain borrowed from the minstrel stage, and while he re-produced stereotypes, he also borrowed tactics of subversive lan-guage use. The particular practice, for example, of talking and never getting around to the point—used repeatedly by Mark Twain, most famously in John Skae's "story" in "The Facts" (1865) and Jim Blaine's in *Roughing It*— had a sure place in minstrelsy (especially, in Twain's experience, in what he called the rambling, "incomprehensible," and "conflicting" monologues of Billy Birch of the San Francisco Minstrels) as well as in African-American language games.[60] Puns, comic boasting, put-ons, and conundrums—all practiced or explicitly admired in Twain's early writing—had their most visible presence on the minstrel stage, but echoed such language use in African-American culture.[61] In general, through verbal masquerade and language play, affinities existed among Twain's performances, minstrel shows, and African-American language practices. But seeing the affinities, of course, should not obscure the differences. Though it is tempting to see an analogy between covertly encoded attacks on "white meaning" in signifying and attacks on dominant middle-class meanings in western male burlesquing, Mark Twain's connection to rather than exclusion from the culture he attacks and the mediation of his burlesquing through minstrelsy require a more complex model. In his attention to minstrelsy exist contradictory stances both toward African Americans and toward bourgeois domesticity and propriety; each was mocked *and* exerted a powerful allure.

Ah Sin, the play Twain wrote in collaboration with Bret Harte, illustrates a similar doubleness.[62] Although the play was finished in 1876, after Twain left the West, it was written with his California friend, and like the "heathen Chinee" from Harte's earlier poem "Plain Language from Truthful James" and the briefly appearing character Hop Sing from his play *Two Men of Sandy Bar*, it drew on racist caricatures from white, male, working cultures and the burlesque and minstrel theaters. Like minstrels, who represented the Chinese especially through a nonsensical jabbering that mocked Chinese language and food (ching ring, chow wow, ricken chicken, and so on), [63] Ah Sin is constantly "jabbering in Chinese" (e.g., 11, 78, 88). And in accord with the racist assumption behind minstrelsy's pretentious interlocutor (who aped white manners), one of the play's characters calls Ah Sin truly a Chinaman in his "monkey faculty for imitating"—by which she means that Ah Sin, a "mental vacuum," ignorantly mimics others without a clue to the significance of their actions (51–52). This white character's aggravation at an apparent idiocy that fails to grasp her meanings is, however, distanced, subjected itself to derision. It arises when she attempts to show Ah Sin, a new servant, how to set the table, and he imitates her every move, including her errors and blunders: she lifts a table leaf and accidentally lets it fall, and so does he, and so on. What looks like empty-headed imitation, in other words, is as easily read as an ignorant mask used against white officiousness and authority, against meaning in the guise of orders.

The latter reading gathers strength in light of the general narrative direction of the play. Like Harte's "heathen Chinee," who euchres a couple of white card cheaters, Ah Sin in this play outsmarts and exposes the villain card sharp and murderer. His "jabbering frantically in Chinese" provides a safety in unintelligibility and apparent stupidity that enables Ah Sin, mainly through subterfuge and trickery, to outwit his adversaries. As in "The Heathen Chinee," which exacerbated anti-Chinese sentiment, there obviously are racist, white supremacist categories in effect, and there may be little profit in distinguishing between the familiar Asiatic stereotypes—inscrutable trickiness and inscrutable idiocy. Yet there is reason not to discount the opposition at work between being fixed in this stylized bundle of racist turns and sounds and eluding, exceeding, and manipulating that mask. Ah Sin's "monkeylike" imitating may suggest, on the one hand, a mimicry that precludes not only intelligence but anything beneath its surface; but on the other hand it also appears to attack and dismantle (white) systems of meaning. In this sense, Ah Sin's expressions hinge on the distinction between "aping" and "jabbering" as objects of ridicule and as tactics of ridicule, as exemplifications of racist attitudes and as undermining mimicries of such racist projections.

That the oppositions hinging on "jabber" or "mumbo jumbo" between idiotically depthless mimicry and disguised intention, and between a racist image and a subversion of that racism, should pertain in Mark Twain's thinking to images of both African Americans and Chinese suggests that race partly became for Twain a generalized category for working out a different problem.[64] It became, that is, a white construction supple enough to give shape to, and slightly to displace, his contradictory relationship to aspects of white American culture.[65] "Monkeylike imitating" had utility as a means of parody and burlesque of middle-class conventions and as a repudiation of the interior of bourgeois subjectivity and its ideally sincere and transparent revelation. Jabber and signifying, in the hands of Mark Twain, could scapegoat both racial others and the parent culture. Instead of grouping "colored traits" as a means only of consolidating and defining a superior whiteness, Twain's conflation is also deployed in a conflict within bourgeois culture, and inside white male identity.

These examples must underscore for us the complexities of racial exchange as they disclose the specific historical uses to which ambivalent racial signs and images in the white imagination can be put. My focus has been on Mark Twain's responses to racial cultures, minstrelsy's responses to them, and Twain's responses to minstrelsy, rather than on African-American or Chinese responses to white culture—the mimicries, signifying, insider talk. But this white man's terrain is nonetheless one of shiftings in racial meanings, where Twain's fantasies of the other come into play, but where they follow various trajectories. Living in a white male culture that had plenty invested in brutal racisms as ways of excluding and subordinating African Americans and Chinese, Mark Twain yet used race, and raided race-associated language and behavior, in his complicated negotiations with middle-class respectability and femininity; as a white male ambivalent about bourgeois norms, he transformed African-American tactics of resistance (affected by their translation through minstrelsy) into his own, in effect using race to attack his parent culture and to articulate his relationship to it. He responded to performances of race and incorporated racial styles into his own performances as a means of contending with and exploring white, middle-class meaning and its expression. This translation, through performance, of race to other concerns, while it cannot obscure the more blatant injuries of racism—and while it still constitutes reassertions of whiteness and maleness—should also find its way back into our estimate of Mark Twain and race relations, thereby complicating our sense of his racial contacts, exchanges, and transactions.

THE BACHELORS WATCH AN "ARTISTE"

Categories of the "feminine" were invariably inextricable from Mark Twain's writings and their reforgings of his identity. In establishing his stance toward middle-class culture he put performances of race, and racial performers, up against a respectability that always had a gendered inflection. He aligned blackness with a vulgar masculinity that, along with its affront, defined gentility as effeminate. The notion of "woman," especially in its meanings of sincerity, expression, emotion, and interiority, always had a role in the self-definition of Twain and his bachelor subculture, most obviously as an exclusion and projection. But with their bohemian ambivalences toward the ideological underpinnings of bourgeois society, Twain and his co-hort also sanctified and preserved the "femininity" so contradictorily necessary to the idea of themselves. Their reactions to Adah Isaacs Menken—probably the best-known and most notorious of the host of female performers in Twain's West, from music-hall *danseuses* to tragedians—especially demonstrated these ambivalences. Having a woman in the role of performer made explicit the gendering of the conflicting terms of performance, particularly those of expression and theatricality. A bohemian woman confounding definitions of Victorian femininity, Menken served as a liminal term over which Twain and his companions could reenact their intersecting dramas of gender and cultural level in relation to their ideas of acting.

Menken forced a rearticulation of the terms of performance be-cause she was a performing woman and a female bohemian. Be-fore she made herself a part of Mark Twain's scene, she had fully established herself in the bachelor and bohemian subculture: she had been a regular among the bohemians of Pfaff's beer cellar in New York, she had had a relationship and a son with boxing "Benicia Boy" John C. Heenan, and she had married the humorist Robert H. Newell (Orpheus C. Kerr).[66] She became a national celebrity after her ap-pearance in Albany, New York, on June 3, 1861, as the Tartar prince Ivan Mazeppa in Henry M. Milner's play *Mazeppa; or, The Wild Horse of Tartary,* her notoriety stemming from the scene in which she was stripped down to a very brief costume and flesh-colored tights, then tied to the back of a horse that ran up a stage mountain. Dressed as a man ostensibly for the opportunity to display her body, Menken was a figure of disruption in the patterns of Victorian gender identity and decorum. Using Byron's character as an occasion for a leg show, she also situated her act between high culture and music-hall titillation. When she played in San Francisco and Virginia City in 1863, she elicited, accordingly, some strikingly clashing responses from Mark Twain, his friends, and his peers.

Many of the remarks among these western journalists divided simply between smirking jokes about Menken's calves or lack of clothes[67] and attacks on her "scandalous, obscene exhibition";[68] the contrasting attitudes of lasciviousness and righteous indignation, of leering and condemnation, posed conventional and familiar male responses—responses that echoed the conflict between errant and respectable masculinity. More interesting (though not unrelated) was a contest over Menken and her meaning that surfaced as a disagreement about her ability to act, but that highlighted the ambivalence in the male subculture about the ideal of sincere expression and the lure of burlesque, as well as an ambivalence about Menken's womanhood. That is, in the responses to Menken surfaces the division I have been sketching in this male subculture between attraction to forms associated with the middle class (especially the expression of tender or "feminine" emotions) and a recoil from such forms to rowdy burlesque. But this ambivalence was complicated by the fact that she was a female performer, and a brazen one at that.

Joe Goodman, Twain's editor at the *Enterprise*, praised Menken in terms that extolled her femininity and expressive capacity:

> It is only in intensely emotional situations that Miss Menken displays those remarkable qualities which prove her claim to the title of great actress. . . . In these she stands peerless as a speechless but eloquent delineator of human passions. . . . When you have watched the dawn of a fresh emotion in her soul, which rises and glows till her whole being is suffused with its spirit, and trembles in her countenance with more than voiceful intelligibility, finding its ultimate expression in some action whose grace and significance scorn interpretation, you feel that words would be a miserable, meaningless mockery. It is no abstract conception of passion that Miss Menken delineates. It is the passion that springs from a profoundly emotional and womanly heart—a heart with all the finest sensibilities, quickest instincts, generous impulses, and noblest purposes, that ever animated or actuated mortal being.[69]

Goodman's judgment rests on a notion of transparent expression that is inextricable from the idea of the feminine as emotional rather than rational, realized through the heart and the body rather than the mind, marking an interior (of soul, affect, instinct) that will not be hidden or obscured but naturally lays itself bare without the mediation of wordcraft. In effect, Goodman's Menken is not acting at all, but is simply emoting, uncontrollably, as any "true" woman might. Far from exercising a calculation in performance, she eschews even the artifice of words.

In pointed contrast are the reviews by Mark Twain. He saw Menken perform twice, first in San Francisco, then in Virginia City. After the San Francisco show he wrote to the *Enterprise:*

Here every tongue sings the praise of her matchless grace, her supple gestures, her charming attitudes. Well, possibly, these tongues are right. In the first act, she rushes on the stage, and goes cavorting around after "Olinska"; she bends herself back like a bow; she pitches head-foremost at the atmosphere like a battering ram; she works her arms, and her legs, and her whole body like a dancing-jack: her every movement is quick as thought; in a word, without any apparent reason for it, she carries on like a lunatic from the beginning of the act to the end of it. At other times she "whallops" herself down on the stage, and rolls over as does the supportive pack-mule after his burden is removed. If this be grace then the Menken is eminently graceful.[70]

Mark Twain's evaluation is the opposite of Goodman's. Instead of a woman whose inner emotion registers automatically in her actions and countenance, Twain's Menken is a bundle of disconnected motions, a flurry of flailing limbs without a directing intelligence, a movement machine expressive of nothing. Part of the contrast at work between Goodman's account and Twain's is a familiar one—a contrast between the serious representation of an emotional interior and the bodily equivalent of mumbo jumbo, between psychological expression and a burlesque cancellation of meaning.

Twain's reading, indeed, may be largely due to a burlesque impulse. In a manner typical of burlesque, it attends most closely to the performative features that foil serious representation, and it thus has a similarity to Twain's illusion-destroying review of Menken's performance in Virginia City, which focuses on her horse—its tendency to be distracted by the theater audience, its walking around the set, its unresponsiveness to Menken's "unconsciously" digging in her heels to perk it up. It echoes, because of this, the host of burlesques of Menken and *Mazeppa* that arose in San Francisco and Nevada, most presenting some version of what the Bella Union Melodeon billed as "Big Bertha on a donkey."[71] Twain's pleasure in the report that another actress, Caroline Chapman, who "must be seventy-five years old, now," would be playing Mazeppa out in Montana came from his imagining "a jolly, motherly old lady stripping to her shirt and riding a fiery untamed Montana jackass up flights of stairs and kicking and cavorting around the stage."[72] Twain recoils into burlesque from the sensation and the reverence that accompanied Menken's spectacle, countering her performance of revelation with his performance of mockery, transforming Goodman's view of her interior to an explosion of seemingly meaningless signs.

The theatrical relationship Menken invited was voyeuristic, but in a way that linked the exposure of the female body with the exposure of feminine emotion—both consumed privately and intimately by the male spectator. The sexual gaze, that is, was paired with the psychological spectacle of sentimentalism, and became similarly prone to burlesque. For private theatrical unveilings of both body and interior clashed with the communal nature of the male ritual of burlesque-irreverent watching. In these burlesques, the scopic sexual relationship is largely sacrificed for the homosocial connection based on mockery and scorn of "the Menken." This switch in the framing of reception links and repudiates voyeurism and domesticity, mass scopophilia and privatized middle-class consumption, in favor of an errant male camaraderie. At the same time that Mark Twain recoils from the private and passive positions of voyeurism and consuming vision, then, he affirms a male ritual that devalues, even discounts, Menken's performance, transforming her from a performer to a token in the forging of male solidarity. The moves to affirm the local over the mass, and the collective over the atomized, also affirm the masculine over the feminine, making Menken an object or effect of male communality.

And in a further discounting of Menken's performance, Mark Twain attributes a theatricality to Menken that is not, like minstrel caricatures, attuned to its own ways of exceeding mimesis (though many late-nineteenth-century actresses, it has been suggested, did indeed "overact" as a means of pressing the bounds of "feminine expression" to which they had been consigned).[73] Instead, in a response whose ambivalence rests on different standards for different genders, Twain on the one hand critiques her acting as violating femininely transparent expression (that is, she is out of line with the Victorian norm of the feminine), and on the other hand attacks that norm with his burlesque (stressing his own manly rebellion against middle-class effeminacy). While Twain seems to have taken pleasure in other female performers—including, for example, the dances, impersonations, banjo playing, and minstrel routines of such women as Lotta Crabtree and the Worrell sisters—his response to Menken may nonetheless be partly a recoil from a performing woman, a reaction that reproduces the prejudice that such a creature is unnatural, because woman by nature is private, her expressiveness flowering only in the home. It is certainly worth noting that a bit later, in 1867, Twain remembered the model artists he apparently saw in New York during his first year away from home as "a pack of painted old harlots," as if performing in public, particularly with an overtly sexual dimension, might necessarily transform true women into false ones, the natural into the painted and artificial.[74]

The contradictions in Menken's performance confronted the contradictory impulses in Twain's bachelor subculture in a way that made the possible meanings of Menken proliferate. Her acting could look like emotion bared as well as like theatrical posturing, and *Mazeppa* had pretensions to be a highbrow and bohemian representation of Byron's poem as well as a spectacle of sexuality, an instance of bourgeois spectacular theater as well as a simple affront to middle-class respectability. When this met the bachelor-bohemian subculture's own ambivalences, the responses included both an appreciation of the strains of respectably feminine expressiveness and an irreverent recoil from them, a spectatorly collusion with the voyeuristic spectacle and a comradely burlesque of it, a characterization of Menken's body as a pellucid medium for emotions and a view of it as hysterically or seductively opaque. There also existed somewhat divergently masculine reconsolidations of power—by making Menken a collective object of scorn or desire and by rebuking her for her sexuality and performance. In effect, Menken's performance was edged out by, or at least the occasion for, male performances and subcultural ritual. Mark Twain, Joe Goodman, and the other journalistic commentators on Menken performed in their interpretive arena, transforming Menken into a token of their contest and once again rehearsing the divisions over cultural level and gender that converged in popular performance. Menken's act and its interpretations and burlesques thus served as stages on which to negotiate cultural disequilibrium.

Peter Stallybrass and Allon White argue in *The Politics and Poetics of Transgression* that, as one of the effects of creating its identity by marking itself off from the popular and the low, bourgeois culture in the late nineteenth century "produced a compensatory range of peripheral 'bohemias' " devoted to symbolically upsetting, transgressing, and inverting the hierarchies of the parent cultures. Far from necessarily subversive, such carnivalesque play with the symbols of otherness served partly to constitute and reconstitute mainstream cultural identities. Bourgeois authorship in this period, they write, "*uses* the whole world as its theatre in a particularly instrumental fashion, the very subjects which it politically excludes becoming exotic costumes which it assumes in order to play out the disorders of its own identity."[75] To a great degree, I have argued, Mark Twain's early writings operate to this purpose. A certain kind of working-class masculinity becomes a desirable fantasy in a way that addresses dissatisfactions with older masculinities precipitated by social change. Chinese and African Americans, their cultures, and their languages are given a symbolic configuration that serves to negotiate tensions in white, middle-class, male identity. A woman and her body provide the theater for these men to rehearse their larger cultural conflicts.

But the effects of this theater, these exotic costumes, and these playings out of identity are not foregone conclusions. If they are not necessarily subversive, neither do they necessarily serve to equilibrate disorder. The diverse concerns of class, gender, race, region, and nation, the competing impulses of the local and the mass, render Twain's performances part negotiation, part reflection of the unnegotiable. Moreover, they depend, of course, upon their particular, historical situations. As a result, their effects are various, conditioned by how they enter into local cultures and national cultures, how they are received by one group or another. This is obviously so even if dominant cultural strains seem to define the identity disorders that dictate the terms and concerns in performances such as Mark Twain's. The play of multiple cultural imperatives, as well as the insistence of middle-class concerns, in the creation and popularity of a performance style—the deadpan style—will be the focus of the next chapter.

2

"Funny Personations"
Theater and the Popularity of the Deadpan Style

The national popularity of Mark Twain began in 1865, when his "Jim Smiley and His Jumping Frog" was published and then repeatedly reprinted; what critics have called his "deadpan style" of performance, a humorous storytelling with no apparent consciousness of the humor, had reached its wide audience. In 1866 Twain began his highly successful lecturing, moving his deadpan to the podium in his talks on the Sandwich Islands, which further consolidated his popularity. Also in 1865 and 1866, Joseph Jefferson III played his first run as the star of *Rip Van Winkle*, transforming what had been a rather simple stage Dutchman into the best-known character in postbellum American theater. More specifically, Jefferson brought a variety-hall ethnic caricature into the play based on Washington Irving's story, and turned it into his fantastically successful, unconsciously humorous Rip. For the rest of the century, Joseph Jefferson and Mark Twain would be associated as two of the men "most celebrated in the country for entertaining others," as the Hartford *Courant* put it—two comedians, I will argue, whose styles struck common chords in American audiences.[1]

I mean to join under the term *deadpan style* not only the platform, standup humor of Twain's "lectures," but also the unconscious humor of his characters from Simon Wheeler to Huck Finn, an unconscious humor also embodied in a range of stage performances, including Jefferson's. The defining trait is the uncertain dividing line in these deadpan styles between self-consciousness and unconsciousness, trick and self-revelation, impassiveness and idiocy, humor and pathos. These dualities, I will argue, not only connect these performances, diminishing the ostensible difference between Twain's sometimes acutely theatrical platform persona and Jefferson's apparently absorbed stage acting; they also had a social resonance that helps explain the simultaneous, fantastic popularity of Twain, Jefferson, and other funny performers of uncertain consciousness in the later nineteenth century. Paul Baender, writing in 1963 of the "Jumping Frog" story, observed that Mark Twain never explained his taste for the deadpan style or suggested what its larger significance might be; Baender did not venture hypotheses about these matters either, and no one since then has addressed the "cultural work" of the deadpan style.[2] My concern here will be with the reasons behind the postbellum, mass-cultural prominence of this style of performance, and particularly with the ways in which cultural and social divisions of these years were acted out in the ambiguities of the deadpan.

In both cases, Twain's and Jefferson's versions of the deadpan style, their mixes of humor and serious innocence, had traveled from minstrelsy and music hall to prominent and proper middle-class entertainments at the same time that "low" theater was being separated from "respectable" theater.[3] In their hands, deadpan performance moved from entertainments mainly for men, burlesque shows that traded in derisive caricature, to performances praised for their realism. This move, of drawing on music-hall buffoons—such as foolish-shrewd Yankees, dandy fops, comic blowhards—in order to create ludicrous characters with "depth," figures who (in the reviewers' cliché) elicited "laughter and tears," was made also by the other comedians who dominated the later nineteenth-century theater, including E. A. Sothern in *Lord Dundreary,* John E. Owens in *Solon Shingle,* and John T. Raymond as Colonel Sellers in Mark Twain's play of *The Gilded Age.* In Twain's work, this deadpan style shifted from caricature in his earlier journalism to *Huckleberry Finn,* a book whose "realism" has always been at issue. Deadpan traveled among, and mediated between, the divisions in theatrical entertainment that powerfully symbolized the strata in the newly developing hierarchies of taste. This migration, this heritage held in common by Twain and Jefferson, can give us a clue to the popularity of the performance style. Poised between music-hall caricature and burgeoning middle-class theatrical entertainments, oscillating between a deceitful deadpan and an unconscious humor, these related methods of performance exemplify the conception that popular entertainments carry contesting meanings and values—and that these embedded antagonisms, and their capacities for echoing differing experiences, are crucial for understanding the prominence of such entertainments.[4] The mere fact that this kind of performance metamorphosed so that it could aptly belong to differing audiences ought to warn us, of course, that there are no essential connections between a style or theatrical practice and a social group or cultural ideology.[5] Yet this caveat cannot prevent us from discerning in a performance elements associated with classes and groups—elements that may resonate with the experiences of those groups and that may (even at the same time) serve to represent those groups to others.

The deadpan style in its various manifestations continued to echo its origins—working-class variety shows, the entertainments of male subcultures, and the status rituals and humiliation anxieties of those groups. But it grew to embody a quite different meaning as it became a privileged mode of psychological spectacle, "revealing" through states of unselfconsciousness a quiet subjectivity suited to a domestic drama, and thereby reaffirming a version of integral interiority and psychology against the disseminations of masking and calculated posing. The doubleness that always lurked in the deadpan stage style between an intentionally blank face and idiocy, or between cunning and naïveté, became weighted toward unconscious revelation rather than disguise as the illusionistic theater appropriated it from music hall. That is, the connections deadpan retained with variety-show caricature, while still resonating with the experience of that venue, also became for the new middle-class audience symbols of a worrisome, masculine, working-class subculture whose threat was defused as these signs became subordinate to the psychology of a character. Any single performance, of course, would yield many more meanings in its context than this basic dichotomy would suggest. But I would like to maintain this general opposition partly because the records of reception—theater reviews and memoirs—so persistently evaluate the performances in its terms and therefore limn a set of widespread interpretive conventions and a certain "horizon" of reception. Many of the performances considered here, indeed, became battlegrounds of taste, alternately denounced as minstrel-show comedy and praised as psychological realism, serving as occasions for the repetition and rehearsal of the terms that conventionally embodied anxiety over social and cultural division.[6]

The performances seemingly had the capacity to affirm those elements of low comedy antagonistic to bourgeois forms. But they also could work to incorporate and contain irreverent burlesque, partly by integrating it into a psychological interior. Undoubtedly, too, in traveling across cultural divides, the style helped soften the hard edges that will jut out from a social breach—thereby allaying some anxieties. As it moved from the devious pokerface to apparently guileless transparency, from the signs of calculation to those of sincerity, it mediated between representations of working-class disrespect and genteel respectability, and between representations of the male marketplace and the feminine home. And for a dominant culture whose values seemed under threat from the peoples and territories seemingly outside its precincts, the style served to resecure notions of an essential psychological self crucial to middle-class identity, in the same moment that older conceptions of "character" were fracturing. It raised the specter of a self fragmented by masks and markets, but revealed there a unified character of psychological depth. While it is important to retain a sensitivity to the style's variety of possible meanings and functions, and to keep an eye on its permutations from audience to audience and from one time and place to another, it is nonetheless possible and useful, then, to offer some generalizations about the import of the deadpan style in nineteenth-century American culture.

In the blank face of the Yankee peddlers so familiar on the stage in the antebellum years, or in the impassiveness and languid drawl of Mose the Bowery b'hoy at midcentury—both of them stage figures important to Mark Twain—the deadpan obviously engaged social conditions that had made trickery and self-betrayal special concerns. The possible value of a deadpan, or a pokerface, to men in the cities and on the frontiers is easy enough to grasp, given the need to operate within a dynamic of concealment and exposure shaped by communities of strangers and men-on-the-make. The deadpan could on the one hand be a protection, a shield for the inexperience, ignorance, fear, or gullibility that if exposed rendered one an easy victim. It could on the other hand be a weapon, a tool of deceit that might enable one to win at poker, or to trick another, or to shame him. In eastern cities and western mining towns, where contact with masses of strangers meant both anxiety and opportunity, to have a face that "gave nothing away" allowed one to keep security and gain advantage. But if a deadpan had a practical benefit for some men in their exchanges, it also had a symbolic dimension, echoing the middle-class culture's worry about and fascination with the world ideologically excluded from genteel and domestic spheres, the world of swindling and deceit. This deadpan figure—as a representative of unruly public territories, of the market, of the street—therefore had a profound resonance for the larger reaches of American culture.[7]

In the male subcultural and working-class context out of which the deadpan style emerged, including the cities Twain visited in the 1850s and the mining towns he lived in during the 1860s, there existed a host of monologuists and comedians who, as it was frequently put, specialized in being funny without seemingly realizing it. As a theater reviewer in Nevada and California, Twain praised Fred Franks, who played comic parts and Yankees in melodramas, for his ability "to do humorous things with grave decorum and without seeming to know that they are funny"; he also admired the "masterly gravity" of the Irish caricatures Billy O'Neil performed in farcical afterpieces; and he promoted the monologues of Stephen Massett, a humorist in the vein of the stage Yankee, who was known similarly for the humor of his oblivious bumpkin persona, Jeems Pipes. Twain compared some of his own efforts at "uncouth burlesques" to the "incomprehensible" and "conflicting" tale telling of Billy Birch, a member of the San Francisco Minstrels who slowly drawled his stage monologues and dialogues in a quiet, lazy, lumbering way. These stage comedians provided a rich resource for the development of Mark Twain's own deadpan style. And Twain was perceived as one of them, with a special kinship to Artemus Ward, Twain's friend and the acknowledged master at that time of the deadpan style, and to Dan Setchell, whose "funny personations and extempore speeches," Twain wrote, made him the best comic actor the West Coast had seen. One of Twain's mentors, Charles Henry Webb, a writer of stage burlesque, declared that "to my mind Mark Twain and Dan Setchell are the Wild Humorists of the Pacific."[8] Within this western locale, dominated by single men, the mockery of others and the release of anxieties about self-exposure set conditions for a comic performer's allure.

The conclusion of various theater historians, for example Richard Moody, that the stage Yankee from whom these deadpan performers descended was always a theatrical contrivance and never a vehicle of "psychological realism," or the generalization by Constance Rourke that the whole congregation of stage Yankees, minstrels, and backwoodsmen provided a theater of mask and disguise rather than emotional expression, will still serve to describe a group of Mark Twain's early unconsciously humorous characters.[9] The "Sarrozay Letter from 'the Unreliable,' " for example, and its revised version, "Inexplicable News from San Jose" wring their humor mainly from the drunken and rambling talk of "the Unreliable"—the low comic character Clemens supposedly modeled on Clement T. Rice of the Virginia City *Union*.[10] Their mockery of a fellow newspaperman helps signal the appropriate interpretive frame—one of public kidding that demands skill in the caricature of the drunk's unconscious absurdities and befuddlement, one of presentation more than serious representation. The kind of caricature of drunks in music-hall variety shows, or perhaps also in the performance Twain saw by Billy O'Neil of a drunken Irishman,[11] would not have aimed at fidelity. The scene of the variety show, with its permeable boundary between performer and audience, and its absence of any pretension to an illusionistic re-creation of an anterior scene, metaphorically characterizes Twain's written performance. A greater stress fell on the rendering itself, on the ritualistic exchange within the subculture, on recreation rather than re-creation. The main appeal of the piece undoubtedly lay in the skillful put-down of a peer, the engagement of a prominent anxiety about making a fool of oneself in public, and the transgressive affront to gentility of displaying public drunkenness.

This dimension of skillful performance, mimicry, and ritual, however, existed always on a variable continuum; the extant written responses even to music-hall deadpan monologuists often enough chose to praise their "pathos" and "expression" rather than their posing. Even the comic drunkenness could add to its silly slurring some moments of unconscious self-exposure, the possibility opened by inebriation's supposed easing of all care in self-presentation. Figuratively straddling the proscenium, neither forthrightly in front of illusionistic space nor fully within it, the most popular deadpan performers also straddled the line between burlesque and serious representation. And this doubleness registered and echoed changes occurring as the middle class resecured the theater for itself—changes that included a stronger demarcation between low comedy and "legitimate" theater and a sharper distinction between a raucously presentational theater and the spectatorship of realism.

In tracing Mark Twain's predecessors, William Burton is especially important in this regard because he clearly became a token in this conflict of cultures and tastes. Although Burton was best known for the burlesques he and John Brougham put on in the 1850s for their mainly working-class audience at New York's Chambers Street Theatre, after his death in 1860 middle-class theater reviewers persistently remembered him for transcending burlesque caricature, for identifying with his characters, and for realistically representing pathos and "homely feeling." Whether or not Twain saw Burton himself in New York in 1853, Burton's famous role as the title character in *The Toodles* lay in the background of Twain's performance style; it was familiar enough nationally to generate imitators across the country, one of which Twain saw in St. Louis in 1853.[12] Especially influential was the best-known scene in which Timothy Toodles, quite drunk and absorbed in his drunken thoughts, mumbles a confused and associative monologue while he acts out other stage business: trying to light his pipe and failing, trying to put on his thumbless glove, dropping it, and falling when he tries to pick it up, and so on.[13] The critical clichés about "laughter and tears" and "humor and pathos," in this case, had special resonance in describing a performance poised between low variety and realism, public drunkenness and private revelation, male-only burlesque and a theater suited for the genteel.[14] Burton's Toodles was especially important, I would argue, for taking the familiar buffoonery of a drunk act and imbuing it with the kind of unconscious revelation and continuity of an interior life that elicited empathic responses. Not, of course, a representation of integral "character" in the older nineteenth-century sense of an identity contained through self-control, fortitude, and sober habit, Burton's Toodles nonetheless depicted a continuous and transparent psychic interior that saved a weaker sense of a unified self—one more fluid than lapidary, a kind of self better suited to accommodate and defuse the attacks on bourgeois selfhood welling up from the precincts of low theater.[15]

It was this kind of contradictory—and mediating—performance that accompanied Mark Twain to his first big national success, the 1865 publication of "Jim Smiley and His Jumping Frog."[16] In 1864 in Carson City, Nevada, Twain saw another performance of *The Toodles*, played by George Marsh of R. G. Marsh's Juvenile Comedians, who, Laurence Hutton recorded, acted "a miniature copy of Burton's Toodles."[17] Twain at this time was also a fan of a somewhat similar role that Burton had made famous, Captain Ned Cuttle in Brougham's dramatization of Dickens's *Dombey and Son*, a role again that was said to combine humor and tenderness, though the humorous absorption was more in old-salt garrulity than in drunken maunderings.[18] In 1865 Twain promoted and defended Dan Setchell's version of Cuttle, discounting the idea that it was not as well done as Burton's.[19] Edgar M. Branch's argument that Setchell's performance constituted a background for "Jim Smiley and His Jumping Frog" is exactly right, except that the theatrical context needs to be conceived more broadly, and we ought to use that context to help explain the popularity and significance of the "Jumping Frog" story.[20]

The traditional argument in the criticism of Twain's story, over whether Simon Wheeler is being a trickster or an innocent, manipulative or unselfconscious, is fundamental to my point. James Cox's assertion that Wheeler is guileless, "so absorbed in his own story" that he is practically unaware of his audience—an argument against the various interpreters who see a sly pose of simplicity used to get the better of a city slicker—puts Wheeler's storytelling in helpful theatrical terms.[21] For it is precisely a contrast between absorption and theatricality (to borrow an organizing opposition from Michael Fried) that is at work here.[22] Wheeler certainly looks as if he is fully absorbed, first in a somatic and nearly somnolent state of regressive, bodily comfort while "dozing comfortably by the bar-room stove" (282), and second in his story and in the associative processes of memory. Such unconsciousness and absorption might certify the "earnestness and sincerity" the narrator discerns in Wheeler. Nonetheless, a genealogy of rustic cunning and devilment would inevitably attach to this piece, a story Twain later called a "villainous backwoods sketch."[23] On the one hand, the frame narrator takes the stance of a detached spectator watching a psychological spectacle, as the associative, digressive, prelogical patterns of Wheeler's consciousness seemingly unfold, and Wheeler's apparent obliviousness to his listener nearly gives the sense of setting up a theatrical fourth wall to peer through. Yet there always hovers the suggestion, given the pokerface swindles and gambling betrayals in Wheeler's stories, that Wheeler's monologue is a conscious game rather than an unconscious self-revelation.

I do not mean to reduce the meaning of Twain's sketch to the ambiguity in it between solitary rumination and public dissimulation. Nor do I want to discount the inevitably multiple and diverse appeals of such a popular performance by overstressing the cultural service it may have performed in conjuring up tensions between interiors and exteriors, cozy hearths and public barrooms, guileless self-revelations and vulgar entertainments. But the patterns of response to the performers I have mentioned, and to Mark Twain's own performances, suggest that some of the most persistent terms through which reviewers, at least, received such acts turned on oppositions between humor and pathos, theatricality and absorption, trickery and sincerity. Whatever the complexities in significance, the meanings activated by reviewers dwelled on questions of representation—whether the act had a serious dimension, whether it inspired belief or not. Because these performances took place at a time of profound cultural change, when the theater graphically epitomized efforts to establish distinctions in taste partly by separating burlesque from illusion, these terms accrue both heightened significance and inevitability. Deadpan performance figured as a transitional form; although any popular performance arguably exists as a cultural battleground where competing ideological forces wrestle, the form of deadpan performance comprised both low humor and high pathos, both music-hall vulgarity and domestic sentiment, and therefore constituted a special terrain for conflict.

This conflict over popular culture emerges even more clearly in Mark Twain's deadpan lecturing and the responses to it. When Constance Rourke asserted that Twain's lecturing "was not truly lecturing at all but the old, spacious form of the theatrical monologue," she meant, properly, to link Twain's performances to stage Yankees and minstrels.[24] As several historians have pointed out, this kind of development—the importing of theatrical comedy, humorous monologuists, dramatic readers, and so on, into the previously staid lyceum lecture course—was new, coinciding with Twain's ascendance in popular consciousness.[25] Promoters and booking agents (especially James Redpath, Twain's manager in the late 1860s and the 1870s) countermanded the previous assumptions about public lecturing and made it a cause of sharp controversy, eliciting criticism from a variety of cultural guardians who deplored the appearance of "showmen," "humbugs and charlatans," and "clowns" behind the podium.[26] Especially noteworthy was an attack by Josiah G. Holland, first editor of *Scribner's Monthly* and a speaker on the lyceum circuit himself. Seemingly directed especially at Mark Twain, who wrote a never-sent rejoinder, Holland's denunciation of lecturing "jesters" and "buffoons" asserted that they had "no higher mission than the stage clown and negro-minstrel" and had therefore a "degrading influence on the public taste."[27]

The theater itself, and theatrical metaphors, had special currency in the battle over public taste and in the maintenance of cultural distinctions. Because Mark Twain situated himself on the border between the low and high, comparing his performances to the theater could cut both ways, serving even to impart respectability. Twain's platform humor was said, for example, to be above "the coarse and stale jests of the endman in the burnt-cork fraternity"; his audience was characterized in another instance as having only a few representatives of "the rowdy or 'fast' element congenial to negro minstrel exhibitions."[28] In any case, his performances made viewers think of stage shows, define cultural divides in terms of them, and take their sides. The terms of genteel evaluation often linked lower levels of class and taste not merely to minstrelsy and music hall, but also to theater itself, to whose level the instructional and edifying lecture was not supposed to descend. Nonetheless, a division endemic to the theater—between serious illusion and burlesque—surfaced continually in Twain's performances and in responses to them. For example, Twain again and again would provide what reviewers called "word pictures"—of Hawaii's Kilauea volcano, or of Lake Tahoe in Nevada—in a serious manner, as if he too were transported by the representation, only to "break the spell," as one reviewer put it, by pretending to forget a word, applauding himself, directing the audience to applaud, or commenting snidely on his skill at "harnessing adjectives together."[29]

Although reviewers persistently complained about the uncertainty in Twain's lecturing between earnestness and burlesque,[30] that uncertainty obviously was part of Twain's allure. James Cox's remark about Twain's deadpan is pertinent: that the anxious question of *"Is—is he humorous?"* and the final turn that puts the joke on us are "not a loss but a gain of pleasure."[31] But in the later nineteenth century that pivot swung between the respectable and the vulgar at a time when a great deal rode on defining the distinction; the cultural capital of an upwardly mobile theatergoer could multiply or go bust depending on where the line of taste was drawn. The pleasures of being entertainingly taken in, or of being uncertainly poised between belief and laughter, must have come partly from treating playfully the uneasiness about the sociocultural division echoed there. The idea that jokes "function" to release social tensions may too strongly imply that culture must work to stabilize social systems, or at least provide imaginary relief; that is, in looking for the comforting, this understanding of humor ignores the pleasures of vertigo, and in looking for versions of equilibrium, it discounts the immediacy of conflict. However, my point about Mark Twain is that, while his performances need not have "functioned" to imaginarily and symbolically ease social tensions—for, obviously, they consistently occasioned conflict—they had the capacity to do so. On the one hand, they echoed the existence and concerns of somewhat marginalized male subcultures; on the other, they did provide an equilibrium that suited more pervasive values. In particular, as we shall see, Twain's deadpan style provided a strong vehicle for easing minds in the northern middle class, one that enwrapped within a representation of a psychological interior the disseminations of burlesque.

In his best-known confessions about lecturing, Twain characterized his platform performances as skillful manipulations full of calculated humorous "effects"—for example, his use of the pause as the foremost "gun" in his "battery of artifice."[32] He might almost lead us to think that his performances exemplified joking effects and theatrical excess. But we must remember that his artifice primarily involved the mimicry of "the stammering amateur" and the "imitation of confusion," as Paul Fatout puts it.[33] Twain impersonated a vacant-minded, rambling, drawling, incoherent bumpkin. As Twain told manager James Redpath, "I rely for my effects on a simulated unconsciousness and intense absurdity."[34] The effects, in other words, issued from miming the effectless. He would walk on stage seemingly absorbed in thought, then startledly notice the audience—and there was the joke. But if apparent absorption was put in the service of effect, effect could also be subordinated to absorption. The seeming somnolence, laziness, drunkenness, and indolence that reporters noted in his drawling, his shuffle, and his lounging brought many of them to characterize his lectures as untheatrical, undramatic, moderate, quiet, subdued.[35] Ultimately the elements of effect, artifice, mimicry, burlesque, and variety could be viewed as embedded within an unselfconscious drawl and a bodily absorption, lessening the sense of vulgarity or theatricality, and heightening the sense of an artlessly unveiled self.

Body and voice served as unifiers in Twain's performances, working against the centrifugal force of comic masks and effects and serving as signs and expressions of a stable, continuous self. Although acknowledging Twain's sometimes abrupt or incoherent shifting from serious description to joke, or from anecdote to anecdote, critics would also remark on the continuously even "manner" or "tenor" of his voice as a means of making his lecture a "whole."[36] Such characterizations also suit Twain's well-known conception of a lecture as a unifying "narrative-plank" into which he could insert serious or humorous "plugs."[37] They suit even better his semifacetious "plan" for a "Patent Adjustable Speech," which would consist of a set of anecdotes, not related to each other or to the supposed topic of the speech. As long as the speaker embedded the anecdotes "in the midst of a lot of rambling and incoherent talk," "filling the air" with "a straight and uninterrupted stream of irrelevancies," the audience would not notice the discontinuities.[38] Apparent unity, continuity, and coherence—in both the speech and the speaker—emanated from the ever-rolling voice. The security of a continuous self rooted in voice and bodily manner, and the sense that it was being expressed despite the joking masks, flowed over the low jokes, the burlesque, the joshing.

The envelopment of vulgar burlesque and comic effects within a continuous "psychology" can perhaps be most easily grasped in its more extreme versions—the popular stage acting of Joseph Jefferson III, E. A. Sothern, and other such stars of the latter half of the nineteenth century. Reaching the heights of their success as theaters finally attracted large portions of the middle class, these actors refashioned variety-show caricatures into representations of psychology. They played characters absorbed in subdued states of reverie, confusion, absentmindedness, and drunkenness. In reaction against the older acting of "points" for "effect," and in accord with newer goals of depicting subtle gradations in interior states and expression, they aimed for a continuous registration of inner life and a "unified" economy of emotions and consciousness, a "consistency in characterization" and a "unity in conception" (to use the critical terms commonly applied). Combing low variety of its "coarseness," moving caricature behind the proscenium and subjecting it to the conventions of illusionistic space—particularly the ban on acknowledging the audience in any way—these actors fashioned a humorous performance that could be watched quietly and politely, that echoed its roots, but did so faintly enough so that the distressing incursions of vulgarity were palliated. And their performances provided models and analogues for Mark Twain's.

At the turn of the century, Laurence Hutton wrote that E. A. Sothern's Lord Dundreary "is no doubt better known in England and America than any other character on the stage or in fiction." Mark Twain gave some weight to that presently unbelievable assertion, remembering in his autobiography that when he first saw Sothern as Dundreary, probably in the late 1860s or early 1870s, it was "the funniest thing I had ever seen on the stage."[39] An eccentric, foppishly dressed Englishman with a lisp and a stammer, Sothern's Dundreary was criticized for being a stage type. Sothern himself, however, claimed "earnestness, intensity, and thorough identification" with his part—meaning, in this case, complete absorption in Dundreary's states of befuddlement.[40] And the weight of critical opinion praised Sothern's enactments of Dundreary's disorganized consciousness. A split hair in his whiskers, or a search for his trousers pocket, would sidetrack and absorb Dundreary, making him forget his own line of talk and the presence and talk of all others. These moments, as well as other instances of distraction, association, digression, "confusions of intellect" and "collisions of trains of thought," while they were received as comedy, were psychologized until they could also be taken as revelations of "a genuine and convincing personality." "Even his extreme eccentricities," one critic wrote, "were soon accepted as innate, unconscious sincerities, not as conscious affectations."[41] The comic artifices that otherwise might have signified caricature garnered the aura that implied expression, individuality, revelation, and a self.

But the greatest success at seemingly unconscious humor through the portrayal of bewilderment and stupefaction belonged to Joseph Jefferson's acting of Rip Van Winkle.[42] Jefferson, as I mentioned earlier, first became famous for playing the unconsciously humorous Rip in the years that Twain's "Jumping Frog" story and his lecturing captured widespread attention. And the descriptions of Jefferson's Rip are remarkably like those of the storytelling Smiley and the lecturing Twain. As he first appeared in the play, the "lazy, good-natured, dissipated, good-for-nothing Dutchman" lounged about, speaking in a "low" and "gentle" voice, and seemingly immersed in bodily comfort and pleasure—partly the product of drunkenness. He would talk "half to himself" and become "plunged in thought." In his conversation with others he would "[lose] the thread of his discourse." Rip even told stories, in a rambling and drunken way, including one about a bull who pitched him over a fence, which resembles the manner and implied incident of Jim Blaine's drunkenly told and maundering "Story of the Old Ram" in *Roughing It,* a story that became one of Twain's platform favorites.[43] Jefferson specialized in representing a lazily unfolding consciousness which, far from a set of comic "turns," attained what Howells called a "unified characterization" that "naturally appealed to the realistic sensibility."[44]

He took what had been a caricatured Dutchman—a shrewd-but-foolish Yankee-like variety-stage figure with an overlay of Dutch dialect and mannerisms—and placed it in the space of illusion. "He has that seeming unconsciousness of his audience which is the peculiar possession of actors of the first class," according to one reviewer. His acting appeared completely real, the critic of *The Nation* wrote in 1869, "as if there were no footlights, no audience, no orchestra, no scenery, no prompter. He seems unaware of his audience's presence. He is thoroughly filled with his part."[45] The centripetal enclosing of this illusionistic space continued with a focus on Rip and his interior. The portrayal of Rip especially after his awakening from his twenty-year sleep was characterized as "an extremely refined psychological exhibition." Jefferson was said to use facial expressions effectively as a means of showing Rip's bewilderment and his efforts to "reassemble his ideas and memories," "to reconcile incongruities," and "to join the past to the present, and to comprehend his prolonged slumber."[46] Jefferson himself said his aim was to show "the condition of [Rip's] mind," and the stage directions of the play stressed Rip's wonderment and puzzlement, his tendency to drift off into dream and reverie.[47]

The issues that the story of Rip Van Winkle always dealt with, especially the tension between a male world of drink and recreation and a domesticated home, were amplified in Jefferson's performance—this time, however, with the signals of raucous male theater subordinated to the values of pathos and sentiment, just as caricature was subordinated to the expression of the interior. "There is much humor in all of this," one reviewer wrote, "but it is of a subdued kind, and tenderly blended with pathos."[48] Rip's imbecility, another wrote, "would excite only ridicule and laughter in the hands of an artist less gifted";[49] but Jefferson accomplished a "transparency" in representation "that, now, is entirely changed from what it used to be in the old days" of low comedy. He managed "to elevate a prosaic type of good-natured indolence into an ideal of poetical freedom."[50] Jefferson's performance became an occasion for distinguishing between higher and lower cultures. Cleansed of vulgarity, erasing its kinship to minstrelsy and variety comedy, "without a suspicion of the least pandering to degraded tastes," Jefferson's acting was even said "to work a refining influence upon the stage and upon the tastes of the dramatic public."[51] Here was a deadpan style with a difference, an unconscious humor distanced enough from its origins really to require a different name.

The simultaneous emergence of Jefferson's Rip Van Winkle and Mark Twain's lecturing persona helps to underscore their kinship, the similar conditions and traditions from which they emerged, and the analogous cultural operations they performed. Even though Twain's "performances" took place in print and at the podium, they were similarly rooted in low-culture caricature, and they made the same trip as Jefferson's Rip to the national stage. The connection, however, can be more surely secured by noting the influence Jefferson's and Sothern's performances exerted over Twain's one successful play, *Colonel Sellers* (1874)—a work that deserves a more central place in accounts of Twain's writing.[52] The play was a transformation of *The Gilded Age* that focused on Colonel Sellers, much in the same way that Sothern transformed *Our American Cousin* into *Lord Dundreary*, and Owens enlarged the Yankee character in *The People's Lawyer* into *Solon Shingle*. And though Twain denigrated it as "simply a *setting* for the one character, Col. Sellers," a framework "to hang Col. Sellers on, & maybe even damn him,"[53] its success, and the money it drew in, led him to fantasize that *Colonel Sellers* would run "twenty years . . . like Jo [*sic*] Jefferson's 'Rip Van Winkle' and John E. Owens' 'Solon Shingle.' "[54]

The cultural importance of *Colonel Sellers* ought to be reiterated. Howells immediately declared, in his 1875 review in the *Atlantic Monthly*, that John T. Raymond's performance put him among the "realistic actors" he most admired, including Sothern and Jefferson.[55] Like Jefferson as Rip or Sothern as Dundreary, Raymond as Sellers was said to be "the most popular comedian on the American stage," or at least "one of the most popular men in the profession," an actor who, in this role, "attained the greatest vogue that any comedian of his day has known."[56] If Jefferson and Sothern derived humor from their characters' absorption in befuddlement, Raymond, somewhat differently, exploited Sellers's absorption in his visions and gar-rulity—though a key scene in which Sellers gets drunk on his patent-medicine "eye-water" surely recalled Jefferson as the befuddled and drunken Rip, and Burton as the befuddled and drunken Toodles. Ul-timately, Raymond's portrayal of Sellers hit a special chord, for re-viewers saw a doubleness in Sellers that matched a doubleness in the acting. Sellers, in the common summary, combined traits of the vi-sionary projector and the swindling exploiter, of the sincere southern gentleman and the con man, but his chicanery was cancelled because he apparently believed in it. As Brander Matthews said of Sellers on stage, he "is as honest as may be and as sincere, and he deceives him-self quite as much as he deceives his neighbor."[57] The quality of be-lieving in one's lies characterized Raymond's performance, too, the reviewers insisted. A "genuine and steady earnestness" pervaded the performance, and, the *New York Times* suggested, Raymond him-self seemed to believe in Sellers's projects, so that both Sellers's lis-teners and the theater audience were deceived into belief.[58]

The doubleness in Sellers between manipulating dissimulator and earnest believer, in other words, corresponded to the doubleness in Raymond's performance between actor and realistic embodiment. A similar resonance, of course, had existed in some degree in all ver-sions of the deadpan style; even the early Yankee performances made cunning and revelation central to both character and enact-ment. In the commentary on Sellers, however, the vocabulary that surrounded deadpan characters and performers was especially persistent and explicit. Some reviewers, including the *Times* re-viewer, saw Raymond's performance as "sympathetic as well as com-ical," the "eccentricities of speech and manner" rendered with so much earnestness, and so little self-consciousness, that the perfor-mance was both "far closer to the truth of nature" *and* "far more en-tertaining than *Lord Dundreary*." Sellers's "wildest exentricities [*sic*]" were subsumed into a believable character.[59] Other critics took the doubleness as occasion to rehearse the conflict over taste, so that Ray-mond was sometimes denigrated as a representative of "the broader phases of American humor" or of "noisy comedy," a comedy of "tech-nical skill" and raucous "by-play" that lacked the subtleties of taste-ful theater.[60] Conversely, he was sometimes praised for a full identi-fication with his role, or rather for such a congruence between his own "sanguine" personality and Sellers's that it was "difficult to tell where art ceases and where nature commences." This quality brought reviewers to characterize Raymond's performance as "of a better and higher type than any humorous part now upon the stage."[61]

Raymond's performance of Sellers helps to clarify the cultural tensions invoked by the oppositions used in theatrical discourse to place and evaluate deadpan performance. "Technical skill," raucous jokes, and caricatures, joined to Sellers's predilection for speculation and patent-medicine salesmanship, would call into play the two territories that, in Victorian ideology, held the greatest symbolic threat to the bourgeois home: working-class male entertainments and the male marketplace. The actor's identification with the character, the unconscious display of psychological spectacle, and pathos, joined to Sellers's sincere belief in his projecting visions and the earnestness of his meandering monologues, would induce associations valuable to middle-class domesticity: interiority, transparency in self-revelation, tender emotion. Mark Twain thought of Sellers in these terms, and criticized Raymond several times for overplaying the humorous "half" of the character, with the result that "the pathos is knocked clear out of the thing."[62] Sellers, in Twain's conception, was "a pathetic and beautiful spirit," whose "big, foolish, unselfish heart" was beyond Raymond's grasp.[63] But, again, the powerful significance of this performance of Sellers lay in the point of contention, in the terms brought into conjunction: humor *and* pathos, heterogeneous comic eccentricities *and* psychological unity, low comedy *and* high realism. And if these terms occasioned and reflected contention, they could also be the opportunity for reassurances. Brander Matthews, for example, asserted that Sellers's excesses, in the hands of Raymond, "were rounded into a harmonious whole, and the character itself was shown to be simple and strong behind all its eccentricities."[64]

It is no accident, I believe, that Mark Twain began *Huckleberry Finn* in 1876, not long after the success of *Colonel Sellers*, and returned to the novel in 1883, around the time he worked on another play about Sellers—*Colonel Sellers as a Scientist*, an unsuccessful collaboration with Howells. Twain's sense, derived from the success of the first Sellers play, of his own gift for creating character and unconsciously humorous monologue, rather than plot, was once again fully realized in Huck's storytelling. Even more significant, Huck reproduces the cultural and ideological stakes I have outlined in deadpan performance. Mark Twain fashioned Huck, a "liminal" adolescent and a representative of hordes of young men newly free of village and family guidance, into a vehicle for worrying the categories the northern middle class used to order its territory—the public and the private, market and hearth, the crowds in the street and the genteel home. Far from being a rogue fully outside of the safe precincts, however, Huck, with Jim, re-creates a home on the raft, a place of tenderness, sincerity, intimate disclosure, and domestic tranquility. Huck's character embodies the contradictions between behavior for crowds and private revelation, lies and sincerity, "masculine" impassivity and "female" expression.

These central dimensions to Huck's character have important implications for his storytelling. A boy with an impulse to dissimulate but a propensity for self-betrayal, and an unconsciously humorous narrator with effects of low comedy embedded in a rolling and self-absorbed monologue, Huck reproduces, both in his self-representation and in the act of representing, the dynamic of the deadpan style crucial to its popularity. But Twain's Huck, perhaps the subtlest rendering of the style, also serves to teach us about deadpan performance. For example, the significance of the prominent *bodily* self-absorption of the deadpan comics—in somnolence, laziness, or drunkenness—becomes clearer in Huck's case, and its own duality surfaces.

Huck's striking absorption in his bodily states—sleeping, eating, dozing, "lazing"—serves, as with Jefferson's Rip and Sothern's Dundreary, to corroborate the unselfconsciousness that in turn helps certify the immediacy of their self-revelations. His predilection to immerse himself in private bodily comforts echoes his similar immersion in memory and in easygoing storytelling; his apparent unconcern in each case for the outside world, including the world of audiences, lessens any sense of artistry or dissimulation. But if this private, bodily self-engrossment seems to collude with the psychological revelation of his storytelling—both of them enhancing Huck's dimension of personal consciousness and domestic intimacy—we also have to remember that Huck's absorptions have a value of excess and irresponsibility. Dozing on the raft is a self-indulgence made possible by escape from Widow Douglas's, by an evasion of the feminine, of "home."

Huck's combination of intimate revelation and rebellious self-indulgence helps to explain the prominence of drunken states in deadpan performance. An apparent guarantee of unselfconscious revelation, drunkenness also signified male excess. A state, in the cases of Rip or Toodles, that allowed an audience to peer into a mind whose self-censorship had been eased, it also signaled unbridled male pleasure. In this light, *any* of the self-absorbed states represented in deadpan performance were two-faced. Intimate, self-revelatory embodiments of individual consciousness that seemed to suit the personal domains not only of the feminine home but also of the newly enclosed space of theatrical illusion, they also invoked a disorderly indulgence that violated the *order* associated with the domestic sphere and the box set of the middle-class theater. They raised the specter of the tavern and the minstrel hall.

The blank face, the unconscious humor, the bodily absorption—*all* of these dimensions of deadpan performance replayed contesting cultural values. Each raised an anxiety about self-exposure, with its imperative to conceal, and an anxiety about dissimulation, with its requirement of sincerity. Each rehearsed the ideological categories that sorted out the American cultural and social terrain, invoking on the one hand a territory of swindlers and jokers, contests of humiliation and dominance, and theaters of vulgar masking and ridicule, and on the other hand safer spaces of domestic tranquility, psychological integrity and depth, and transparency of expression. These categories resonated with divisions of class, gender, and taste. Because the various versions of deadpan performance conjured up these worrisome divisions, this style of unconscious humor secured its gigantic place in late-nineteenth-century popular entertainment. A supple form, it could be put to various uses for its various audiences. If, in the hands of Twain, Jefferson, Sothern, and the other mass-cultural stars, the vulgar mimicry and disrespect of the deadpan seemed ultimately to embed itself in proper unities of character and psychology, thereby smoothing the cultural rifts invoked, laughter was still possible. The example of Mark Twain demonstrates both the powerful consolidation of middle-class self-consciousness in the 1860s and the pockets of trouble and difference that resounded in the deadpan style.

3

"Absorb the Character"
Acting and "Authenticity"

In the 1880s and the 1890s, when dramatic readings by authors had been established as a fashion and a staple of the lecture circuit, Mark Twain frequently "acted" his works at the lectern. This was especially the case during his reading tour with George Washington Cable in the 1884 to 1885 season. As he polished his delivery, Twain later recalled, he kept in the back of his mind the readings he had seen by Dickens in 1867—highly theatrical events, with the black-suited Dickens against a red background, brightly lit while his audience "sat in a pleasant twilight," a separation further underscored by Dickens's refusal to acknowledge his audience. "It will be understood," wrote Twain, "that he did not merely read but also acted," gesturing, modulating his voice, riveting his spectators. After a week of readings with Cable, however, Twain decided that it was not sufficient "to do like Dickens—get out on the platform and read from the book." Instead, Twain memorized his passages. When reading from a text, he explained, "You are a mimic, and not the person involved; you are an artificiality, not a reality; whereas in telling the tale without the book you absorb the character, just as in the case of an actor."[1]

A different aspiration from that of deadpan performance, this aim of obliterating the gap between artist and creation, performer and character, had pertinence for Twain, of course, beyond the genre of dramatic readings. This was especially true for the Mark Twain of this period, who by the 1880s had a claim to literary credentials, but could still be beset with the anxiety, as he reportedly (perhaps apocryphally) said to Cable, that he was "demeaning" himself on the lecture platform, "allowing myself to be a mere buffoon" instead of a serious artist.[2] The concerns here—between mimicry and identification, detachment and absorption, and the artificial and the real— were crucial questions now for Mark Twain as a "realist" writer, as a depicter of characters he evaluated according to their "authenticity," and they were rehearsed again and again in his writings, especially in the 1880s and thereafter.

These concerns bore upon a host of questions about representation: how an actor or writer could represent another person, what conscious or unconscious processes enabled such representation, what kinds of selves were best suited to represent other selves, and whether an artist could represent people of other classes, genders, and races. They resurrected, of course, old arguments over whether acting (or dramatic reading, or writing) properly flowed from the heart or from the head, from inner resources of emotion and character or from fabrication and calculation. Mark Twain's versions of these disputes, however, drew upon contemporary reconceptualizations of emotional expression and "character" and, ultimately, on changing cultural conceptions of the self. The ways in which habit, repetition and "practice," automatisms, and other unconscious processes constituted both expression and character, and circumvented mimicry and artificiality in art, became preoccupations, as we shall see, in *Huckleberry Finn* (1884), *A Connecticut Yankee* (1889), and *Pudd'nhead Wilson* (1894). Not coincidentally, the 1880s saw a renewed and heightened debate over these questions among actors and critics Mark Twain knew and in the magazines of the middle-class and genteel cultures he was embracing. The debate over acting reverberated with Twain's concerns about realistic and credible representation.

For a long time before this debate of the 1880s, Mark Twain seemingly subscribed to the general tenets of absorbed acting—that serious actors ought to feel the emotions they portray, should identify with the characters they embody, and must dramatize parts of themselves on stage. In 1853, when the young Samuel Clemens saw Edwin Forrest in *The Gladiator,* he thought the last part of the play was "splendid" because, in portraying "the fierce pleasure of gratified revenge" as Spartacus battles the Roman murderers of his family and then falls mortally wounded, Forrest's "whole soul seems absorbed in the part he is playing; and it is really startling to see him."[3] Through at least the 1860s Twain remained a staunch defender of Forrest and his acting, though by the mid-1880s he agreed with the general opinion that Forrest's "startling" moments displayed theatrical overexertion rather than convincing absorption.[4] By the 1880s, of course, the "quieter" and "realistic" style of the sentimental comedians—Joseph

Jefferson as Rip Van Winkle, E. A. Sothern as Lord Dundreary—had supplanted Forrest's romantic style in the premier theaters as well as in Twain's esteem. But the terms of identification remained in force as criteria for evaluating such performances. Importantly, these terms shaped the understanding Twain had of the performance of his own effort in sentimental comedy, the wildly successful play *Colonel Sellers* (1874). As noted in the previous chapter, scholars have not pursued the impact of its success on Mark Twain's work, perhaps because the play has not been readily available.[5] But, I would like to reemphasize, because it set Twain off on a course of playwriting—five plays between 1877 and 1884, often written with particular actors in mind, plus several unhatched playwriting projects—it deserves reevaluation as a formative moment in Twain's career.[6]

The remarks of Twain and his friend William Dean Howells about the performance of Colonel Sellers by John T. Raymond hinge on the opposition that would garner so much attention in the 1880s: whether actors ought to efface themselves, indeed suppress themselves, so that they might serve as transparent mediums for an artist's conception, or whether they must draw on their own experience, character, and emotion, capitalizing on personal resources in order to "realize" the text. In the first flush of success of *Colonel Sellers,* both Twain and Howells praised Raymond for subordinating himself to Twain's conception, erasing himself for the sake of Sellers. Twain acknowledged that Raymond had "faithfully reproduced the Sellers that is in the book."[7] And Howells, in his review of the play in the *Atlantic Monthly,* declared that Raymond "does not merely represent; he becomes, he impersonates, the character he plays. The effect is instant; he is almost never Raymond from the moment he steps upon the stage till he leaves it"; Raymond's "assumption of Sellers" is "perfect," with the result that Twain's conception of the character is "interpreted without loss by the actor."[8]

But when, as Twain put it, Raymond adopted the idea from reviewers that *he* had "taken a vague suggestion from the novel & by his genius created a fine original character from it," both Twain and Howells emphasized different terms of evaluation.[9] Howells, to console Twain, pointed to the part of his review criticizing Raymond for overplaying the "absurdity" of Sellers and missing "the tenderness of the man's heart"; "We are loath to believe," the review said, that Raymond "is not himself equal to showing it" (751). Twain seconded

Howells's remark; Raymond *"can't* do a pathetic thing," he declared, for "he isn't man enough."[10] And Twain later asserted that "only half" of Colonel Sellers was portrayed on stage—the laughable, not the pathetic, half. "Raymond could not play the other half of him; it was above his level."[11] The idea that an actor must subordinate himself to an author's conception remains in place, but instead of mediumistically erasing the self, the actor here must dramatize the proper inner resources in order to realize the author's conception. If the author's conception is larger than the actor's self, if it includes features of character or aspects of experience the actor lacks, the representation will fail.

These were essentially the terms around which the debate of the 1880s waged. The most important instigator of this debate was the English translation in 1883 of Denis Diderot's *Paradox of Acting* (written 1773–78). Diderot's basic view—that an actor ought to remain unmoved in order to elicit emotion from an audience—was elaborated, with more or less agreement, in essays by two French actors, the 1881 English translation of Benoit Constant Coquelin's 1880 essay, "Art and the Actor," and the English reprinting in 1883 of François Joseph Talma's 1825 essay, "Reflexions on Acting." Diderot's view was contradicted, however, by the English actor Sir Henry Irving, who argued in his prefaces to the 1883 editions of Diderot and Talma that actors, at least to some degree, must experience the emotions they represent. Four years later, in 1887, Coquelin, Irving, the actor-director Dion Boucicault, and Henry James (the actors, at least, were friendly acquaintances of Twain's during the late 1880s)[12] published essays—in *Harper's Monthly, Nineteenth Century,* the *North American Review,* and *Harper's Weekly*—engaging the question of whether actors should identify with their roles. And William Archer wrote a series of important articles in *Longman's Magazine,* collected in 1888 into *Masks or Faces? A Study in the Psychology of Acting,* which countermanded Diderot's argument and placed these questions of acting into a more modern frame—by introducing into the debate contemporary theories of the unconscious, automatism, and multiple levels of consciousness.[13]

Mapping the positions in this argument is necessary for understanding Twain's deliberations over acting in his fiction and composing. For Diderot, absorption in a role and actually feeling the emotions portrayed were the road to failure not only because emotions unleashed were undisciplined by art, but also because actors who relied on their own feelings and character would have a narrow repertoire. They would fall short, as Twain and Howells thought Raymond fell short, of being able fully to embody a great writer's conception. The best actors, in Diderot's view, would be able to mimic any of "the outward signs of feeling" (19), even if they were incapable of feeling them, and could therefore realize conceptions created by authors who had experience and imagination beyond their own. The crucial faculty for imitation works best when the actor's "own special shape never interferes with the shapes he assumes" (41), and such interference is best surmounted by people who do not have much of a self to begin with (46). Diderot's endorsement of the emotionless and characterless mimic raised objections, naturally enough, from the actor Irving, who thought that emotion and character were most realistic when they were expressions of inner condition; felt emotion, sympathy, strong "personality," and full "being" were assets for an actor.[14] Instead of effacing themselves, actors benefited from relying on their own characters. The more there was to a person—the more experiences, emotions, observations, and impressions that had become "a part of his being" (Talma, *Reflexions,* 2)—the better the actor.

While this outline of the debate provides my frame for grasping Mark Twain's engagement of acting in his fiction of the 1880s and 1890s, Twain pushed these issues in more complicated directions, directions that are best laid out in Archer's *Masks or Faces? A Study in the Psychology of Acting.* Although I have no particular evidence that Twain read *Masks or Faces,* Archer serves as the perfect template for configuring Twain's ideas about acting and representation, because Archer was so attuned to the developments in physiology and psychology that were imbuing Twain's conceptions of representation and performance.[15] The strongest line of argument Archer presented against Diderot's contention that the best actor consciously and detachedly manipulates the body to mimic emotion lay in his assertion that human means of emotional expression are not all subject to conscious control. Drawing on Charles Darwin, who characterized most emotional expressions as innate, products of inbred survivalist habits, Archer wrote that our "simple emotions" (grief, joy, rage, terror, shame) are expressed "directly and unmistakably," and often irrepressibly, in "physical manifestations" (101), and many of these bodily symptoms "cannot be imitated by mere action of the will" (219). In addition, because the more "complex" emotions, those of learned rather than instinctual habits, are often expressed "through the medium of the simple emotions," the more or less involuntary manifestations of these emotions are "the raw material of expression" (101–2).

Because of the direct and automatic nature of much emotional expression, Archer concludes, most actors believe that feeling the emotion, then letting the expression flow from it, is more effective than trying to mimic and police all the facial and gestural details of expression (220). Imaginatively felt emotion, he writes, "can readily bring about minute yet expressive changes, muscular and vascular, which the unaided action of the will is powerless to effect" (225), and without which the expression is easily detected as mechanical and artificial (115). Moreover, the process by which imaginatively felt emotions "communicate themselves to the nerve-centres of the actor" and "affect his organs of expression" so closely resembles the action of actual feeling "that it is surely illogical to deny the 'reality' of this mimetic emotion" (224–25). Archer ends his study by distinguishing between "mimicking tricks or habits and yielding to emotional contagion." "Roughly speaking," he concludes, "the one is an affair of the surface, the other of the centres" (218).

Clearly enough, Mark Twain's concern with such automatisms, with unconscious mechanisms of expression, preceded Archer's exposition of them. An instance in *The Adventures of Tom Sawyer* (1876), for example, exemplifies the point that imagined feeling generates expression that far surpasses mimicry. Disinclined to go to school, and having heard of a patient whose "mortified" finger laid him up for a couple of weeks, Tom Sawyer lies in bed in the morning groaning and fancying "that he began to feel pain in the toe." Moaning away, *trying* to wake his brother Sid—sharply attuned, in other words, to his mimicking and to his audience—Tom finds himself "panting with exertions"; fabricating the false outer expressions of inner pain is work, and unconvincing partly because of the transparency of this labor. But this condition changes after he has awakened Sid and sent him for help: "Tom was suffering in reality now, so handsomely was his imagination working, and so his groans had gathered quite a genuine tone." Tom's efforts at acting the part ultimately lead to identification and an imaginative self-deception that change the reality of

Tom's inner condition and render the false expression seemingly authentic (though in this case Aunt Polly, initially worried about the groans, immediately laughs at the story of mortification).[16]

A somewhat similar instance occurs in *The Prince and the Pauper* (1881), as Tom Canty's boyish play of imagining himself a prince ultimately works "such a strong effect upon him that he began to *act* the prince, unconsciously"—in a kind of automatic response to his imaginings—and he gains the admiration of his fellows.[17] And the circumstance reappears in *Huckleberry Finn* (1884), as the king, disguised as Harvey Wilks, tries to explain why his handwriting and that of his brother fail to match letters from the Wilkses, and he "warmed up and went warbling and warbling right along, till he was actly beginning to believe what he was saying, *himself.*"[18] In each case, after some warmup, these actors submerge in their roles, deceive themselves into believing in their new characters, and gain in credibility (even if they cannot manage to fool everyone). As William Archer argued, it is precisely the *automatic* expression of a newly imagined subjective reality that makes the role-playing credible. Emotion finds expression in ensembles of symptoms that exceed the supervisory capacities of consciousness and the will.

But if this idea seemed clear enough to Twain, a host of problems nonetheless accompanied it. What, after all, were the limits of such imaginative identification? None of these characters—Tom Sawyer, Tom Canty, and the king—had experience in their roles. Tom Sawyer had merely heard about the intense pain from a mortified finger; Tom Canty had merely read about being a prince; and the king had launched off into full-blown fabulation, starting from a flimsy, secondhand sketch of the Wilks brothers. If credible emotional expression involved automatic, unconscious, habitual bodily manifestations—symptoms of inner condition that could be activated by imaginative identification—then were there not limits, both in one's capacity to imagine another person and in one's repertoire of habitual circuits of expression? In the well-known instances of Huckleberry Finn's role-playing, Twain exactly sets out to examine these questions. At issue, seemingly, is whether an irreducible bodily and psychological self can be located—as a complex of emotion, memory, nerves, reflex, and habit—that would both enable and limit the imaginative identification of acting. Twain sets up extreme cases for Huck—acting a girl and acting runaway boys—in order to clarify the matter.

When Huck decides to masquerade as a girl as part of his recon-
naissance mission ashore, he makes his project one of conscious effort and mimicry. Dressed in a girl's gown and bonnet, he "practiced
around all day to get the hang of the things," and, thanks to Jim's
coaching, learns to walk less like a boy and manages to repress his
impulse to pull up the gown to get at his pants pocket (67). When
he finally gets to Loftus's, Huck tells us, "I . . . made up my mind
I wouldn't forget I was a girl." But Huck's conscious resolution
does not stop him from automatically blurting out a defense of Jim
against the charge that he murdered Huck (though he stifles this before Loftus seems to notice). He also fidgets because he is uneasy,
looks afraid and uncomfortable when Loftus eyes him suspiciously,
shakes like a leaf when she accuses him, and, of course, decisively betrays himself by his boy-gestures of catching the bar of lead between
his knees rather than in his lap, throwing the lead overhand, and
threading a needle by bringing the eye to the thread. The point,
clearly enough, is that conscious mimicry does not work, and the automatic and habitual expressions of emotion and character *do*. For as
hard as he tries, Huck cannot consciously police his automatic responses, and Loftus is able to discern, in his involuntary fidgeting
and shaking and in the habitual boy-movements that flow automatically from his identity, that he is a male in female clothing. Huck's
experience and habits are far enough away from a girl's to prevent
him from identifying and then letting the expressions emanate from
that identification. The fact that Huck is more believable as George
Peters (the identity he adopts after Loftus finds him out) further suggests that credible role-playing is enhanced by imaginative identification enabled by common experience; "George's" orphanage, his
escape from cruel treatment, his traveling by night, and so on, resonate with Huck's identity. Indeed, whenever Huck can identify so
that his expression, be it physical or verbal, can "flow" automatically,
whenever he can rely on "instinct" to put words in his mouth (279)—
as when he plays the roles of George Jackson and Tom Sawyer—he
elicits belief.

In *A Connecticut Yankee in King Arthur's Court*, Mark Twain again
explicitly revives these issues, most particularly in the section in
which, with Hank Morgan as acting coach, Arthur prepares to travel
the kingdom disguised as a peasant.[19] The structure of the situation—which echoes Jim's serving as Huck's acting coach—helps to

signal us that Twain is returning to similar problems of expression and representation. And, indeed, the section begins exactly with the opposition between a drilled and self-conscious mimicry of external signs of identity and an automatic and unconscious revelation of inner being. But, almost as if Twain had indeed read Archer's recent writings, the terms and implications of this opposition between mimicry and absorption, drill and identification, are here more fully laid out. And before the section is over, the issues are complicated in an Archer-like way, as Twain introduces notions of analogous, rather than identical, sympathetic states, and multiple, rather than exclusively absorbed or detached, states of consciousness.

Hank Morgan insists at the start that if Arthur is to travel England incognito, he must be "deliberately and conscientiously drilled," or "the very cats would know this masquerader for a humbug and no peasant" (320). But Huck's problem pops up: disguise, drill, and practice do not suffice, because the obscured and repressed interior persists and resurfaces. While Hank can get Arthur's clothes and face to look properly bedraggled, his "soldierly stride" and "lordly port" betray him. "You stand too straight, your looks are too high, too confident," Hank explains. "The cares of a kingdom do not stoop the shoulders, they do not droop the chin, they do not depress the high level of the eyeglance, they do not put doubt and fear in the heart and hang out the signs of them in slouching body and unsure step. It is the sordid cares of the lowly born that do these things" (320). As Hank has it, in other words, inner, "sordid cares" are directly and reliably manifested in the bodily signs of a peasant. This is a question of natural expression; droops and stoops unconsciously and automatically expose doubt and fear. Although Hank declares that Arthur "must learn the trick; you must imitate the trade-marks of poverty, misery, oppression, insult, and the other several and common inhumanities that sap the manliness out of a man and make him a loyal and proper and approved subject," the "trick," if it merely involves consciously imitating trademarks, apparently will not work. A peasant's body will express a peasant's inner being, and Arthur's body will persistently, and unconsciously, betray his kingship.

Hank eventually makes a distinction that reproduces Archer's contrast between "mimicking tricks or habits" as "an affair of the surface" and "yielding to emotional contagion" as an affair "of the centres." After more efforts to train the king to lower his chin, look at the ground, and shamble, Hank declares:

"Now then—your head's right, speed's right, shoulders right, eyes right, chin right, gait, carriage, general style right—everything's right! And yet the fact remains, the aggregate's wrong. The account don't balance. Do it again, please. . . . *now* I think I begin to see what it is. . . . You see, the genuine spiritlessness is wanting; that's what's the trouble. It's all *amateur*—mechanical details all right, almost to a hair; everything about the delusion perfect, except that it don't delude." (321)

Even when Arthur's conscious efforts actually succeed in policing the expressive details in his deportment, he fails to be credible. Only the unconscious and automatic expression that integrates expressive details by linking them all to an inner core of identity and feeling promises success. Arthur presents externals unconnected to a "genuine" source, studied bodily signs unanchored in interior life, a body-machine without the ghost, or spirit—or spiritlessness—that would animate it.

Hank's solution, in order to transform the king from an "amateur" actor into one who will delude, is to work on Arthur's interior—to get the right feeling and to hope that the external details will come by themselves. "Now, make believe you are in debt," he exhorts the king, "and eaten up by relentless creditors; you are out of work— which is horse-shoeing, let us say—and can get none; and your wife is sick, your children are crying because they are hungry" (323). This work of the imagination, however, proves equally unsuccessful. Tom Sawyer may be able to imagine himself into real suffering, and Tom Canty may be able to imagine himself into a credible version of a prince. But, like Huck's failure as a girl, Arthur cannot "be" a peasant. He simply does not have the inner wherewithal, the experiences and memories, that would enable identification. Hank concludes that his coaching of Arthur's imagination "was only just words, words,— they meant nothing in the world to him, I might just as well have whistled. Words realize nothing, vivify nothing to you, unless you have suffered in your own person the thing which the words try to describe" (324–25). Here, successful acting *does* depend on the actor's self, on its resources and limitations, rather than on its ductility and imitative skill. But having to draw on one's self in order to embody another does, too, quite practically limit the repertoire.

Arthur's ensuing misadventures as a peasant would seem at first simply to underscore this lesson. Hank must always worry that the king will unconsciously betray his identity by saying something "in a style a suspicious shade or so above his ostensible degree," and

Hank must deal continually with instances in which the king "had forgotten himself again" (316); as an actor, Arthur simply "can't remember more than about half the time" that he is "letting on to be something else" (355). Continuously effective conscious control over his bearing eludes Arthur, and uncontrollable expressions of his identity constantly glimmer through. But the king *does* have a success, one that follows partly from an automatic response of sympathy, of identification. When Hank and Arthur, in the peasant hut, watch the smallpox-infected mother kissing her young daughter and cooing over her, both Hank and the woman see "tears well from the king's eyes, and trickle down his face." The old woman says, "Ah, I know that sign: thou'st a wife at home, poor soul, and you and she have gone hungry to bed, many's the time, that the little ones might have your crust; you know what poverty is, and the daily insults of your betters, and the heavy hand of the Church and the king." Hank notes that the king "winced under this accidental home-shot, but kept still; he was learning his part; and he was playing it well, too, for a pretty dull beginner" (332). What he has "learned" and "played" well is partly the conscious suppression of his own kingly, automatic response to insult; he keeps still and does not betray his true identity. But he has also been mistaken for a genuine peasant because of his sympathetic, unwilled tears. He *does* delude here.

The larger implication for acting and fiction making is at least twofold: first, that credible role-playing indeed involves identification in which "real" emotion, upwelling practically unconsciously, manifests itself in those small, not completely voluntary, and therefore seemingly authentic "signs" such as tears—but that such identification need not rest on absolute identity. Arthur apparently can elicit the response of a tearful parent without being an oppressed, peasant parent by generalizing and analogizing his feelings. Talma had declared that "the man of the world and the man of the people, so opposite in their language, frequently express the great agitations of the mind in the same way. . . . Each puts off the artificial man to become natural and true." As an illustration, he noted, the emotional expression of a mother "looking on the empty cradle of a child she had just lost" will "represent the sorrow of a woman of the people the same as that of a duchess" (*Reflexions,* 16). While Mark Twain may have entertained such an idea that at the extremes of emotion humanity is one—Hank Morgan's frequent moments of sympathy with tortured slaves (199, 245, 390) and cruelly divided families (246, 337, 403) might suggest this—he clearly enough would have agreed with Archer that there can be "a close analogy between personal and mimetic emotion" (222), and that the memory of an emotion can mingle with and enliven a representation it (merely) resembles (130–38). That Arthur's fatherly emotion could be mistaken for empathy with the oppressed points the way to possibilities in duplicity that Twain would more fully explore in *Pudd'nhead Wilson*, as we shall see in a moment.

The second important implication of Arthur's successful "playing" of his "part" is that the conscious suppression of his kingly wince occurs along with his sympathetic emotional identification. The idea that in acting there is a dual consciousness, with felt emotion existing alongside a detached consciousness that can suppress discrepant signs and shape a performance, can be traced back for centuries in the persistent formulation that an actor ought to have a balance between spontaneity and premeditation, nature and art. Prior to writing the *Paradox*, Diderot, too, had believed in a balance between calculation and emotion and, in a conception based on the mind-body split, he thought that detached observation could coexist with bodily automatisms.[20] Both Coquelin and Talma wrote of an actor's "double personality" or "dual consciousness," both detached and involved, and in the 1880s it was an actor's commonplace to claim to act with a "warm heart and a cool head," with emotion and restraint, passion and composition.[21] But the later decades of the nineteenth century brought a new twist to the cliché as an emergent psychology and psychophysiology was brought to bear on the problem. Archer wrote of "double or treble strata of consciousness" (190) and of "the multiplex action of the mind whereby the accomplished actor is enabled to remain master of himself even in the very paroxysm of passion" (224). Automatic action of the nervous system coexisted with (and was often hard to distinguish from) "conscious or subconscious mental activity" (185–87). Claiming that "the total absorption in one mode of feeling which numbs the intellect and deadens the sense is of very rare occurrence in real life, and still rarer, of course, on the stage" (196), Archer argued that it was, however, a common thing to have "double and treble strata of mental activity" (224), detached and involved, rational and emotional, conscious and unconscious. His articulation of this psychology with theories of creativity and acting formed part of the discursive context for the division in King Arthur's successful acting between the flowing tears and the suppressed wince.

These uncertainties of representation and character seem to have loomed larger and larger for Mark Twain. His stretching of the bounds of resemblance in sympathetic identification, so that whatever basis Arthur may have had to weep can be mistaken for actual experience of oppression, clouded the aura of "authenticity." The search for the realism of the "genuine" by requiring that an actor's (or writer's) embodiment of it draw on actual experience and inner resources was undermined because the whole enterprise was based upon resemblance, upon analogies whose similarities could be stretched further and further, until the connection between the artist's reality and the represented reality was tenuous and weak. In addition, the security of identity that lay in the absorbed mode of acting was weakened by the acknowledgment of multiple "strata of consciousness." The irreducible core of identity that both Huckleberry Finn and King Arthur had, the basic substratum that prevented Huck from embodying a girl and Arthur from portraying a peasant, was shaken through this fragmentation of the self.

Pudd'nhead Wilson (1894) pursues these uncertainties doggedly, particularly through the role-playing of Roxy and her son and in ways that exacerbate Twain's shifting sands of character and representation.[22] Identities that are deposits of habit show themselves capable of erosion and reconfiguration. The capacity Mark Twain discovered in his dramatic readings of the 1880s for memorizing a part so that he "absorbed the character" is reproduced, with the effect that memorization, drill, and practice troublesomely transform artificialities into realities, transform one habit-based identity into another. The exhilaration in this for credible acting and fiction making—that one could *adopt* a role in such a way that it *became* an "affair of the centres" and would issue in natural and automatic expression— brought with it anxiety about the durability of the self and the fragility of reality. In the possibilities for believable role-playing lay anxieties about the effectiveness of duplicity.

Huck practices to be a girl only to find that his boy-self will come irrepressibly to the surface; Hank drills Arthur in the gait and attitudes of a peasant only to discover that such exercise fails to cover up the king's durable and insistent kingly self. But Roxy's experience seems completely to contradict the assumptions about character that underlie the unsuccessful role-playing of these fictional predecessors. In her case, after switching Tom and Chambers, she spends the night "practicing," treating her son like the master, the other baby like a slave:

> As she progressed with her practice, she was surprised to see how steadily and surely the awe which had kept her tongue reverent and her manner humble toward her young master was transferring itself to her speech and manner toward the usurper, and how similarly handy she was becoming in transferring her motherly curtness of speech and peremptoriness of manner to the unlucky heir of the ancient house of Driscoll. (16)

This is a virtual reprise of the drilling and practicing Huck and Arthur go through, but in Roxy's case the drilling works. It is true, of course, that Roxy has had "training" at being both slave and mother, and therefore has resources Huck did not have in playing a girl and Arthur did not have in trying to be peasantlike. It is nonetheless significant that Twain accentuates Roxy's *practice* and makes her "awe" transfer itself as a result of rote action and manner, rather than insisting that action and manner flow automatically from inner condition or a reimagined interior.

This causal reversal is underscored later, when Twain, in a well-known passage, reviews Roxy's accomplishment of installing her son in the role of Tom Driscoll:

> By the fiction created by herself, he was become her master; the necessity of recognizing this relation outwardly and of perfecting herself in the forms required to express the recognition, had moved her to such diligence and faithfulness in practising these forms that this exercise soon concreted itself into habit; it became automatic and unconscious; then a natural result followed; deceptions intended solely for others gradually grew practically into self-deceptions as well; the mock reverence became real reverence, the mock obsequiousness real obsequiousness, the mock homage real homage; the little counterfeit rift of separation between imitation slave and imitation master widened and widened, and became an abyss, and a very real one—and on one side stood Roxy, the dupe of her own deceptions, and on the other stood her child, no longer a usurper to her, but her accepted and recognized master.
>
> He was her darling, her master, and her deity all in one, and in her worship of him she forgot who she was and what he had been. (19)

The success of practicing "outward forms" is striking. Even if we consider Huck's and Arthur's selves to be no more solid than a set of habits, their characters prove much more stable, capable of resisting drills, and ready to maintain a less mutable reality. What, then, might account for Roxy's susceptibility to change in her reality and identity? I would like to argue that in the model of absorbed acting, as Mark Twain and his contemporaries conceived of it, reemerged the tension between tapping the resources of a durable self in order to play a role and transforming the self in order to do it. But the tension was transformed by newly subtle ideas of self and expression that eroded distinctions between durable and transformed selves, and that complicated the representation of switched identities in *Pudd'nhead Wilson*. And Mark Twain's pursuit of the implications for "character" of the suggestible self proceeded straight into the problems of race, training, and identity that so preoccupied Twain in *Pudd'nhead Wilson*, and have so occupied critics ever since.[23]

Citing the anecdote about the English tragedian William Charles Macready's shaking a ladder in order to work up the feeling of anger in his role as Shylock, William Archer in *Masks or Faces* noted that many actors will physically perform the signs of an emotion in order to generate it inside, a practice that verifies "the undoubted tendency of outward expression to react upon emotion" (171–72). In a section titled "Autosuggestion and Innervation," Archer invokes Darwin to support the idea that "the simulation of an emotion tends to arouse it in our minds" (Archer quoting Darwin, 172). By relating this phenomenon to Darwin's idea of innervation, in which physical stimulation excites sensory cells, which excite nerve cells, which produce a response (including emotional expression)—all by reflex and apart from consciousness and will—Archer gave the matter a scientific basis. Archer took the term "autosuggestion" from Eduard von Hartmann's *Philosophy of the Unconscious* (1868; translated into English in 1884), and he used it to support the same basic principle, that physical or "mechanical" activity could work through a physiological circuit, apart from the will, to effect changes in emotion.[24]

In attending to this phenomenon in relation to acting, Archer presented it as another way to generate "genuine" emotion, a way inferior, perhaps, to conjuring the emotion less mechanically, but a way nonetheless of creating an inner condition that would then manifest itself in the full complex of physical and involuntary details that convincingly signal emotional expression. The basic assumption, that felt emotion would express itself in physical expression, could remain intact if this mechanical, physical activity was thought merely to awaken the inner "centres" and memories of emotion. Nonetheless, a distinction lurks in the mechanics of autosuggestion between the more essential self that could be drawn upon to stage a reality and the more ductile self so susceptible to suggestion, between the affective self as fount of expression and the malleable emotional self as epiphenomenon of the body.[25] Intertwined in the relative unconsciousness of absorbed acting, in other words, was, first, a notion that freedom from a shaping and censoring consciousness would enable "genuine" and unmediated expression of the "centres," but also, second, a sense of surrender to processes, such as autosuggestion, liable to erode a central identity.

This doubleness in the processes of imaginative embodiment helps explain the apparent vacillation in Mark Twain's writings between characters highly susceptible to autosuggestion, so susceptible, in fact, that their realities can be fundamentally changed—such as Tom Sawyer when focused on his mortified finger, Tom Canty acting as prince, and Roxy—and characters with residual selves resistant to such changes—such as Huck and Arthur. Mark Twain, arguably, was working through conceptions of the self as they relate to capacities for representation. This thinking was connected to intellectual developments, especially those Darwin precipitated in *The Expression of the Emotions in Man and Animals* (1872). And it was related to cultural developments as well. As I suggested in the previous chapter in reference to the uncertain and emergent conceptions of the self and its continuous psychology that the deadpan style invoked, the older notions of "character" (which historians such as Joseph Kett, Karen Halttunen, and Warren I. Susman have situated in the earlier and middle nineteenth century) were losing their hold in mainstream American culture; by the 1890s, clearly enough, the common idea of character as a relatively sturdy, acquired structure contended with widespread ideas of it as malleable and multiple. And this contest marked Twain's conception of an actor's absorbed representation of another, as the necessity of drawing on one's inner resources for identification clashed with the idea of reshaping one's reality through practice and drill. For Twain, the correspondence between this actorly concern and cultural conceptions of the self had sharp social ramifications—especially for racial identity.

It was in *Pudd'nhead Wilson* that Twain most pointedly brought these conflicting ideas in contact with questions of race, and particularly with the racism that declared blacks both characterless and highly imitative. Susan Gillman may be right to suggest a connection between the role-playing of Roxy and Tom Driscoll and the fact that "as mulattoes their identity is, more radically than any white person's, tampered with by social fictionalizing." They are indeed "the novel's only explicit manipulators of identity" (73), and their malleability may be due to a social victimization of character structure, a violation of identity that Mark Twain's King Arthur and Huckleberry Finn never endured. But that hypothesis is undermined by the contrast drawn between Roxy and Tom. Roxy, who has lived all her life with the violence of the social fiction about her identity, nonetheless has a "strong character and aggressive and commanding ways" (46); "her face was full of character and expression," and a seeming inner vitality of character appears to manifest itself in her "majestic form and stature," her "imposing" "attitudes," and the nobility and "grace" of her "gestures and movements" (8). Within her, as Twain has it, there is a formidable inner core that magnificently radiates outward in all her bodily and habitual actions. When the same kind of familiar, nineteenth-century notions of strong and durable character are applied to Tom, he is found wanting, largely, it seems, because of his lax upbringing. Judge Driscoll accuses himself of not "training him up severely, and making a man of him" (67). Pudd'nhead Wilson decides Tom "hadn't character enough" (98) to kill his uncle, and the fact that Tom *did* kill the judge after all does not quite redeem him on the character scale—it was not the effect of premeditation or will. And Roxy has trouble truly loving him "because there 'warn't nothing *to* him' " (46). An idea of character as a built-up structure, and as inner fortitude, is operating here, and we are clearly invited to think that Tom's flaccid character emerged from his easygoing ways, and that Roxy's strength, perhaps, may have come from adversity, from having weathered the humiliations of slavery.

I would propose, that is, that as part of the argument in this novel between race and training as determinants of identity, Twain invokes assumptions about the "natural" imitativeness and characterlessness of blacks in order to discount such racisms and to emphasize instead the effect on role-playing of "character" as a deposit, a structure, an accretion of habits. Consider Tom's instant transformation from a white man to a black, his immediate identification with the plight of the slave. The day after learning he is Roxy's son, Tom wakes up thinking, "How hard the nigger's fate seems, this morning!—yet until last night such a thought never entered my head" (44). And from that instant Tom unconsciously and automatically acts like a "nigger," his identification so complete that aspects of bodily expression that are not or cannot be controlled by the will constantly declare his new identity: blushing before old white friends, "involuntarily giving the road, on the sidewalk, to the white rowdy and loafer," "shrinking and skulking here and there and yonder," feeling "ashamed to sit at the white folks' table," and manifesting other symptoms of "the 'nigger' in him asserting its humility" (44–45). Roxy thinks the manifestations of the "nigger" in her son are the result of black blood (70). But Tom's transformation into a "slave" is both so quick and so temporary—we are told that, quite suddenly, "the habit of a lifetime," that is, all the habits of behaving like a white man and slave owner, "had in some mysterious way vanished" (45)—that it is much more satisfactorily explained by Mark Twain's understanding of character, identification, and the psychology of acting. Tom has a character flimsy enough to be powerfully susceptible to suggestion.

Tom appears to be a textbook example of thorough identification that, through the automatisms of bodily expression, produces the details that guarantee authenticity. Because of his conviction and belief, his imaginative identification, "the 'nigger' in him" is expressed automatically, unconsciously, and "involuntarily," in signs ranging from uncontrolled blushing to all the minutiae of gait, gesture, and attitude. The contrast to King Arthur is sharp, and perhaps purposeful. For, although Tom and Arthur have similar role changes—each goes, without experience, from being a ruler to being a subject, from being a master to being a slave—Arthur never identifies with slavehood. Whereas Arthur has to guard against unconsciously revealing himself as king, Tom has to worry about betraying his new inner condition of blackness and slavehood. He fancies he sees "suspicion and maybe detection in all faces, tones, and gestures," and people *do* notice his conduct, and give him "puzzled expression[s]"; he "feared discovery all the time" (45). So convincing is his portrayal that Judge Driscoll says, "What's the matter with you? You look as meek as a nigger" (45). The novel retains the faint, racist suggestion that Tom's black blood has predisposed him to characterlessness, to a self so unstructured that it is quite vulnerable to being possessed by a new identity—so that, even though he has no more inner grasp of slavery than Arthur, his ductility enables him to surrender to the conception of it. But when we remember that Roxy, who *does* have experience in her slightly altered role-playing of slave and mother, finds it hard to adopt her new roles, Tom's malleability cannot easily be ascribed to race.

I would like to suggest that, in the cases of Roxy and Tom, Mark Twain is focusing on oppositions between character and character-lessness, and between ductile actorly selves and strong actorly personalities, in order to find middle terms. In the process, the racial charge that the opposition between character and characterlessness could carry is also complicated, its terms confused, in a movement that meshes with Twain's general undoing of racial difference. Roxy has a strong character, *and yet* she can transform her identity through the autosuggestion of practice and drill. Tom has a weak character, readily transformed through imaginative identification, *and yet*, the narrator tells us, though "Tom imagined that his character had undergone a pretty radical change," this was not so: "the main structure of his character was not changed, and could not be changed." His opinions had changed, and a couple of "features" of his character "were altered." Nonetheless, we are told:

> Under the influence of a great mental and moral upheaval his character and habits had taken on the appearance of complete change, but after a while with the subsidence of the storm both began to settle toward their former places. He dropped gradually back into his old frivolous and easygoing ways and conditions of feeling and manner of speech, and no familiar of his could have detected anything in him that differentiated him from the weak and careless Tom of other days. (45)

In a way typical of Mark Twain, oppositions are presented to be confounded. Here, sturdy character turns out also to be malleable, and pliant character is nonetheless structured. Moreover, Tom's character structure is pliancy; when he stays the same he returns to malleability. The confounding of these oppositions had a meaning that resonated widely through conceptions of the self. It also dovetailed with the confounding of race, with the damage that *Pudd'nhead Wilson* enacts on the boundaries of "whiteness" and "blackness." And, in the idea that a strong character like Roxy's could be altered by memorization and drill, and a changeable character like Tom's would only momentarily undergo complete metamorphosis, Mark

Twain invested possibilities for fiction making as well as anxieties about mutability.

Accompanying this dissolution of the sureties of character, race, and identity is an undermining of certainties of expression. The moment in *A Connecticut Yankee* when Arthur's sympathetic, fatherly tear serves to verify him as a peasant has numerous analogues in *Pudd'nhead Wilson*, especially in the successful role-playing of the novel's primary dissimulator. For example, after his mother returns from downriver slavery and explains that she fled because her owner's jealous wife ordered the overseer to work her especially hard, Tom seethes with anger at "that meddlesome fool" who drove Roxy to escape. "The expression of this sentiment was fiercely written in his face," we are told, but Roxy happily and affectionately mistakes it for grief for her wrongs and resentment toward her persecutors (86). Even more telling, perhaps, when Tom grieves for the man he murdered, he "was playing a part, but it was not all a part"; he keeps seeing the image of his bloody "alleged uncle," and the grisly picture gives him a "quiet and sorrowful" demeanor that is mistaken for proof of his sensitive nature and his adoration of his uncle (99). The sources of the emotion in such playing of a part are unverifiable. If it is "genuine," even if it is also actually the opposite of what it seems, it certifies authenticity. Tom is angry that Roxy is free, not because she was mistreated; he is dismayed because his dead uncle's image persists, not because Driscoll is dead and buried. But the sympathy he invites through such expressions of feeling persists almost to the end; as Tom looks more and more distressed at the trial, because of the way Wilson's argument closes in on him, the audience takes the distress as a further sign of his supposed bereavement and pities him (109, 111). Such misperception obviously has plenty to do with the frames of interpretation and the prejudices of the perceivers—the same ones who scrutinized David Wilson's face and misdiagnosed irony as pudding-brains. But the combination in the performance situation of the perceptual predilections of the spectators and actorly emotions once-removed could obviously provide a profound basis for mistakes—and fictions.

Part of Mark Twain's preoccupation with these cases had to come from a fiction writer's agenda. The grasp Twain had of an actor's multiple strata of consciousness (as in King Arthur's successful acting) accommodated his own practice, which involved identifying with his characters and allowing them to use him as an "amanuensis," at the same time that it demanded conscious shaping. Coquelin had used writers to explain actors, because, he said, writers must be both involved and detached, and are apt to write "under the dictation of some spirit" only to revise later and shape their writings more carefully (*Art of Acting*, 5–6, 85). Boucicault also invoked the writer as a model—of one who can lose self-control and be transported, becoming "an actor, not a spectator in the scene," allowing the writing, including grammar and spelling, to be "instinctive" (*Art of Acting*, 56–58). Such nineteenth-century models may, then, relieve us from arguments over whether Twain was a "jack-leg" novelist, submitting willy-nilly to his unconscious, or a scrupulous craftsman and reviser. The consistent returns, however, to absorbed, identifying, and virtually unconscious acting are crucial, for they echo Twain's conviction about his fictional practice that, as he said in his autobiography, "if *I* tell a boy's story, or anybody else's, it is never worth printing; it comes from the head and not the heart, and always goes into the wastebasket. To be successful and worth printing, the imagined boy would have to tell his story *himself* and let me act merely as his amanuensis."[26]

But within this dynamic—of necessary identification, of writing as automatic and therefore as heartfelt and authentic as a blush or a tear—there remained the question of the limits of identification. Not only in the case of a boy's story, but also, Twain claimed in the autobiography, in "the 'Horse's Tale,' the horse told it himself through me." *Joan of Arc*, too, he claimed in 1894, seemed to write itself. As he later recalled, Joan knew what she had to say without intervention from Mark Twain, and "she said it, without doubt or hesitation."[27] Such problems of stretched identifications—across species, across gender—had in effect been broached and to some degree solved in *Pudd'nhead Wilson*. For a man who liked to joke about the weakness or absence of his own character, the example of Tom Driscoll, who could *momentarily* undergo a radical transformation, long enough for some absolutely convincing performances, and yet return to his old identity, provided a model. For a man who knew well enough that his habits, and the identity they preserved, could not be "thrown out the window," but only "coaxed down-stairs a step at a time" (*Pudd'nhead Wilson*, 27), the possibility Roxy held out that drill, memorization, and imagination could enable one to "absorb the character" held promise for both dramatic readings and writing. For a writer doubly committed to authenticity and fiction, there must have been a welcome prospect in the sense that analogous experience and emotion could root writing or acting in reality, yet enable the artistic embodiment of identities quite different from the performer's. But if these questions of acting helpfully infused Twain's notions of realistic writing, the concomitant uncertainties about character and reliable representation persisted. The dubious identities of Tom Driscoll and Chambers at the end of *Pudd'nhead Wilson* attest to this, as they attest to the uncertainty of race and the unreliability of its representation, and as they subtly undermine the certainty of any other categories of identity and its expression.

4

The Expressive Body, Gesture, and Writing

For Mark Twain as a writer profoundly concerned about authenticity in representation, but constantly troubled by uncertainties and unreliabilities in expression, the expressive body became a locus of concern and a theater for experiment. Nineteenth-century theories of acting enhanced this interest as they elaborated conceptions of the body as the actor's medium, and especially as they drew on advances in physiology and biology to characterize the body and its processes as privileged vehicles of expression. William Archer's *Masks or Faces? A Study in the Psychology of Acting* exemplifies this tendency; as I observed in the previous chapter, its assertion that credible acting is grounded in involuntary (and therefore unfeigned) expressions of emotion, in processes of stimulus and response shaped more by neural networks and evolutionary habit than by the mind, drew directly on an emergent psychophysiology. Archer's mingling of acting theory and biological science was only an instance in much larger confluences of thought that sought continuities between emotion and corporeal expression, mind and physiology, identity and legible signs of it in the body. At stake were radical reconceptions of expression and representation.

The gesturing, blushing, weeping body became for Twain a means for raising questions about the immediacy of representation, especially about the directness of connection between emotion and expression. Especially consequential, I will argue, the bodily processes of expression provided Twain with a model for conceiving of representation generally in terms of physical registration. The somatic circuit between, say, an emotion and its expression offered a model of reference based on something more than resemblance or mimesis. When Hank Morgan, in *A Connecticut Yankee*, sees the look of gratitude on the face of a condemned mother when a priest pledges to care for her baby, he says: "You should have seen her face then! Gratitude?

Lord, what do you want with words to express that? Words are only painted fire; a look is the fire itself" (403). This alternative to mimesis or "painted fire," this sense of the presence of the actual thing, became his model for expression and representation. The extension and testing of this model as analogy, measure, and ideal for any kind of representation—including writing—occupied Twain throughout most of his career. While this is a pursuit of reference and reality quite unlike that of the more widely recognized theorists of realism, such as Howells or James, it should nonetheless resituate Twain as a kind of "realist," sophisticatedly in quest of "sincerity," "the genuine," and "the real," focused on connections between the body surface and its interior, gesture and emotion, sign and referent.[1]

The problem, as Twain most immediately grappled with it, was put squarely by Darwin in *The Expression of the Emotions in Man and Animals* (1872)—a book Twain read and annotated. The "movements of expression," Darwin asserted, "reveal the thoughts and intentions of others more truly than do words, which may be falsified."[2] Was this the case? The question was a crucial one for a writer in pursuit of genuineness and sincerity. For Darwin, bodily expressions of emotion were more reliable because they tended to be involuntary, unconscious, reflexive. For Twain, such features fixed a reference point. To the degree that bodily registrations of emotion, thought, and character were unconscious, they promised truthful revelation—and raised the threat of self-exposure. To the degree that bodily signs were automatic, results of a chain of physical processes, they overcame the seemingly unbridgeable gap between such arbitrary signs as words and their referents. Twain's fiction became an arena for testing the reliability of bodily signs, as well as for investigating whether verbal expressions could aspire to the status of the unconscious, automatic, or reflexive.

Twain addressed the automatism of the bodily expression of emotion as early as 1869, when in chapter 28 of *The Innocents Abroad* he wrote about sorrow scientifically analyzed:

> There are nerves and muscles in our frames whose functions and whose methods of working it seems a sort of sacrilege to describe by cold physiological names and surgical technicalities. . . . Fancy a surgeon, with his nippers lifting tendons, muscles, and such things into view, out of the complex machinery of a corpse, and observing, "Now this little nerve quivers—the vibration is imparted to this muscle—from here it is passed to this fibrous substance; here its ingredients are

separated by the chemical action of the blood—one part goes to the heart and thrills it with what is popularly termed emotion, another part follows this nerve to the brain and communicates intelligence of a startling character, the third part glides along this passage and touches the spring connected with the fluid receptacles that lie in the rear of the eye. Thus, by this simple and beautiful process, the party is informed that his mother is dead, and he weeps." Horrible!

The clinically scientific nature of this account of bereavement would supposedly also be repellent, at least to aesthetic sensibilities, in a physiological account of creative activity, or in a biological rationalization of an actor's emotional expression. Nonetheless, in it lay both repulsion and attraction for Mark Twain, the attraction derived partly from a view of expression as a circuit coursing through a physical "machinery," unimpeded by a dissimulating consciousness. The stimulus travels, by quivers, vibrations, and chemical action, to the tear ducts; a direct response of bodily mechanism, weeping is therefore uncensored, uncensorable, an involuntary effect of a nervous disturbance.

This "analysis" of sorrow must bring to mind Twain's better-known account of beauty destroyed by "scientific" knowledge—his story in chapter 9 of *Life on the Mississippi* (1883) about learning to read the "face" of the river, so that it "told its mind to me without reserve, delivering its most cherished secrets." Being able to see in this surface the hideous underlying secrets of treacherous rocks and wrecks killed "the grace, the beauty, the poetry" of the Mississippi, just as the surgeon's understanding defiled the sanctity of sorrow. But there is another similarity. The signs that make up "the language of this water" and turn it into a "wonderful book" are not arbitrary and symbolic, like words. The "faint dimple" on the surface physically registers the presence of a wreck or a rock. When Twain asserts that "those tumbling 'boils' show a dissolving bar" and "that slanting mark on the water refers to a bluff reef," "referring" and "showing" identify direct and concrete transmissions. The signs are made by contact, by a material circuit, much as the vibrations and quivers in the body physically connected weeping to its nervous stimulus.[3]

When, in the last paragraph of this chapter on the Mississippi, Twain more explicitly compares the face of the river to the face of a woman—whose "dimple," "boils," and "marks" are symptoms of a hidden interior—the metaphor of the river's surface as a "skin" is secured. "What does the lovely flush in a beauty's cheek mean to a doctor," he asks, "but a 'break' that ripples above some deadly disease? Are not all her visible charms sown thick with what are to him the signs and symbols of hidden decay?" These symptoms, too, are physical, the effect of natural processes. The mysterious, and apparently horrible, interiors of the woman and the river are there to see, registered on the surface. I would like to leave aside, but only for the moment, the sharply gendered dimensions of these images—the familiar, voyeuristic relation of male analysts and experts diagnosing female bodies and unveiling female interiors as legible and controllable, this conjunction of prurience and the pursuit of truth—in order to focus temporarily on another point.[4] Implicit in Twain's comparison, I would suggest, is a distinction that Charles S. Peirce, at the turn of the century, would describe as that between arbitrary and conventional "symbolic" signs, such as words, and nonarbitrary "indexical" signs, which signify through a physical relationship, are caused by their referents, and exist as traces of the material presence they point to.[5] Mark Twain became fascinated, I will argue, by the possibility that physical transmission was the most faithful means of representation; he tried to locate a reliability for signification in physical contact, in tracks and traces, a pursuit that ultimately focused on the issue, or expression, of the body's material circuits—skin, flesh, muscles, nerves, electric charges, physical force.[6]

But from the start, problems beset and bedeviled Twain's investment in the reliability of these physically registered signs. As the foregoing examples suggest, embracing the natural, fleshly, automatically functioning body as a medium for emotion or thought meant embracing a passivity—and, ultimately, a "femininity"—in the processes of representation. Ways of confronting the femininity culturally superimposed on the creative body, but also evading it, repeatedly occupied Mark Twain's attention in his stories and prose as he embraced for himself the certainties that bodily expression, free of conscious dissimulation, appeared to offer, but then retreated to the companionate position—that of the "masculine" mind, the conscious observer and detached interpreter, the surgeon, the riverboat pilot, the physician, the knowing recipient of unwitting bodily self-betrayal. From the latter position, separated from the physical chain of signification, another difficulty emerged: even natural, indexical signs lost their certainty, became a language that had to be learned, accessible to the expert, but subject to his misreadings, and liable to be misread by everyone else. Yet, if in his thinking such signs were liable to lose their certainty and justify the metaphor that they too were a "language" and an "alphabet," Mark Twain also held out the possibility that words and language themselves could in some ways aspire to the automatism and naturalness of the index. Writing and speech, that is, could be partly the results of habits, reflexes, unconscious processes; they could be uttered automatically, without censorship; they could have a residue in them of the body. My concerns in this chapter, then, are Twain's versions of the language of the physical, especially of the body, and the ways in which the body might infuse language. The alphabet of gesture and the physiology of writing meet to shape this territory.

PHYSICAL CIRCUITS

Mark Twain's pursuit of certainty in representation—an earnest enough undertaking—was nonetheless persistently accompanied by destabilizations of the grounds of such certainty. His early study of phrenology, which helped set the stage for his interest in the reliability of bodily registrations of one's interior, was perhaps the least vexed instance of his long-standing inquiry. For the eighteen-year-old Samuel Clemens, the allure of phrenology lay in the certainty associated with the indexical. If the material surface of the body registered—as a mold would, through physical impression—the qualities of the interior, the science of phrenology could secure not only the knowledge it promised about dissimulating or dangerous strangers but also the surety of Clemens's own identity.[7] The strain in phrenology of materialist science that reduced the incomprehensible human mind to the potentially mappable brain promised to sweep away the uncertainties of representation by certifying the reliability of physical transmission from cerebrum to cranium and from inner character to body type.

But Twain's subsequent considerations of indexical signs, and his pointed juxtapositions of bodily signs and other indexical signs, served in a thoroughgoing way to map the limits of their reliability and to undo the opposition between the natural and the conventional on which this reliability rested. In the process of doing this, he also invoked, and at the same time undermined, the social security that rested on the promise of indexical signs—as he used such signs to identify, but not always positively, kings and criminals, innocents and murderers. Let us take the striking example from one of Twain's later stories, "Tom Sawyer's Conspiracy" (1897–99), in which traces of the body function at the melodramatic moment of revelation as the assurance of the truthful plumbing of mystery.[8] Detective Flacker, who has convinced the townsfolk that he "could read every little sign he come across same as if it was a book, and you couldn't hide nothing from him" (230–31), nonetheless wrongly makes Jim out to be a murderer. His "circumstantial" evidence pales next to Tom's indexical evidence—the king's bootprint, the false teeth of the duke—which verifies the familiar impostors as the culprits partly because its physical fit does not seem to require "reading" or interpretation, because these signs do not have the drawbacks of those in a "book" (242). As Peirce later characterized the relation between the indexical sign and its referent, "the interpreting mind has nothing to do with this connection, except remarking it, after it is established" (114). Flacker's "expert" reading of his "book" of signs is discredited by the signs verified through their fit rather than their interpretation.

But if the bootprint and the teeth register their referents in a way analogous to the imprint of the phrenological brain on the cranium, we nonetheless see instability among the oppositions on which indexical certainty lies—oppositions between imprint and symbol, physical process and interpretation, the body and the mind, the natural and the artificial. Tom points, after all, to the imprint of a boot, not a foot, and to the fit of false teeth, not real ones. Such toying with these "natural" signs could only have been intentional. Breaches have been made in the chain of material signification, unleashing confusions between the "naturally automatic" and the artfully manufactured, and raising doubts about the reliability of such signs for deciding identity, character, and event.

Far from an incidental or occasional concern, this moment in "Tom Sawyer's Conspiracy" has a long prehistory. The most familiar echoing instance is the sign that assures Huck Finn that his father, Pap, has returned to St. Petersburg—a bootprint with a devil-repelling cross made with nails in the left heel.[9] Pap's presence is verified not only through the print of a boot rather than a foot, but also through the imprint of an iconic, cultural symbol (what calls attention to its status as icon and symbol more than a cross does?). Peter Wilks's tattoo works to similar effect. More permanent, like a fingerprint, than other bodily features, an indelible mark on the skin with a kinship therefore to the indices of phrenology and palmistry, it is nonetheless a cultural sign, iconic or symbolic—a thin blue arrow, according to the king, or the initials "P-B-W," according to the real Harvey Wilks (255). Twain further twists this sign by using it to identify the live Wilkses, rather than the dead, tattooed one, as if the entire project of identifying marks has lost its anchoring and has been set adrift in a sea of indirection. At the same time that symbols with some features of indexical signs are used as "surer" identifiers, indexical signs imprint conventional symbols and thereby lose their precultural immediacy. Mark Twain repeatedly rehearses versions of this problem, invoking, yet foiling, the oppositions that might clarify signification.

The text in which Twain most directly engages the question of the reliability and informativeness of signs on the body's surface and of indexical imprints is, of course, *Pudd'nhead Wilson*. And there he again experiments, testing links in the chain of physical transmission. As Susan Gillman, Michael Rogin, and David R. Sewell have pointed out, the best-known moment in Twain's writing of revelation and betrayal by the body—Wilson's use of fingerprints to expose the slave identity of the supposed "Tom Driscoll"—says nothing about inherent racial identity.[10] Indeed, the whorls and ridges express nothing about character, temperament, or psychological interior. The integrity of indexical transfer between glass pane and fingerprints remains intact, but the fantasy of the equally reliable transfer between one's psychological or biological interior and the skin surface (the unrealized hope of both Mark Twain and his source, Francis Galton's *Finger Prints* [1892]) pointedly fails.[11] Yet palmistry in this novel works differently. The traces of character, experience, and even future deeds demonstrably exist in the lines of Luigi's palm. It is Wilson's *reading* that falls short—a problem the fingerprints seemingly are not subject to, with their indisputable, point-by-point correspondence between imprint and pattern.

Contrary to Rogin's argument that the representational reliability of the palms compositionally predates the later crisis of representation exemplified by the failure of fingerprints to express categories of identity, I would argue that these two moments are instances of an ongoing inquiry. They are distinguished primarily by the slightly different impediments to representational immediacy. The fingerprints provide a certain sign (easily legible) but an uncertain referent (the uncertainty of identity); the palm produces a certain referent (Luigi's character) but an uncertain sign (it is hard to read). The difference lies in the location of the break in the material chain of transmission. Near the end of the novel the kind of difficulty posed by the juxtaposition of palmistry and fingerprinting is repeated. There the prosecutor Pembroke Howard, like Detective Flacker, has a "chain of circumstantial evidence" convicting the Capello twins. While the chain is "without a break or fault in it anywhere" (100), it is nonetheless unattached to the physical realities of the case. This circumstantial evidence, by definition indirect and enabling only inference, falls before Wilson's fingerprints in a moment that seems to repudiate truth based on chains of logic and interpretation and to uphold truth based on material circuits. But, of course, if Howard's chain of logic is unchained from physical realities, Wilson's material signs are connected only tenuously to the elusive "identity" of "Tom Driscoll." It is precisely this metaphor of the *chain* of representation that crystallizes the problems Twain engages, a metaphor that privileges physical connection, and provides the model of the broken link to conceive of failures in the "sign."

To reiterate and underscore the problem Twain has defined, the entry in Pudd'nhead's "Calendar" at the head of the first chapter about the trial casts doubt over Wilson's surer evidence at the same time that it (though somewhat facetiously) reconsiders the registration in one's "marks" of inherent identity: "Even the clearest and most perfect circumstantial evidence is likely to be at fault, after all, and therefore ought to be received with great caution. Take the case of any pencil, sharpened by any woman: if you have witnesses, you will find she did it with a knife; but if you take simply the aspect of the pencil, you will say she did it with her teeth" (99). Preceding as it does Wilson's triumph with the fingerprints, which are *opposed*, seemingly, to Pembroke Howard's "circumstantial evidence," these marks, like fingerprints, ought to provide a perfect match—with either knife or teeth. Instead they are confoundingly *equated* with circumstantial, indirect evidence rather than with direct and essential proof. The physically transmitted sign yields its certainty to testimony, seemingly because the power of gynephobic interpretation (perhaps preferring the dental threat to that of the knife) shrouds the truth of the indexical marks. The problem of palmistry, of reading, resurfaces. On the other hand, however, these marks do reliably identify the gender of the sharpener. "Any pencil" sharpened by "any woman" will look like this, as if the peculiar movements of the female body will always reliably register themselves in this predictable pattern. The matter of the expressiveness of the body, in other words, is far from resolved, as Twain invokes and destabilizes the clarifying oppositions between direct and indirect proof, essential and circumstantial evidence, and material and hermeneutic circuits.

GESTURE, REVELATION, AND
"NATURAL LANGUAGE"

If the detective story of Pudd'nhead Wilson moved purposefully from a universe of potentially meaningful signs to a sign rooted (though perhaps not so securely) in the body, it also submitted the body itself to this process, winnowing its reliable surfaces from the possibly dissimulative. Wilson discounts face, hair, height, and "form" as bodily signs that can be counterfeited, duplicated, disguised, hidden, worn away, or otherwise rendered illegible; fingerprints, quite differently, are "physical marks which do not change their character, and by which [one] can always be identified—and that without shade of doubt or question" (108). Wilson's purpose here parallels a nineteenth-century tradition that pursued both certainty of meaning and stability of character. The still influential physiognomy of Johann Caspar Lavater declared that stature, gait, bearing, gesture, and handwriting revealed the inner self, but were less reliable than more permanent facial features—forehead, eyes, nose, mouth, chin, profile—which he thought indicated unchanging mental powers and character.[12] Phrenology, too, put its greatest store in the skin surface that contoured the sturdy skull, and in enduring signs of character rather than in the fleeting and potentially manipulable symptoms of interiority manifested in movement and facial expression.

Why, then, do Twain's fictional moments of revelation hinge as often on gesture as on the more permanent bodily indices? In *The Prince and the Pauper,* while the bodies of Tom Canty and Prince Edward are apparently indistinguishable, finally throwing the official proof of royalty onto the shaky grounds of memory, Tom's mother, having sensed that there is something strange about her "son," devises a convincing test. Knowing that ever since some gunpowder burst in Tom's face he casts his hand before his eyes when he is startled out of his dreams or musings, she tries awakening and startling the boy a number of times, only to find that the "habitual gesture" is not there (115–17). Later, during the aptly named royal "recognition procession," the real Tom suddenly spies his mother in the throngs along the route, "and up flew his hand, palm outward, before his eyes; that old involuntary gesture born of a forgotten episode and perpetuated by habit!" Mrs. Canty, assured of his identity, runs to him, embraces his leg, and kisses it (304). A similar gestural revelation occurs in *Tom Sawyer, Detective* (1896), in which a convoluted network of lies, mistaken identities, misperceptions, and legal argument that pins the murder of Jubiter Dunlap on Uncle Silas Phelps is exploded when Jubiter, attending the trial disguised as a "deef and dummy," reveals himself to Tom by nervously and unconsciously engaging in his idiosyncratic habit of drawing an imaginary cross on his cheek with his finger.[13]

These two characters' disguises are undone by involuntary, unconscious gestures, and certainly Mark Twain's interest lies in the contrast between their calculated disguises and their uncontrolled, gestural self-betrayal. Habitual gesture functions here as a hallmark of truth because it escapes the control of conscious feigning. Ultimately, however, such gestures resembled indexical signs not only because they bypassed consciousness, but also because, according to the scientific theory Twain avidly read, gestural circuits too were physical and physiological, a kind of bodily chain.

Darwin's *Expression of the Emotions in Man and Animals*, whose sections on gestural expression as habit and reflex action Twain had heavily underscored and annotated, had the general aim of identifying what Darwin called "true expression," by which he meant expression neither conscious nor conventional, expressions that are automatic responses of human organisms and no longer prompted or fully controlled by the will.[14] *Most* expressive movements, Darwin ultimately claimed, were innate, inherited residues of movements useful for survival—as a sneer is the residual effect of baring the canine tooth (352). Gestural expression was "natural" in this sense, universal and automatic rather than acquired and willfully used as a language is, difficult to suppress or falsify, and therefore apt to expose people's real thoughts and emotions.

One of Darwin's concerns was to make distinctions between emotionally expressive actions that were "reflexive" in the sense of being actions purely and simply of the nervous system—relays from sensory to motor nerves—and more complex actions that happened similarly outside of volition but were the products of habit. His study, however, effectively weakened this distinction as it argued that in the evolutionary process habits useful for survival were implanted into reflexes (39–40), that habitual actions had a physiological basis in the tendency of nerve force to travel in well-worn channels (69–71), and that habitual gestures were difficult to distinguish from reflexive ones (35–36). For Mark Twain this muddling—the confusion between signs relayed by physical circuits and habitual signs whose origins presumably lay in consciousness—obviously demarcated a territory of concern. The genesis of Tom Canty's gesture of both protection and fear clearly enough lay in reflex. But Twain roots it equally in habit, pointedly foregrounding the uncertainty.[15]

When in 1896 Twain read William James's version of emotional expression in *The Principles of Psychology* (1890), he would have had even more reason to class gestural emotional expression with indices in the category of physically transmitted signs.[16] In James's theory the body does not actually "express" the emotions; rather, emotion is simply how our adaptive, survivalist, bodily, reflexive responses feel: anger is what it feels like to hit someone, fear is what it feels like to tremble. Emotions have physical causes, are directly linked to the body—indeed, consist solely of bodily symptoms, and come "from parts below," without the mediation or interference of ideas, cognition, or any "cerebral processes" (II, 472). Here lay a justification for a materialist rooting of signification and for elevating gestural "expression" above any conscious dissimulation. Yet this version of the body's revelations still failed, it seems, to gain Twain's full consent. Jubiter Dunlap's gestural index of fear is the tracing of a *cross* on his cheek. In the same way that Twain complicates the index by placing the cultural icon of the cross in Pap's bootprint, he questions the innate circuit of gesture by making it issue in this most familiar example of a cultural symbol.

Gesture becomes a site for questioning the possibilities of representation, for separating and melding the categories at stake in Twain's concern over reference and realism: the physical and the conventional, materialism and language. In his play *Cap'n Simon Wheeler, the Amateur Detective: A Light Tragedy*, written in 1877, Twain presses the Darwinian suggestion that most expressive gestures are innate by ranging this universalism up against conceptions of codification and language.[17] Amateur detective Wheeler, eager to mimic the professionals, imitates the pacing, frowns, and gestures of a detective thinking out a problem. When his admiring wife, Jenny, tells him that he goes "through the motions as elegant as any detective I ever saw," Wheeler responds:

> It's a big part of the business, too, to do it right.—I mean when there's people looking at you. Ah, when a detective's under the public eye, it's *beautiful* to see him go through the motions—beautiful! Why Jenny dear, you watch a detective, and you can follow his line of thought right straight through, just the same as a deef and dumb scholar can foller his teacher's meaning when he stands on the school platform making *signs*. Now here—I'll do the head-shakes and nods, and so on, and I'll give you the language of each one as I make it. (271)

And Wheeler does perform a series of head-shakes and nods, all the while providing Jenny an interpretation of the thoughts and thought processes these gestures signify. However, the meanings he attributes to his gestures are preposterous, involving the impossible divining of his incoherent theories about the crime and detecting from the way in which he puts his nose in the air or slaps his forehead. The legibility and reliability of gestural signs are cancelled not only because they apparently rely on expertise and artifice—business, elegance, and theatrical beauty, as Wheeler suggests—but also because no concrete connection exists between Wheeler's babble of words and his babble of gestures.

A humorous send-up of stage detectives, of the detective-story tradition that a careful observer (like Poe's August Dupin) can discern another's private thoughts from facial and bodily expression, and of the notion that the signs of the body (both detective's and criminal's) could be reduced to a key, the Wheeler play nonetheless seriously engages the proposition that language and codification can infect and derail gestural expression. In a scene near the end of the play, the presumably murdered Hugh Burnside returns to town disguised as a deaf-mute tramp. He encounters a group that includes a character, Charles Dexter, who has studied "deaf and dumb signs," and Burnside *"proceeds to make absurd signs and say 'Goo-goo' etc."* Dexter, unable to make any sense of Burnside's "extravagant signs and noises," laments that his "noble dream is dead!"—for he had imagined that sign language might serve as a "universal language," a natural language that would allow communication with "Christian and savage, learned and ignorant." Millicent Griswold, however, the heroine of the play, rejoins that "there *is* one sign that is universal—the symbol of compassion," and she puts a coin in the "tramp's" hand, and he makes "*signs and 'Goo-goo' of gratitude*" (270).

As gesture moves toward language, Twain seems to suggest here, and toward codifications that lose gesture's corporeal grounding, it falters. Darwin had distinguished between expressive gestures rooted in practical survival and other gestures which, while perhaps seeming "natural," have actually "been learnt like the words of a language"—including "the finger-language used by the deaf and dumb" (352–55).[18] The problem with Wheeler's "head-shakes and nods" is that he must teach "the language of each one," and the problem with sign language is that it *is* a language, and requires "a deef and dumb scholar" to make sense of it. Yet, the legibility of the isolated gestural sign, Millicent's sign of emotion, of compassion, apparently persists. We must infer, it seems, that such an act as her almsgiving, in which a deed and its meaning become indistinguishable, successfully roots the sign of the interior in its practical expression, much as Darwin rooted "true expression" in acts of survival. It is as if representation in languages is surpassed by both enactments and literal embodiments. Security of meaning then lies in materialism and pragmatism, in circuits of physical impression and concrete issue instead of in the resemblance of metaphor or the arbitrariness and relational meaning of language.

It is no accident that Mark Twain joined the question of the meaningfulness of gesture and language to the "deef and dumb" acts of Hugh Burnside and Jubiter Dunlap. Peter Brooks, in *The Melodramatic Imagination*, argues that nineteenth-century melodrama, in its attempt to negotiate what people were experiencing as a crisis in meaning precipitated by a perceived deficiency in language, turned both to gesture and to a generic deaf-mute figure. Melodrama took the body as a natural, universal medium whose expressions existed prior to the corruption and alienation worked upon meaning by words, Brooks argues, and it designated gesture as a means to recover immediacy, purity, and clarity of meaning (66–67). It concomitantly took the mute role as the repository, or embodiment, of unspoken, nonverbal sense, as "the virtuoso emblem of the possibilities of meaning engendered in the absence of the word" (62).

The prominence and import of the mute figure on the nineteenth-century stage heightens the significance of the duke's claim, in *Huck-*

leberry Finn, that he has special skill in impersonation because he has played "a deef and dumb person on the histrionic boards" (208). But, of course, like Hugh Burnside's "deef and dumb" impersonation, and Jubiter Dunlap's, and Injun Joe's in *Tom Sawyer*, the duke's performance as the deaf-mute William Wilks takes this melodramatic emblem of truth as a *mask*. True, Jubiter Dunlap, in accord with the natural eloquence of muteness, exposes himself through unconscious gesture; but the other characters successfully hide behind their veil of silence. And in the case of the duke, the supposed capacity of the deaf-mute figure to render meanings that words otherwise obscure is pointedly used itself to swindle the Wilkses.

Through the king's explanations in *Huckleberry Finn*, Twain introduces the idea that the feelings of the heart are more important than those of the head, and that words somehow obscure those feelings— with the implicit suggestion that other means of expression do not. The king's thanks for the sympathy and "holy tears" of Peter Wilks's townsfolk, he claims, come "out of his heart and out of his brother's heart, because out of their mouths they can't, words being too weak and cold" (213). And although the king makes no claims for the universal expressiveness of "deef and dumb signs," which he acknowledges must be learned (250), after he "signs" to the duke the suggestion that they turn all of Peter Wilks's money over to the nieces, the king declares that the duke's joyous hugs will "convince anybody the way *he* feels about it" (216). This apparent emotional outpouring is supposed to surpass words, but Huck knows not only that the duke's deaf-and-dumb language is just "a lot of idiotic signs" (209), but also that the gestural expressions of emotion are "rot and slush" (213). In this case, the arbitrariness of deaf-mute language is underscored by the duke's signs, and the emotional gesture is rendered specious by its theatricality. However, as evidence of Twain's continuing preoccupation with both the promise and the uncertainty of gestural expression, the same novel supplies Huck's well-known moments of self-betrayal by the body.

GENDER, GESTURE, AND
PUBLIC EXPOSURES

Dressed as a girl, Huckleberry Finn simply cannot help but expose his masculinity. For the spy mission ashore, Huck disguises himself in a dress and bonnet and rehearses girl behavior, but he betrays his gender, as Jim points out, because he walks like a boy and because he keeps pulling up his gown to get at his britches pocket. Though he resolves that he must not "forget I was a girl" (67), he exposes himself on shore by unconscious movements which Loftus says are typical of boys. Like the gestural exposures of disguise and truthful identity in the cases of Tom Canty and Jubiter Dunlap, Huck's movements are unconscious, and his gestures are similarly poised ambiguously between natural and learned behaviors. But Huck's movements do not identify him as Huck. They identify him as male.

Gender figures prominently in gestural revelations throughout Mark Twain's writing, partly because the exposure of gender is so wedded to the fixing of identity, but even more because gendered identity conditions exposure. Men and women in Twain's work differ in their capacities for disguise and in their susceptibilities to self-betrayal, and the dynamic of exposure has different effects on masculine and feminine terrains. Mark Twain reproduces and tests that version of the Victorian ideological system in which the social, and therefore the dissimulative, is associated with masculinity and contrasted to the domestic sphere of intimacy, sincerity, and transparency. Corporeal signs, for example, tend to expose imposture in men, who are typically masking themselves in the public sphere, and to expose, for voyeuristic pleasure, the interiors of women—who, maskless and incapable of masking, already display their identities for all to see. More generally, exposure and revelation hinge on the profoundly gendered distinctions between the public and the private, exteriors and interiors, experience and innocence, and the mind and the body.

Mark Twain's girls and young women are especially likely to betray themselves by uncontrolled facial expression. In *Tom Sawyer*, for example, after Becky Thatcher has torn the picture in Mr. Dobbins's anatomy book, Tom knows their teacher will ask each student to confess, "first one and then t'other, and when he comes to the right girl he'll know it, without any telling. Girls' faces always tell on them. They ain't got any backbone. She'll get licked" (149). Given Dobbins's pastime of peering into anatomical secrets, there is the implication of voyeuristic pleasure as he tells Becky to "look me in the face"— where, presumably, she will see nothing, but will yet, in looking, expose her own sexual guilt and desire. The pallidness and terror in her face are about to betray her, until Tom—in a successful and manly lie—confesses to the crime (151). The character most fully on his way to a masculine adulthood of "backbone" and "character," Tom dissembles promisingly. Girls, on the other hand, despite their best efforts to "act," tend to broadcast their true feelings. So, when Tom ably hides his feelings and responds coolly to Becky's pointed failure to invite him to her picnic, "Becky's lip trembled and the tears came to her eyes; she hid these signs with a forced gayety and went on chattering, but the life had gone out of the pic-nic, now, and out of everything else" (139).[19]

Female romantic affections, especially, are difficult to keep under control, and Twain takes pleasure in their exposure. Sophia Grangerford in *Huckleberry Finn*, for instance, turns pale when she learns that her beau, Harney Shepherdson, has been shot at, but, as Huck notices, "the color came back when she found the man warn't hurt" (145). This of course is not an innocuous sign, since open knowledge of the nature of her love for this enemy of the Grangerford clan would have dire consequences. But she cannot help it. Later, after Huck retrieves the note Harney left for her in the church pew, "She was mighty red in the face, for a minute, and her eyes lighted up and it made her powerful pretty" (149). Mary Jane Wilks is similarly transparent. When, out of sympathy for Mary Jane and her sisters, Huck first decides to "blow on these frauds" and betray the swindle of the king and the duke, he wonders, "Shall I go, private, and tell Mary Jane? No—I dasn't do it. Her face would give them a hint, sure" (225–26). When he finally does tell Mary Jane about them, he asks her to go to the Lothrops' *before* breakfast, "because you ain't one of these leather-face people. I don't want no better book than what your face is. A body can set down and read it off like coarse print." She would give herself away when the duke and the king came to kiss her good morning, or when she greeted her sisters, or if she saw *anyone*, because "if a neighbor was to ask how is your uncles this morning, your face would tell something." And, given that Huck, during their conversation, fully registers the way she "reddened up very sweet," the way "her nostrils spread," and the way her face looked "afire like sunset," we might conclude that Mary Jane's unwitting emotional exposure is also "powerful pretty" and enticing (240–42)—in yet another confluence of male prurience and truthful exposure in the female body.

The revelation on the surface of the body of the feminine interior is both titillating to a masculine eye and a sign of weakness, vulner-

ability, and ineptitude in the ways of manly double-dealing. Meld-
ings of emotion and body, females, and especially innocent girls, lack
the "backbone"—the self-control and mental discipline over the
body—to insure secrecy and emotional clampdown. When Tom and
Huck make a blood pact to "keep mum" about Injun Joe's murder of
Dr. Robinson, they are glad that they are not "gals, 'cuz *they* go back
on you anyway, and blab if they get in a huff" (*Tom Sawyer,* 79). Even
so, the boys are intensely worried about unknowing self-betrayal,
and, for example, when the town is gathered at the murder site and
the boys meet each other's eyes, "both looked elsewhere at once, and
wondered if anybody had noticed anything in their mutual glance"
(87). Partly a moment for readers to shudder over general anxieties
about self-exposure in public, the boys' worry is also about "feminine" weakness in the male, about personal failings of self-control
and mental dominion over body and impulse.

Twain's self-exposing males tend to be situated on the boundaries
between maturity and childhood, experience and innocence, mind
and body, and masculinity and femininity. Huck exposes himself as
a boy while he is passing as a girl; the cross-dressing has much to do
with this instance of masculine self-betrayal. Near the final battle
with the English knights in *A Connecticut Yankee in King Arthur's
Court,* Hank Morgan, anxious about the loyalty of his corps of hand-
picked cadets, "watched [his] fifty-two boys narrowly; watched their
faces, their walk, their unconscious attitudes: for all these are a language—a language given us purposely that it may betray us in times
of emergency, when we have secrets which we want to keep"
(473–74). While this attests to the general doctrine that the unconscious "language" of the body most reliably registers one's interior,
this group is especially susceptible to such self-betrayal because they
are *boys,* not men, and because, as Hank says, "Ah, they were a dar-
ling fifty-two! As pretty as girls, too" (476). Morgan, who declares
himself masculinely unsentimental and seems indeed to be the epitome of the swindling, Barnumesque performer, feels secure against
self-betrayal through bodily indiscipline (although, as I will argue in
my next chapter, his masculine duplicity is finally inverted).

Tom Driscoll in *Pudd'nhead Wilson* similarly suits the profile of the
effeminate self-betrayer, and he is pointedly contrasted to David Wilson, the master of both the pokerface and the theatrical effect. A boy

without "character," in Wilson's estimation, and a male who cross-dresses to disguise himself (as a young girl, as an old woman), Tom is eminently susceptible to self-betrayal. For example, though he thinks that Roxy knows merely about his secret gambling debts, when she first threatens to expose him his "cheek blenched, and she saw it," despite his effort to cover up his worry with "a gay laugh and a hollow chipperness of manner" (38). Later, when she shows up infuriated that Tom sold her downriver, Tom is at pains to hide the arrangements he has made for her recapture, but Roxy knows what to do: "Turn up dat light! I want to see yo' face better. Dah now—lemme look at you. Chambers, you's as white as yo' shirt!" (88). As he reads aloud the runaway slave poster—deleting his name—she detects the omission in his face. And when he asks to step outside for some air, she realizes her master is in the hotel: "Yo' ornery eye tole on you" (91).

Even more dramatic, of course, is the revelation of Tom's guilt at the trial. He was rightfully worried about Pudd'nhead's palmistry: "Why, a man's own hand is his deadliest enemy! Just think of that—a man's own hand keeps a record of the deepest and fatalest secrets of his life, and is treacherously ready to expose him to any black-magic stranger that comes along" (52). But it is not only handprints and fingerprints that betray. Wilson in the trial tests his guesses about "the origin and motive of the murder" against Tom's face, and verifies his "hits" by Tom's involuntary signs of worry. When he says he will produce the murderer in court, he sees Tom "flying signals of distress" (109). And when accused, Tom's face turns bloodless and ashen, his lips make some "impotent movement," and he "slid limp and lifeless to the floor." In response to this mute, involuntary, bodily response, Wilson declares: "He has confessed" (113). Indeed, this moment, rather than the fingerprint revelation, constitutes the crowning effect of the trial, serves as the ultimate revelation. Unlike the manly Injun Joe in *Tom Sawyer*, who "tore his way through all opposers" at the trial "and was gone" after Tom Sawyer revealed him as a killer (172), the limp Tom Driscoll faints, his girl-boy body usurping the office of words in verifying his guilt. It is necessary to acknowledge, as I argued in the previous chapter, that many of Tom's emotional expressions are misread or easily misreadable; Twain seems invariably to undercut moments of clear legibility with uncertainty. But it is also important to notice that the moments of apparent reliability in Tom's emotional expression are also moments of his "effeminate" helplessness.

This preoccupation with the certainties of expression in the feminine/effeminate body had large implications for Mark Twain's own practice of realism. If "the movements of expression," in Darwin's phrasing, did indeed "reveal the thoughts and intentions of others more truly than do words" (364), and if the feminine was the further guarantee of such transparency, was Twain not doubly distanced from representational fidelity, a dissimulative male working in a falsifying medium? The question posed a serious problem. The possible solutions lay in crossings of the boundaries between masculinity and femininity and between the body and words. Mark Twain was demonstrably fascinated with confusing the clear division between natural indexical signs and cultural symbols. He similarly melded distinctions by affirming both the reliability of physically transmitted signs and the inevitability of interpretation. He provided instances of emotional gesture turned theatrical as well as instances of gesture as self-betrayal. These strategies of combination pointed the way.

PHYSIOLOGIES OF VOICE AND WRITING

Metaphors of trace and reflex that Mark Twain employed to describe writing attest to his impulse to ground inscription in material processes. When he draws analogies between photography and realist writing, for example, he emphasizes physical and mechanical transmission. "It is all such truth," he wrote to Howells in praise of *The Lady of Aroostook*, "truth to the life; everywhere your pen falls it leaves a photograph"; and of Howells's *A Boy's Town* Twain wrote, it "is perfect—perfect as the perfectest photograph the sun ever made."[20] The vocabulary of leavings and of photographic process—another indexical process in Peirce's categorization, the physical tracing of light (106)—furnishes writing with a material mechanism, as if life registered itself through the writer onto the page in a manner akin to the exposure of a photographic plate, and almost as if the intervention of interpretive subjectivity were eliminated. But Twain was even ready to subsume certain mental operations under the rubric of photographlike registration; he compared the unconscious processes of fashioning a literary character by blending memories of real people to the making of a "composite photograph," the practice which Francis Galton made famous, of exposing several portraits on a single plate in order to get an "average" image, a "type."[21] Galton himself made the analogy between this technology of mechanical "averaging" and the creative artist's ability to generalize, undoubtedly further blurring for Twain the distinction between the physical and mental. Automatic, physical registration of reality emerges as a privileged process, and Twain seems to invest more and more in those writerly operations rooted in the physical. He takes a position quite contrary to that of his one-time collaborator, Charles Dudley Warner, who discounted the indexical as the proper pursuit of the artist by declaring that a "photograph of a natural object is not art," nor is "the plaster cast of a man's face."[22] For Twain, such typical declarations that art surpassed automatic registration failed as prescriptions for realism.

Possible registrations of the body in writing or words (as I shall be arguing here and in the next chapter) served as a special area of concern, since the proximity to its words of the speaking or writing body promised a connection, or reduced the gap, between person and expression, referent and sign. In his courtroom speech on "sure identifiers," Pudd'nhead Wilson's likening one's fingerprints to "his signature, his physiological autograph" credits signature with features of the fingerprint, as if the habitual gestures of handwriting similarly left traces of the body (108). And for Twain, I will argue, an irreducible residue of the material and physiological seemingly could linger in the written word. Script becomes akin to Becky Thatcher's ribbon—found by trackers as a sure sign of the doomed children's presence in McDougal's cave, and cherished by Mrs. Thatcher "because this one parted latest from the living body before the awful death came" (*Tom Sawyer*, 207).

But it was easiest, it appears, for Twain to discern the living body in the *spoken* word. A language of bodies permeates his comments on lecturing—a commentary organized around the poles of the living word that issues from the mouth, the tongue, the lips, and the written word whose mediation so distances the moment of life as to render the utterance a cadaver. Speeches which "carried away all my wits & made me drunk with enthusiasm" were disemboweled when put in print; their "still sentences seem[ed] rather the prone dead forms of a host whom I had lately seen moving to the assault in the fire & smoke

& tumult of battle, with flags flying & drums beating & the clarion voice of command ringing out above the thunder of the guns."[23] He was amazed at how "pale" speeches looked in print, "but how radiant, how full of color, how blinding they were in delivery!"[24] Of the orator Robert Ingersoll, he wrote, "Lord, what an organ is human speech when it is played by a master! All these speeches may look dull in print, but how the lightning glared around him when they were uttered, and how the crowd roared in response!" After reading some of Ingersoll's writing, Clemens wrote to him, "I wish I could hear you *speak* these splendid chapters before a great audience—to read them by myself and hear the boom of the applause only in the ear of my imagination, leaves something wanting—and there is also a still greater lack, your manner, and voice, and presence."[25]

The bodies of dead soldiers, pallid complexions, the absence of voice and presence; this vocabulary of living presence and bloodless, absent, or dead bodies is even more pronounced in Twain's remarks about his own speeches. An evening's "warbly" and charming "little talk" looks "miserably pale and vapid and lifeless in the cold print of a damp newspaper next morning. . . . You do not recognize the corpse. You wonder if this is really that gay and handsome creature of the evening before. You look him over and find he certainly is those very remains. Then you want to bury him. You wish you could bury him privately."[26] Newspaper reports of his own lectures and readings generally left out their life and "charm," for such things "cannot be put upon paper—& whosoever reports a humorous lecture *verbatim*, necessarily leaves the *soul* out of it, & no more presents that lecture to the reader than a person presents a *man* to you when he ships you a corpse."[27] He rather similarly thought that giving voice to words on paper restored their life and sense: "Lord," he wrote, "there's nothing like the human organ to make words live & throb, & lift the hearer to the full altitudes of their meaning."[28]

Mark Twain may not have intended the double entendre of the human "organ"; that is, he may have meant to invoke a wind instrument and not fleshy tissue. But the ability of this organ to make words "live and throb" suggests otherwise. The body here invests words with life. Words are made to register the life of the body. It is the material contact of words with muscle, tissue, moisture, or membrane that makes the difference between "presence" or "soul" and a pale, cold corpse. The circuit of "life," voice, and speech approximates the other lines of transmission—such as that from character through brain to cranium, or that from the unconscious to outward expression in gesture—which implant the surest signification in the flesh.[29]

If words could begin to approximate indexical and gestural signs because they physically issued from the body, and came all the closer to this ideal the nearer they were in space and time to the body itself, they also could approximate bodily expression if they were unconsciously, involuntarily uttered. Words, of course, could be unconscious slips, and therefore could have a relation to concealed truth similar to that which bodily symptoms were likely to have. In *Tom Sawyer*, for example, when Tom is preoccupied with keeping his troubling secret about the murder of Doc Robinson, his uncontrollable bodily signs—his hand shakes, he spills his coffee at breakfast—may actually be less revealing than the mumbling Sid hears when he hovers over the restlessly sleeping Tom (90). Huck, also, is inclined to unguarded verbal outbursts. And he, too, in *Tom Sawyer*, betrays secrets about Injun Joe, truths he and Tom had sworn to suppress. He unwittingly reveals that the deaf and dumb stranger can speak; though he was trying to keep Injun Joe's identity secret, "his tongue seemed determined to get him into trouble in spite of all he could do," and his auditor immediately grasps that "you've let that slip without intending it; you can't cover that up now" (214). The wagging of the tongue, in this case, resembles the self-exposing movements of arms and legs that betray Huck in *Huckleberry Finn*, as if speech truly might have a kinship with unconscious and habitual gesture. And indeed, in *Huckleberry Finn*, as the disguised Huck pumps Judith Loftus for information, he only barely stifles his protest that Jim is no murderer, despite what the St. Petersburg townsfolk think (69); his tongue and his boy-gestures are juxtaposed as unconscious betrayers. The gap between body and word is diminished.

These examples must suffice for the moment to support my point—that for Twain there existed a gestural, bodily dimension to words, and that this dimension helped credit utterances with a degree of immediacy inasmuch as they were automatic and unconscious. In Mark Twain's thinking, especially of the 1880s and 1890s, the gaps of representation might be bridged by linking thought and word, emotion and language, through physical mediums; a problem of realism and reference had a possible solution in this more direct and concrete connection. *Our* contemporary concern with the body, Elaine Scarry has suggested, emerges largely from an anxiety and preoccupation about reference; efforts to reconnect language to the world have moved inevitably to "the most extreme locus of materialization, the live body," in order to imbue language with the corporeal, or tie it to the materialized voice.[30] The similar doubts about reference that plagued the realists, and the realist desire to *embody*, to give palpable form, to provide the physically real and not just the imaginatively true, drove Mark Twain to the juncture of the somatic and the semiotic as the most easily bridgeable gap between the material world and meaning.

This conception led Mark Twain much more deeply into contemporary psychology and "mental physiology"—led him, indeed, to work out much more elaborate, physiological accounts of the creative process and of writing. And it was in these investigations that he most fully confronted the difficulty that, by taking the natural, fleshly, automatically functioning body as a medium for thought and emotion, he necessarily had to acknowledge something "feminine" in creation and composition. It is to these issues that the next chapter will be devoted.

5

Mediumship, "Mental Telegraphy," and Masculinity

In "Clairvoyant," a fragment of a story written probably in 1883 and 1884, Mark Twain tells of John H. Day, a man who, in addition to being able to tell the future, can learn everything about a person's character and intimate thoughts and feelings—each man "as he is," not merely "as he seems to be"—by looking into the ears, under the guise of checking for deafness. That Day's eyes in repose look like "smouldering fires" and when stirred brighten to brilliance echoes the popular belief, still common enough in the late nineteenth century, that mesmerists could project magnetic fluid (or bodily electricity, or some other "vital force") from their eyes into their subjects' eyes or ears and read minds via this medium. Apprehension of a person's reality beneath the bodily surface is sexualized and masculinized by the metaphor of penetration and invasion through the ear. But Day in turn himself serves as a kind of medium for the narrator of the story, who surreptitiously watches the clairvoyant while Day dreams about the people whose secrets he has plumbed. Occasionally Day, asleep, mutters such things as, "People who think they know him would say the thing is incredible." Generally he functions as an expressive image, inviting identification from the narrator: "Smiles would flash across his face; then the signs of sharp mental pain; then furies of passion. This stirring panorama of emotions would continue for hours, sometimes, and move me, excite me, exhaust me like a stage-play."[1]

A "medium" himself, Day links together two physical mediums as channels of representation: the ethereal medium that penetrates the ears, carries to him the private and secret information, and grounds his perception in a material relay; and the medium of the face, the body surface that expresses Day's interior. As such, Day echoes two kinds of popular, mediumistic performances—the spiritualist performances that were in such vogue in the second half of the nineteenth century, and the unconscious and absorbed "stage-play" actor's automatic and bodily expressions of emotion. He also combines his penetration of others with the passive and unconscious expression that the narrator voyeuristically watches; both Svengali and Trilby, the spirit control and the channel, Day condenses invasion and openness, conscious surveillance and unconscious revelation. For Mark Twain, I will argue, Day is a figure of the artist as authentic representer, a figure specifically of the writer as a medium, receiving his subject matter from "elsewhere" (a process usually bound to a seminal flow) and expressing or unveiling it automatically, almost unconsciously (a femininely passive operation). Just as mediumship in nineteenth-century America was insistently cast and recast in gendered and sexualized terms, so Mark Twain could theorize his own creative processes as active and passive, as "masculine" and "feminine." The move launched this "manly" writer into a difficult territory of gender confusion.

The invocation of clairvoyance and mediumship as analogues for writerly representation rehearsed, but also reconfigured, Mark Twain's concerns about performance. From his recollections of itinerant mesmerists in Hannibal and his journalism on spiritualist performances in San Francisco to the representations in his fiction—the king as mesmerist in *Huckleberry Finn,* Joan of Arc as a channel for holy voices, the ambiguous treatment of spiritualism in *The Mysterious Stranger Manuscripts*—mediumship always held for Mark Twain a set of uncertainties.[2] There usually lurked a suggestion of charlatanry or theatricality that promised ultimately to discredit the veracity and fidelity of medium-conveyed representations, partly because public exhibition of mesmerists, telepaths, clairvoyants, animal magnetists, spiritualist mediums, table-rappers, and so on, had become common currency in popular entertainment. I do not want to discount this skeptical dimension of Twain's attention to mediumship. In this chapter, however, I will be more concerned with the possibilities he saw in mediumship for representation. Mediums themselves tended to defend their legitimacy by downplaying the publicly exhibitive dimension of their performances and stressing the non-theatrical; mostly young women, they used as credentials their femininity, their passivity, their unconsciousness, and their predilection for summoning spirits into small, intimate, family-sized groups.[3] Twain pursued similar means of authenticating his writing processes

and his fiction, and overstressing his skepticism obscures his territory of concern—the distinctions and connections between expression and performance, the private and the theatrical, "feminine"
transparency and "masculine" publicity.

I will focus attention first, however, on the ways in which Twain's
interest in mediumship meshed with his interests in the body as a
medium and, more generally, in physical circuits for representation.
John H. Day's juxtaposition of mediums epitomizes a connection that
preoccupied Twain. Day's "stage-play" primarily involves the unconscious expression of emotion in his face. Automatic and uncensored, these expressions of emotion are reflexive, effects of the nervous system, seemingly direct registrations of Day's dreams, the
results of bodily machinery. The medium of his clairvoyance, emitted
from his eyes, is apparently physical, or material, too. Franz Mesmer,
of course, had posited the existence of a "superfine fluid" as the
medium for gravity, electricity, heat, light, magnetism—and also, finally, for empathy, thought transference, clairvoyance, and communication with the dead.[4] As the nineteenth century progressed, electricity, or some physical substance akin to it, took the place of vitalistic
fluids as the force used to give a material basis and explanation to a
host of still puzzling phenomena, ranging from the nervous system,
the body's economy of energy, and virility to artistic creation and
spiritualist communication.[5] "Mental physiologists" emerged who
placed on a material continuum the reflexive gesture that expressed
emotion, the hysteric's symptoms, unconscious processes of creativity, and spiritualist trances. It is to these traditions of the physical and
the physiological that we should relate Twain's interest in mediumship.[6] And it is through these traditions that mediumship became
for Twain a crucial vehicle for representation, a means of physically
registering reality, a way for a referent to express itself.

PHYSICS OF MEDIUMSHIP/
HYSTERICS OF REALISM

For a writer who was fascinated with the reliability of gesture, bodily signs, and physical circuits, such "scientific" theories—physical or
physiological—for operations of the human psyche held a great deal
of allure. The implications Twain saw for his own art in physical
explanations of mediumship come out most tellingly in his essay

"Mental Telegraphy"—a piece begun in 1878, finished in 1881, and finally published (with an addition) only in 1891.[7] Here, among various instances of thought transference, Mark Twain recounts a case directly pertinent to writing, a case, moreover, that reproduces and elaborates the (sexualized) model for artistic invention and representation implicit in John H. Day's example. One morning in the 1870s, Twain tells us, while he was "lying in bed, idly musing," "suddenly a red-hot new idea came whistling down into my camp, and exploded with such comprehensive effectiveness as to sweep the vicinity clean of rubbishy reflections" (379). The idea—that his Nevada friend Dan De Quille (William Wright) ought to author a book about the 1860s silver rush. Twain quickly outlined the book, but before he got a letter off to De Quille suggesting the project, he got a letter *from* De Quille proposing just such a book. The two letters were the same "in substance," though differently worded. De Quille, Mark Twain concluded, had "*originated* that succession of ideas," and "telegraphed" them to Twain's "receiver" (380–81), "fill[ing] my head with them, to the exclusion of every other interest" (383). Twain had then translated the ideas into his own words.

Twain favored *telegraphy* as the term for thought transference because he believed that "the something which conveys our thoughts through the air from brain to brain is a finer and subtler form of electricity," and therefore analogous to telegraphy (389). In his 1875 correspondence with De Quille about this instance of thought transference, Twain refers to this force as "mesmeric current," a physical fluid capable of establishing "mesmeric sympathies." Relatedly, in notes made in 1878 he mentions "dyllic" and "odic" auras, which apparently refer to the "od" or "odylic" force similarly thought to connect minds and spirits. De Quille described the "subtle fluid or force" that connected him to Twain as "some all-pervading element like electricity, but even more subtle, that circulates through all things."[8] Especially telling for Twain's preferred terminology, however, is his reference in "Mental Telegraphy" to "Mr. Brown, the 'mind-reader' " (384), because it clearly refers to Jacob Randall Brown, who became nationally known in 1874 through well-publicized mind-reading performances, whose abilities were tested at Yale University and recounted in journals of neurology, and who, in a stunt that may have helped generate Twain's electric-telegraphic metaphor, once attached a Western Union wire to his head in order to read the mind of another man similarly attached to a wire and sitting miles away in a telegraph office.[9] Twain thought Brown's mind-reading might indeed be legitimate. However, he was convinced that this medium of thought was superior to electricity and its wires; hence, mental telegraphy would sometimes outrace a telegram, and one's addressee would respond by wire even before Western Union reached him; the message apparently went "straight from your brain to the man it was meant for, far outstripping the wire's slow electricity" (391). Now, Twain fantasizes, if someone would only invent a "*phrenophone;* that is to say, a method whereby the communicating of mind with mind may be brought under command and reduced to certainty and system," just as electricity has been put to use in telegraphy (389).[10]

Part of the reason for the fantasy of the phrenophone was to enable communication and representation whose fidelity was insured by the physical circuit. Embodied in the electricitylike medium, De Quille's idea can travel pellucidly to Twain's brain, remaining the same "in substance." But when Twain puts the idea into words, it does not match De Quille's written description. While, Twain asserted, "I *know* now that mind can communicate with mind without the slow and clumsy vehicle of speech," in the absence of phrenophonic mastery of this physical medium, communication was relegated still to the faulty connection between referent and word, to the modes of translation and resemblance instead of physical transmission. Ultimately, Twain declared, "We must have the *thought* itself shot into our minds from a distance; then, if we need to put it into words, we can do that tedious work at our leisure"—though, in the conscious labor of words, the circuit of substances and the fidelity of representation go awry.

The distinction Twain makes between immediate, automatic, electrical transmission of thought and the mental labor of wording is fundamentally that between indexical signs and symbols, between reflexive gestures and calculated ones, between physical transmission and its break. Yet, while he has imported the familiar gap between word and referent into his account of mediumship, he has also fashioned a basis for crossing that gap. His materialist account of brains and physical force (rather than minds and spirit) participated in a late-nineteenth-century extension of the principle of conservation of energy (the first law of thermodynamics) and the "correlation of forces"—that not only were light, heat, mechanical energy, magnetism, and electricity correlated and convertible one to another, but "vital force," "nerve force," and mental energy in animals and human beings were part of the same economy of energy.[11] By suggesting that the medium for thoughts was a finer form of electricity, Twain connects physical and mental events in a way that profoundly affects representation, opening a route to conceive the expression of thought and emotion as a physical circuit not unlike that of the index. If telegraphy and thought were thus of the same order—that is, if mental force was akin to electrical energy, and electricity was part of the physical world—then this scientific erasure of the distinction between spirit and matter pointed a new way toward understanding literary creation. The familiar problematic, in which artists tried to "realize" or "materialize" ideas—and always failed, to some degree, in giving material form to inner or spiritual significance—could be rethought as a matter of physics, as material transmission. The gap between idea and realization, or mind and body, or spirit and matter—all resonating with the gap between concept and representation—could be bridged on the continuum that joined mental force to substance.

Emerging theories of mental physiology provided Twain with conceptions that further blurred distinctions, not only between thoughts and their expression, but also between processes of thought transference and processes of unconscious creativity (or between interpsychic communications and intrapsychic communications). The disposition of scientists and popularizers of science to use the telegraphic metaphor to describe both telepathy and the human nervous system itself (the brain often acting as the central office, telegraphing electrical messages throughout the body) implies the common explanation. One of the most prominent of the mental physiologists, William Carpenter, made frequent use of the telegraphic metaphor as a way of grounding mental phenomena in the material world, and took spiritualist mediumship as a special object of study. He thought it possible that "Nerve-force as a special form of Physical energy" might be able to "exert itself from a distance, so as to bring the Brain of one person into direct dynamical communication with that of another, without the intermediation either of verbal language or of movements of expression."[12] Despite this legitimation of Twain's type of mental telegraphy as a means of communication superior to words or gestures, Carpenter thought it more likely that mediums'

communications were "nothing else than products of their own automatic mental operations," internal flows of nerve force operating
outside consciousness, as *reflexive* responses to stimuli, whose automatism made them feel like communications from another (303).
Carpenter called such automatic operations "unconscious cerebration" to identify them as activity of the cerebrum (the physical brain)
rather than the "mind."

Twain similarly linked, as cases of "unconscious plagiarism," both
the "telegraphic" communication from De Quille (101–2) and the unconscious processes of memory and writing that made him un-
knowingly reproduce as a dedication in *The Innocents Abroad* Oliver
Wendell Holmes's dedication to his *Songs in Many Keys*.[13] That is to
say, unconscious plagiarism (the "happy phrase" he borrowed from
Holmes) blurred distinctions for Twain between subconscious communications from others and subconscious communications from
memory. These phenomena were associated not only because both
occurred outside of consciousness; Twain's idea of mental telegraphy as a matter of physics corresponds to Holmes's conception of unconscious plagiarism as a "mechanism of thought," a function of the
physical brain. This coupling is important for two reasons: first, because it forwards mental telegraphy as a general model for literary
creation, and second, because it subsumes a certain kind of "unconscious" *writing* within the physical model. Through avenues akin to
Holmes's explanations of certain kinds of writing as emissions of the
body, I would like to suggest, Twain found a way to certify some of
his *wording* as immediate, like a gesture, like a reflex.

In *Mechanism in Thought and Morals* (1871), Holmes describes unconscious mentation as a material process.[14] He writes of the "inscription" of memory "in the very substance of the brain tissue" (71),
of the coursing of impulses along the nerves ("the telegraphic cords
of the system" [12]), and of the development of an idea when one "is
least conscious of it" through the organic alterations inevitably occurring to "an impression made on a living tissue" (57). Unconscious
plagiarism, Holmes suggests, is an instance of "unconscious cerebration" or "reflex action of the brain"—terms he borrowed from the
mental physiology of Carpenter and Thomas Laycock (33–37). But so,
more generally, is the writing of poetry a process "automatic and im-
perceptible" (44), unwilled and passive, as if the poet were receiving
"dictation *ab extra*" (51). Borrowing a figure central to those psy-

chophysiologists interested in establishing mental events as reflex phenomena—that of the hysterical woman whose mental condition was still thought by many to be an effect of uterine irritation or ovarian malfunction[15]—Holmes characterized poetry as "hysterics of the intelligence," an emission "as automatic, involuntary, as entirely self-evolved by a hidden organic process, as are the changing moods of the laughing and crying woman" (51).[16]

Carpenter similarly thought that the processes of artistic genius and invention were "essentially *automatic*," especially when, as in the work of Wordsworth, Coleridge, or Mozart, ideas flowed spontaneously and poems or sonatas seemed to be composing themselves (510–13). Such creation was so much like "the mysterious performances of a *clairvoyante* or a *medium*" that he pointedly wondered how parapsychological dictations *ab extra* "are related to those glorious creations, which have sprung from the legitimate exercise of the imaginative faculty in a Shakspere [*sic*] or a Milton" (612). It is through this frame, which joins apparent dictation from outside with an internal reflex of uncontrolled cerebration, that we should grasp Mark Twain's familiar descriptions of his authorial passivity. He would write in 1884 to the Society for Psychical Research that he had often thought "that all my powerful impulses come to me from somebody else. . . . [I] feel like a mere amanuensis when I sit down to write. . . . I consider that that other person is supplying the thoughts to me, and that I am merely writing from dictation."[17] But this is only an instance in his longer history of attributing his writing more generally to an unknown, upwelling force, which made it necessary only that he hold the pen while the writing "went by itself."[18] Twain characterized himself repeatedly as an amanuensis, passively taking dictation *ab extra*, with "no cogitations, no attempts at intervention" (*Mark Twain in Eruption*, 243). And, he declared, "As long as the book would write itself, I was a faithful and interested amanuensis and my industry did not flag, but the minute that the book tried to shift to *my* head the labor of contriving its situations, inventing its adventures, and conducting its conversations, I put it away and dropped it out of my mind" (196).

While these pronouncements invite association with contemporary investigations into psychic phenomena and the psychology associated with them, as Susan Gillman has shown, they ought also to be connected to mental physiology. The well-known story of how he surmounted an impasse when *Tom Sawyer* shifted its writing to Twain's own contrivances securely relates authorial passivity to the reflex activity of the brain that so occupied Oliver Wendell Holmes and William Carpenter. When Twain reached page four hundred of the manuscript of *Tom Sawyer,* he claimed, "the story made a sudden and determined halt and refused to proceed another step. . . . I could not understand why I was not able to go on with it. The reason was very simple—my tank had run dry; it was empty." When this happens, "when the tank runs dry," Twain concludes, "you've only to leave it alone and it will fill up again, in time, while you are asleep— also while you are at work at other things, and are quite unaware that this unconscious and profitable cerebration is going on" (*Mark Twain in Eruption*, 197). Elsewhere he referred to the "mill" of "unconscious cerebration," "whose helpful machinery never stands idle," and he testified that, whenever his tank had run dry, he could simply wait until "U. C." (his abbreviation of the familiar "unconscious cerebration") had refilled his creative reservoir.[19]

Although Mark Twain's delight in his "U. C." seems focused on sheer production, it is a production grasped as an unconscious making, as an uninterrupted mechanical circuit, rather than the production of signifying products cut off from their signified causes. To an important extent, unconscious cerebration and physiological mechanism promised a guarantee for the realism Twain was pursuing. Although his medium here is that of words rather than expressive bodily gestures, because the writing has the character of reflex, avoiding both the contriving mind and will and the tedious labor of translating ideas into sentences, it attains the immediacy of index and gesture.

At the same time that the abyss between body and words is crossed by the physical bridge of these cerebral processes, I would argue, distinctions grasped in terms of masculinity and femininity are breached. To the extent that Mark Twain thought his ideas came from somebody else, he was penetrated and feminized; he functioned—as he did when, lying idly in bed, he caught De Quille's mental ejaculation—as a passive "receiver" for seminal ideas. To the extent that his writing was an internal dynamic of unconscious reflex, it amounted to "hysterics of the intelligence," and therefore to feminine spasms of bodily indiscipline. Mark Twain relaxes the masculine control and dissimulation that aimed to plug any truthful exposure through the cracks of protective armor. Its effect is the immediate speaking of what amounts to a masculine-feminine body, a writing equivalent to hysterics, blush, or jabber that carried with its femininity a certification of the truthful and the real.[20]

As a precaution against the threat of full feminization, I would suggest, Mark Twain theorizes a masculine-feminine intrapsychic economy that follows popular scientific accounts of the relation between physical and vital force. Late-nineteenth-century science, that is, posited body and mind as a relatively contained energy system, in which physical activity depleted mental reserves or, as G. J. Barker-Benfield characterizes the "spermatic economy," in which a limited reserve of seminal force could be expended in—or hoarded for—sexual activity, physical labor, or mental labor. Metaphors of the body as a battery, or galvanic cell, proliferated.[21] In Mark Twain's version, apparently, unconscious cerebration amassed a reserve of creative force that sent telegrams to a passive consciousness. In much the same way that it took Twain a period of not-quite-conscious worrying about something to get his own mental telegrams "up in good shape" ("Mental Telegraphy," 377), he testified that it took periods of unconscious cerebration, sometimes lasting for years, to refill his creative tanks. Though giving up the masculine will and controlling awareness, this model celebrated masculinity in the form of seminal-mental upwellings of energy from below (suppressing the associations of reflex with "female" hysteria). Twain enacted a kind of autoeroticism, became an actually procreative bachelor machine, his automatic, electrical cerebrations ejaculating telegrams to his passive consciousness. He transforms the interpsychic model, in which he is the feminine receiver for De Quille's mental force, into an intrapsychic model more akin to John H. Day's, in which he is both the source of seminally creative fluid and its passive conduit. This saved him from feminization, and yet annexed reflex action and passivity as guarantees of realism. But we must consider, quite clearly, that this ultimately narcissistic and masturbatory move aimed to efface the problematic connections among passivity, the body, and femininity.[22] As I shall try to show in a moment, however, the gender troubles in analogizing mediumship and authorship far outstripped this solution of autoeroticism.

Twain managed to press the model of physically transmitted representation to limits that revealed its shortcomings as well—most pointedly, I think, in the play *Colonel Sellers as a Scientist* (1883), a work that brings us back to the year Twain probably wrote "Clair-voyant," and back again quite explicitly to issues of mediumship and representation.[23] Twain collaborated on the play with William Dean Howells, but the main character was Twain's (from *The Gilded Age* and *Colonel Sellers*), and according to Howells it was Twain's idea to make Sellers a scientific inventor and "a spiritualist, whose specialty in the occult was materialization"—that is, the embodiment of de-parted spirits.[24] Readers of the play have found the materialization theme simply ludicrous.[25] In the context of the foregoing discussion, however, it will be obvious that *Sellers as a Scientist* is a reconsidera-tion, albeit in a farcical way, of possibilities of representation, the spiritualist aim of bringing dead spirits back to life serving as a metaphor for art, reproduction, and realism.

Sellers promises an up-to-date *electrical* version of materialization. "No spiritualism about it," he says; "A purely scientific operation" (223) based on "natural forces," not the supernatural (226). His mate-rialization contraption, a congeries of "poles and batteries" (220), somehow uses "stored electricity" (225) as a means for "absorbing and condensing the enormous waste of vital force with which our at-mosphere is filled from the dissolution of the human race" (226). Thus gathered together, this "vital force"—also referred to as "unor-ganized matter"—gives substance to the spirits of the dead. Embody-ing an understanding of vital forces unmistakably modeled on ther-modynamics, and particularly on the conservation and convertability of forces, Sellers's facetiously presented materializer echoes Twain's serious concerns about economies of energy and representation. Al-though the materializations Sellers plans may superficially sound like those of other popular spiritualist exhibitors, he claims they will not be like "ordinary mediumistic arms and feet and things that don't amount to anything—no substance in them—you strike a light or fetch in a skeptic, and pff! They disappear" (221); his materializations will be translated to the flesh through electricity and matter. More-over, Sellers's aim is nothing "so paltry as an *exhibition*" (215). He will materialize spirits in the *mass:* "The spiritualists materialize one little pitiful spectre—or part of a spectre—a leg, or an arm! Or a forefinger, or a big toe!" He, on the other hand, will materialize the dead on a grand scale, hundreds of thousands of whole bodies a year, for the purpose of filling out the ranks of police, politicians, and public ser-vants (215). Lafayette Hawkins, Sellers's auditor and admirer, ap-

provingly exclaims that Sellers's plans will be "a much bigger wonder than materializing a mere plaster of Paris leg in a dim light" (215).
The crucial distinction is that Sellers is a scientist rather than a spiritualist, stressing electricity and the *substance* of "vital force" as his
means of materialization. But, if this resembles the transmigration of
ideas in Twain's mental telegraphy, then the play nonetheless repudiates this model of artistic creation. Sellers himself discounts his
own vaunted process. After a typically Twainian confusion of identities, an astonished Sellers concludes that he has actually materialized someone: Reginald De Bohun, the heir to the earldom of Dover
and a man reported to have just died in a fire. Yet Sellers belittles this
apparent success by declaring his belief that the man before him is
without substance, that he is liable to float away or disappear (221).
And when the prospect looms that this "materializee" might marry
his daughter, Sellers strenuously objects that the man is a mere "sim-
ulacrum," a "spectre," a "miserable fraud of an apparition" (233), not
the substantial, warm, living body that a husband must be. But the
final blow to the entire undertaking of representation—whether it be
through simulacra and facsimile or physical transmission—comes
with the revelation that this materialization never took place after all.
Sellers, as an artist and reproducer of reality, failed completely.

   As echoes and analogues of Sellers's translation of the dead, the
play introduces other media that promise the technofantasy of the reproduction of reality, notably a telephone and a phonograph—each
of which raises questions about the reliability of physical transmission. As Nicholas Royle has persuasively suggested, telepathy in the
nineteenth century was related to a more general "tele-culture" of
communication through invisible channels—"in telegraphy, photography, the telephone and gramophone"; and if Alexander Graham
Bell and, especially, Thomas A. Watson, the inventors of the telephone, joined their thinking about telephonic communication to spiritualism and occult forces, it should be no surprise that Twain links
telephony and Sellers's materialization.[26] But like the electrical
medium for reproducing the dead, the electricity of the telephone
misfires. It serves merely as an occasion for a long passage of mis-
communication between Sellers and the "call-boy" of a hotel. The
telephone finally fails to convey any information and elicits from
Sellers a curse on "that deaf and dumb machine" (234).

   Another medium that mechanically listens and mechanically reproduces what it hears, that translates the voice through a malleable

substance, is the phonograph, in this case "the Sellers Ship's phono-graph for the application of stored Profanity to the working of Ves-sels during storms. Adapted to the use of Foremen in Boiler Manu-factories and Large Press-Rooms" (223). When "loaded up" with "sailor profanity" by a hired "expert," this invention is supposed to aid first mates by relieving them of the responsibility of doing all the swearing at the sailors. Used as Sellers means it to be used, then, the phonograph would represent skillful swearing, but mainly for effect rather than for the purpose of realistic reproduction. However, "if you leave it open, and all set," the phonograph will also "eavesdrop, so to speak—that is to say, it will load itself up with any sounds that are made within six feet of it" (241). Akin to the mediumship of John H. Day, who in a sense reproduces eavesdroppings, the phono-graph's registration and conveyance of the talk of unsuspecting peo-ple is even less satisfactory than Day's face, with its incomplete and puzzling representations. The physical and direct medium of the phonograph plays back fragments of language as collage or as bur-lesque. For example, a conversation recorded between Mary Sellers and Aunt Sally, a black servant, comes out as juxtaposed snippets of Mary's weeping over her lover and Sally's cursing him, and more gen-erally as a sentimental language of love discomposed by blackface minstrel dialect (224). Later, when Colonel Sellers tries to demon-strate some profanity, he gets only a sentimental ballad by an un-known singer interrupted by cats wailing and *"warming up towards a fight"* (241). The phonograph simply cannot represent transparently. Its mediation rearranges reality into noise, nonsense, and burlesque.[27]

Huckleberry Finn—which, because it was started a couple of years before "Mental Telegraphy" and finished in 1883, the year of "Clair-voyant" and *Sellers as a Scientist*, understandably echoes mediumistic concerns—reiterates the message that any medium for communica-tion transmits but also impedes. Consider the fog, which makes Jim's panicked whoops indistinguishable from other raftsmen's and causes sounds to "dodge around" and "swap places," much as Sell-ers's phonograph does. As Huck concludes, you "couldn't tell noth-ing about voices in a fog" (100–101). Huck later juxtaposes the fog, in which confusedly disembodied voices sound "like spirits carrying on that way in the air," to clear atmosphere, in which you could eas-ily see a raftsman at a distance chopping wood: "You'd see the axe flash, and come down—you don't hear nothing; you see that axe go up again, and by the time it's above the man's head, then you hear the *k'chunk!*—it had took all that time to come over the water" (157). The effect of this observation, though, is to underscore the airy medium as both channel and impediment for distant reality. In Huck's superstitious world, similarly, leaves may try to rustle a mournful message, owls may whoo-whoo about a spirit, dogs and whippoorwills may cry about the dying, but all of these fall short of full communication, just like the wind, which tried "to whisper something to me," but with so much noise that "I couldn't make out what it was, and so it made the cold shivers run over me." The failure of communication itself causes terror and grief: "Then away out in the woods I heard that kind of a sound that a ghost makes when it wants to tell about something that's on its mind and can't make itself understood, and so can't rest easy in its grave and has to go about that way every night grieving" (4).

As if he were embodied fog, or a version of Sellers's profanity phonograph, Huck as a representation mechanism also works as both channel and impediment. When Huck goes on automatic, that is, and trusts to "instinct," as he puts it (279), or relies on "Providence" to put words in his mouth (277) (an important conflation, by the way, of scientific reflex action and spiritual mediumship), what comes out are "lies" that are worked-over versions of his experience. His lies to Judith Loftus, to the Grangerfords, to the duke and the king, to the Phelpses—which contain elements of his experience, such as being orphaned, being treated cruelly, rafting down the river, secretly traveling at night—all come off better than when he consciously has to fabricate stories, say about being an English "valley." As with Mark Twain, in other words, when the mental labor of storytelling is made a conscious task, it goes awry; but the automatism that might promise truth turns out to be bound to a mechanism whose corporeality, and circuitry, and sheer physiological functioning cancel the promise of a simple and direct conduit. Like the fog, Huck as a medium makes his realities dodge around and swap places. Like the profanity phonograph, Huck will register a variety of external stimulations through different channels, and his circuitry relays them back quite revised. Mechanical reproduction guaranteed by physical transmission is replaced by production as a reconstruction.[28]

Even so, Huck has other, mediumistic qualities that help to authenticate his narration. In contrast to Jim, whose mediumistic prophesying through his hairball is transparently a money-making hoax, and whose tale of being entranced and ridden by witches serves mainly a purpose of extravagant theater, Huck and his story-telling have that aura of general somnolence, absorption, and un-selfconsciousness, a kind of feminization and passivity, and an asso-ciation with the sincerity and intimacy of the domestic circle he fashions with Jim—all of which he reproduces in his intimate narra-tion. These qualities situate him as a kind of amanuensis of reality, at least to the extent that he is removed from the realm of theater, hoax, and public performance. It is to these dimensions of mediumship in Twain's writing that I now turn.

"ADDLE-HEADED, FEMININE MEN"

The analogy between mediumship and writing, as our current schol-arship demonstrates it, was most obviously pertinent for women. As historians of nineteenth-century women's writing point out, many women writers in effect denied having written, in order to avoid the suggestion that they were stepping onto the public stage in an un-feminine and unseemly way. They characterized themselves, in-stead, as mediums, "instruments" who operated unconsciously, mouthpieces of God, nature, or home—vehicles for larger forces that submerged the individual female identity and that redeemed this writing from any taint of aggression, competition, ambition, or writerly manipulation.[29] Historians of mediumship and spiritual-ism similarly point out that acting as a medium allowed women to take to the stage as public performers, to act out a variety of roles, to lecture as "trance-speakers," or to publish as "spirit writers" with the understanding that these events were really enacted by absent people, supposedly dead ones.[30] The spectacle of female passivity served as an alibi for the gender crime of public performance: the real perpetrators were supposedly somewhere else. A condition for suc-cessfully taking the stage was to abjure both ambition and agency.

Wedded to this dynamic, however, was a more general logic of representation. If one pattern in the Victorian ideological system credited women with expressive authority—with sincerity and truthfulness because what they said was private and domestic—and thereby posed for them the problem of somehow bringing this au-thority before the public without losing it, another pattern posed for male authors the problem of annexing that authority in their public writing without becoming too "feminized." These twin difficulties gained an institutional prominence in the 1850s through the 1880s when "feminine" novels so dominated the writing of fiction. Alfred Habegger, in *Gender, Fantasy, and Realism in American Literature*, has argued that, as male novelists coming of age during these years, William Dean Howells and Henry James "seized a popular women's literary genre" and "entered deeply into the feminine aspirations it articulated."[31] Mark Twain, I will argue, also grappled with this doubleness of embracing a femininity of privacy, transparency, and domesticity while preserving a masculinity (a preservation Habegger accomplishes for James and Howells through his metaphors of seizure and penetration). The prescription for women—that they could enter the "masculine" public sphere chiefly by exaggerating their private and passive "natures"—resonated for men, too, who gained public credibility by amplifying the intimate and private features of their performances.[32] The paradoxes of the female medium, the sincere male author, or the published private writing all participated in the larger Victorian cultural dynamic that closely wedded, constantly confused, but strove to distinguish between inside and outside, domestic secrecy and masculine publicity.

Mark Twain's automatisms of mental telegraphy and amanuensis were embedded in and related to the larger, longer-standing conceptions of feminine mediumship. If automatism could, in its most obvious initial impulse, save representation from the division between sign and referent, or signifier and signified, by collapsing the difference, feminine mediumship promised to save representation from the alienation of expression and the dissimulations of exchange in the masculine marketplace by undoing the strict opposition between public and private. Ultimately, automatism and mediumship came to share features, feminine mediumship gaining (through nineteenth-century scientific explanations of unconscious cerebration) the character of automatism, and automatism, because of its private and unconscious character, gaining the aura of transparency, passivity, and domesticity that belonged to mediumship. They became related partly by joining their ostensible opposites—the theatricality that presupposes a division between expression and inner reality, and the marketplace self-presentation associated with aggressive cheating and male duplicity. They also became related through the similar services they performed, joining inner and outer, public and private in a way that promised possibilities of expression without theatricality or alienation.

The constellation of values that seemingly repudiated theatricality and marketing by privileging automatism, mediumship, and domesticity—and yet allowed for publication and audiences—appears perhaps most obviously and consciously in Twain's autobiographical dictations. There he announces, first, that he is "speaking from the grave, because I shall be dead when the book issues from the press"—a stipulation for publication which allowed him, he thought, to speak his "whole frank mind." He functions in the present, in a sense, as a medium, a spirit writer, for his own voice from beyond, the voice of that future self who will no longer care enough about what an audience thinks to tailor his remarks; in a typical twinning, Twain himself provides us with both the irreverent truth-teller and his passive amanuensis. Enough distance exists, he suggests, between the performed truth and the theatrical occasion of publication to alleviate any impulse to reshape the truth for its audience. He then connects "speaking from the grave," and its occult and spiritualist overtones, to his other model for the autobiography, the love letter, for as the "frankest and freest and privatest product of the human mind and heart," unburdened by the sense that any stranger would see it, such a letter allowed free and truthful expression.[33] The privately and intimately domestic utterance, the "frank" transparency, and the mediumistic are clustered here under the nontheatrical, joined in their freedom from having to solicit and attend to an audience, though the point of the autobiography is to broadcast (eventually) these unfettered opinions.[34] Presiding over this mediumship and domestic intimacy is Twain's *dictation* of the autobiography, in which his talk emerges freely, and it is transcribed automatically, so that the links from brain to voice to paper are preserved as continuous. In one remarkable confluence, Twain annexes privacy, intimate sincerity, and automatism, all as a means of certifying to a future public the unalienated and uncensored nature of his writing.

Twain explored over the course of his career various dimensions of this configuration, both "antitheatrical" and devoted to publication. Here I would like to attend especially to *A Connecticut Yankee in King Arthur's Court*, which operates explicitly with the oppositions between mediumship and theatricality, domesticity and marketing—and attempts to keep them intact. (The next chapter will discuss

ways in which these oppositions are complicated, and the final chapter, in its discussion especially of *Joan of Arc,* will show how Twain
pressed these distinctions to their confusion.) The Hank Morgan of
our critical tradition, of course, is quite lopsided, far from being
a femininelike medium; he is instead the sly manipulator, the embodiment of theatricality and market-mindedness (the version of
Hank to which I will attend more fully in the next chapter). But it is
important to note that he is also the medium who connects the nineteenth century to the sixth, whose narrative is supposed to carry
some weight in 1889 and not exist simply as a stunning flourish.
When Hank compares his experience of the "transposition of
epochs—and bodies" to the spirit traveling (and spirit possession) of
the "transmigration of souls" (48), he invokes a kind of connecting
medium ostensibly akin to that which might materialize absent bodies. And, significantly, it is only after having been rendered unconscious with a crowbar (51) that Hank can serve as the medium for
representing the nineteenth century to the sixth. Even more important, it is only after having been put into a deep sleep that he can serve
as the medium for representing his sixth-century story to the modern Mark Twain (and by relay, through the medium of Twain, to us).

While Hank's representation of the sixth century to the nineteenth
carries an aura of authenticity, his representation of the nineteenth
century to the Arthurians is a poor translation. Hank is a poor
medium because in Camelot he is still the prototypically masculine
inhabitant of the business marketplace and the factory bureaucracy,
and as a result a manipulator and a performer. Everything he produces, therefore, is a show, a theatrical spectacle whose "effects" are
carefully calculated and marketed, and therefore fabricated rather
than mediumistically conveyed (a condition which, as I shall argue
in the next chapter, Twain thought was indeed a vexingly endemic
condition of public representation in the late nineteenth century).
The representation of the nineteenth century that he produces in
Arthur's court, in short, is an effect in form and ruthlessly effective
in substance. As if he meant to highlight this underside of the realism that, like Hank, is "barren of sentiment" and of "poetry" (50),
Twain draws a sharp contrast between this theatrical Hank and the
narrating Hank of the story's frame. The Hank Morgan that Mark
Twain meets in the frame has an attractively "candid simplicity," and
"he talked along, softly, pleasantly, flowingly," seeming to "drift
away imperceptibly out of this world and time, and into some remote

era and old forgotten country" (47). Hank has changed from a manufacturer of theatrical effects into a teller of flowing stories, and from
a consciously theatrical manipulator to a man somehow in touch
with, and inclined unconsciously to float off into, another era. The
author invokes this quality, and reestablishes the distinction between
medium and manipulator, precisely to endow Hank's story with authenticity; Hank in the end seems to be a proper medium who transports Twain to another time and place, who "gradually wove such a
spell about me that I seemed to move among the spectres and shadows and dust and mould of gray antiquity" (47).

If, in the frame at the start of the novel, Hank puts "Mark Twain"
into contact with specters and shadows, in the closing frame an entranced and delirious Yankee, whose "mutterings and ejaculations"
carry on with an obliviousness to Twain's presence, thinks he is communicating indeed with the dead. Semiconscious, he can be heard
mumbling:

> O, Sandy, you are come at last,—how I have longed for you! Sit by
> me—do not leave me—never leave me again, Sandy, never again.
> Where is your hand:—give it me, dear, let me hold it—there—now, all
> is well, all is peace, and I am happy again—*we* are happy again, isn't
> it so, Sandy? You are so dim, so vague, you are but a mist, a cloud,
> but you are *here*, and that is blessedness sufficient; and I have your
> hand; don't take it away—it is for only a little while, I shall not require
> it long. . . . Was that the child? . . . Hello-Central! . . . She doesn't an-
> swer. Asleep, perhaps? Bring her when she wakes, and let me touch
> her hands, her face, her hair, and tell her good-bye. (492)

In a nice touch that joins the medium of telephone communication to
this mediumistic transmigration across epochs, Hank calls for his
daughter, Hello-Central, whom Sandy named after his earlier unconscious muttering, when, in his dreams, he had "wandered thirteen
centuries away" in search of his telephone operator girlfriend (453).
More important, however, this communion takes place on Hank's
deathbed, the ultimate symbol of sincere Victorian feeling, and the
vague entities conjured up from the dead (perhaps even materialized)
are Hank's family.[35] That this spirit communication re-creates inti-
macies between husband and wife, father and mother, parent and
child, points toward the conditions which so transformed the Yankee.

Much of the change in the Yankee as a communicator, that is,
comes with his marriage to Sandy. His new model, intimate communication within the family, which has the same kind of sanctity for
Hank that it does for Mark Twain, undergirds Hank's telling of his

story. For he writes the story—"turning my old diary into this narrative form" (or this *novel*)—during the week in which, besieged in his cave, he also devotes time to "writing letters to my wife." The letters are "almost like talking," a kind of intimate, family communion undefiled by revision, censorship, or theatrical effect, enabling Hank to imagine "it was almost like having us all together again" (473). Mingled as it is with love letters, the novel is plainly meant to resemble the easy talking of the family circle. And the novel further resembles the letters—which Hank cannot, and will never, send, though he does not know it yet—because it, too, like spirit writing, is a writing from the grave, a writing that will see the light only centuries after its composition. Like Twain's autobiography, Hank's story garners an aura of "frankness" through association with mediumship, unconsciousness, somnolence, domesticity, and intimate talk.

This is not to say that Twain uncomplicatedly resolves his problems with representation and simply affirms this mediumship. In the last lines of the novel, Hank has returned to theatricality, busy "getting up his last 'effect' " (493). And at various points in the novel the ease with which mediumship is tinged with hoax or transformed into theater is underscored. Hank attributes charlatanry to mediums, noting that "a crowd was as bad for a magician's miracle in that day as it was for a spiritualist's miracle in mine" (252). He transforms bona fide communication through the medium of the telephone into a magic show and an "effect" when he is "clairvoyantly" able to say what the distant Arthur is doing (282). And he makes "prophecy" sound, too, like something of a hoax: "A prophet doesn't have to have any brains. . . . It is the restfulest vocation there is. When the spirit of prophecy comes upon you, you merely cake your intellect and lay it off in a cool place for a rest, and unship your jaw and leave it alone; it will work itself: the rest is Prophecy" (315). The point, however, is that Twain grapples with—and tries in *A Connecticut Yankee* to retain—an opposition troublesomely defined in terms of gender, demarcated according to masculine and feminine spheres, according to consciously calculated performance and unconscious expression. His inability to keep them sharply distinct testifies to their cultural interrelatedness and sets an agenda he will necessarily return to.

Among the masculine-feminine contrasts of nineteenth-century Anglo-American culture traced in Sandra M. Gilbert and Susan

Gubar's *The Madwoman in the Attic* is the opposition between a masculine writing as seminal outflow through the pen-as-penis and a somnambulistic "trance-writing" typical of many nineteenth-century women.[36] Obviously enough, such an opposition operated pervasively in defining authorship. Rather than simply dividing men and women, however, these conflicting categories also obviously constituted individual writerly subjectivities—including Mark Twain's. This is not meant in any way to discount the special difficulties women writers faced, for, obviously, male writers had a degree of freedom to adopt both active and passive roles which was denied to women. I do mean to suggest, however, that we can look even to Mark Twain, supposedly one of the more "manly" of the classic American authors, for symptoms of cultural confusions and anxieties about gender and their "separate spheres," anxieties continually heightening over the course of the nineteenth century.

In their historical accounts of gender and authorship, such critics as Terry Lovell, Rachel Bowlby, Elaine Showalter, and Michael Davitt Bell have outlined the difficulties posed for late-nineteenth-century male novelists.[37] With culture and artistry often associated with the feminine, and with novel writing and reading frequently understood as womanly and domestic pastimes, the male novelist, as Bowlby puts it, "might be in something of an ideological bind; neither pure artist nor fully masculine, and unable to alter one side of the pairing without damaging the other" (11). The stratagems for overcoming the difficulty of "unmanliness" were various. Men could, of course, insist on the pen as penis, and similarly characterize creativity as a product of masculine vitalistic force. Or, as Showalter has noted, "One defense against the mother's reign is to appropriate her power by repressing the maternal role in procreation and creation, and replacing it with a fantasy of self-fathering. . . . Male writers constructed a new myth of creativity in which the work of art was the product of male mating and male inspiration, totally independent of even metaphorically feminine cross-fertilization" (77–78).[38] As I have suggested, Twain's conception of writerly creative force, whether exchanged between himself and De Quille, or circulated within his own bodily economy, suits these models for expelling the femininity with which novel writers and writing were imbued. Certainly his initial attempt at novel writing, in which he and Charles Dudley Warner joined forces to improve upon the sort of novels their wives were reading, followed this pattern—two men bonding in order to invade female territory and to usurp a womanly vocation.[39]

Clearly enough, too, men struggled to masculinize the novel and to depose the women novelists who dominated the field during the middle third of the century. Both the writing of "boys' books" and the touting of "realism" were part of this tendency. Michael Davitt Bell, for example, argues that Howells used "realism" to transform art into a manly activity by pitting his focus on facts and the representation of plain reality against "feminine" preoccupations with style, form, literariness, and "art." Howells thought that the best writing was "unconscious" writing in which "there is no thought of style" or of calculated "dramatic effect."[40] And he included Twain's writing in this category, as when he called Twain "dramatic and unconscious."[41] A strategy that replaces feminine sincerity with feminine artifice in order to reclaim unconsciousness for masculinity and male realism, it nonetheless registers the problem of "male femininity" as much as it solves it.

Mark Twain's fellow humorist Q. K. Philander Doesticks called female mediums "crack-brained masculine women" and male mediums "addle-headed feminine men"—a transparent enough effort to resecure an endangered difference.[42] He might have said the same about novel writers. When we consider a time when women came before the public by mediumistically impersonating men, and men adopted passivity as they recoiled from the masculine territory of the market and pursued the powers of the unconscious and of "truth" in art, we have to reconsider the gendering of writing, realism, and the possibilities of representation in a way sensitive to the contradictions and tensions of this transitional period—and in a way suspicious of Victorian fantasies about the fixity and stability of gender identity. Mark Twain's ruminations on mediumship and his implicit notions about the gender ambiguity of writing echo anxieties about and shifting definitions of masculinity and femininity. They may help us revise our picture of American realism, of the power of the "feminine" novelistic tradition, and of the "masculine" wing of American literary history.

6

"It's Got to Be Theatrical"
Spectacles of Power and Products

If Mark Twain pursued "authenticity" in expression and reliability in reference—through notions of identification in acting, indices in bodily expression, and mediumship—he did so with an insistent sense of the impediments to such representation. And if he sanctified, along with much of his culture, a sincerity linked to private and intimate expression, this came with an awkward sense of a theatricalized mass culture that so avidly consumed it and thereby made any publicly visible expression look like a performance. The rapidly transforming public realm, with its "laws of conspicuous and performed identity," as Philip Fisher has phrased it, was Mark Twain's constant stage, and its seemingly corrosive effects on representation became one of his preoccupations.[1] Twain's writings provide us with a self-reflective diagnosis of the cultural operations of magnified performance and spectacle. Especially as his writing and his theatrical self became American institutions, Twain called into question their representational possibilities.

His assessment focuses partly on the performance of power and the politics of performance, weighing the possibility of "authentic" *public* symbolism and, in the texts I will examine in this chapter, drawing rather pessimistic conclusions about the reliability of symbols and expression when the display of authority and popularity is at stake. Twain turns also to the effect of the marketplace on both "serious" theater and burlesque, partaking of an emergent myth about mass-marketed culture that discerned a new, pervasive degeneration in the capacity of performance to root itself in experience—and degeneration, too, in the ability of joking and derision to overturn regimes of mass deception. He anticipates the modern argument that commodification invades signification, obliterating referents through fetishization, and neutralizing subversive humor, thus transforming any kind of "Mark Twain absurdity," as Max Horkheimer and Theodor

Adorno put it, into another version of market amusement, always with a persistent undercurrent of "the sales talk, the quack's spiel."[2] Though Twain's terms of understanding belong to the late nineteenth century, the critique of mass deception and market dissimulation is one we have inherited. However, Twain's sense of market and theater, I intend to show, moves toward a wider view than the typical Victorian recoil to the home or our familiar critical distaste for commodification.

I will turn first, however, to a pattern of thinking pertinent especially to *The Prince and the Pauper* (1881), in which Twain analyzes and criticizes national spectacles, invoking medieval conceptions of the king as a divine representative in order to dispense with any such transcendent security in signs of power. Kingly authority becomes instead an effect of its public display, and by extension, symbols of national identity or communal meaning appear without moorings—a worry pertinent, I would suggest, for a man beginning to conceive of himself as a national author. The theatricalization of prominence and power, rather than common symbols, constitutes the public spectacles Twain depicts. This extends, in Twain's critique, to otherwise seemingly serious and resonant public symbols, compromised by their association with cultural hierarchy and powerful interests.

Then, *A Connecticut Yankee in King Arthur's Court* (1889) takes a world whose public theater is already fashioned in the interests of power rather than "truth" and introduces into it not only Hank Morgan's market-mindedness and commodification, but also the nineteenth-century split between the private and the public, the home and the market, on which Morgan's theatricality depends. On the one hand, for example, Hank introduces the notions of "private parts" and "indecent exposure"; his shame and embarrassment at his nakedness and at "undressing before folk" is alien to the Arthurians (57, 80, 153). On the other hand, he is the impresario of the most public spectacles and magnificent self-presentations that medieval England has ever seen. This division puts in place distinctions between intimate and public expression, the sincerely frank and the theatrically calculated, which recapture the possibility of transparent representation, though the oppositions are also defamiliarized by an Arthurian context that makes no such distinctions. Through these distinctions, we are invited to see the inauthenticity of Hank's public, marketed spectacles—especially by contrast to his confidential revelations. Mystification and demystification make each other possible; they are among the most basic innovations that Hank brings to Arthur's court.

As part of this portrayal of Hank's theatricality, Twain provides us with a critique of market value and the fate of the commodified sign. That is, Twain's criticism of the publicity of Hank's theater is inextricable from the criticism of its commerciality. The dissociation of public spectacles from origins in frank expression meshes with the dissociation of spectacular commodities from their causes. Spectacles of Hank Morgan's sort, as Twain presents them, are products of the late nineteenth century, effects of commodification and industrialization on the sign, in which referents are hidden, the resonance of symbolism is corroded, and both official spectacle and burlesque are absorbed into the continuum of market display. But the criticism undertaken in this vein—and much of *A Connecticut Yankee*, I will argue, is devoted to it—is eventually undermined, in a typically Twainian move, when Hank theatrically reveals what he has hidden, not only exposing the secret but also turning revelation into evasion, exposure into profit. Moving beyond the recoil from the market and its production of fetishized signs, Twain suggests more various processes of displacement, evasion, and reemphasis, which color not only the machinations of the state and the market, but also the intimate revelations that seemingly define themselves against such public stratagems.

SYMBOLS AND SHOWS

In 1897, in the essay "Queen Victoria's Jubilee," Twain declared that a public spectacle or "procession" "has value in but two ways—as a show and as a symbol," the first insignificant splendor, referring to nothing, merely a delight for the eye, the second weighted with meaning, apt to "compel thought" and "inflame the imagination," with a "moving history back of it."[3] As an example of the first, he cited Mardi Gras, "a mere show, and meaningless." To epitomize the second, he described a parade of Civil War veterans in New York shortly after the war, with spaces left in the ranks for the war dead. This procession had "no color, no tinsel, no brilliancy, yet it was the greatest spectacle" he had seen, because "it had history back of it, and because it was a symbol, and stood for something" (193–94). The oppositions Twain invokes are familiar enough, between frivolity and seriousness, the superficial and the deep, spectacles without referents and spectacles secure in their meanings, appeals to the senses and appeals to the imagination. But they serve merely as a starting point, as Twain more complicatedly thinks through the values of public spectacles and performances, and the opposition between symbols that stand for something and images that do not.

Having posed this contrast, Twain appears to shift the terms of his essay, refocusing it on a comparison between Queen Victoria's Diamond Jubilee and the 1415 procession through London celebrating King Henry V and the English victory over the French at Agincourt. The description of the latter political spectacle, presented through the mouth of a young man at the event (conveyed "through a competent spirit medium" and translated into modern English by Twain's own hand, in a kind of relay that, as I argued in the previous chapter, Twain associated with authenticity and transparency), has an internal contrast that corresponds to "symbol" and "show." On the one hand, there is the solemn spectacle of Henry V's power, a spectacle of English victory in the array of soldiers and prisoners, and a spectacle of divinely sanctioned kingly authority. The alignment of divine order and monarchical order is spectacularly highlighted as Henry bows and lifts his shield when he passes the church, and the procession follows suit in a tremendous flash as the sun glints off their shields. On the other hand is Sir John Oldcastle (also known as Falstaff, Twain notes): fat, drunken, leering, blasphemous, lying about his battle glory and about the number of men he killed, and followed by his "mumming and blethering" lieutenants (200–201). The opposition between show and symbol is reproduced here, of course, in the contrast between Oldcastle's carnivalesque, Mardi Gras–like playing with meaning and Henry's serious and pellucid symbol of king, nation, and church, a symbol of their identity and of their transparent translation one into the other.

The distinction Twain makes explicit between the 1415 and the 1897 pageants, however, is in what he calls their "symbolic" dimensions; in this pairing neither seems, at first, to be the "show" to the other's "symbol." Their relation rests in the "thought-breeding" contrast between the backwardness of the fifteenth century and the progress made by 1897 in liberty, democracy, and the English people's well-being. Victoria's Jubilee, "in its major function, its symbolic function," "will stand for English history, English growth, English achievement, the accumulated power and renown and dignity of twenty centuries of strenuous effort" (194). Twain does not dwell on the "showiness" of the queen's parade; "meaningless" magnificence, at least in Twain's initial, manifest concern, seems hardly pertinent.

Yet even as Twain suggests that the "unexpected splendors" and "variety" of the Jubilee spectacle have symbolic meaning, "stand[ing] for the grandeur of England," in his description of the many-colored uniforms and complexions of the representatives from the empire—from Asia, Africa, India—a different note is implicitly struck, one that undermines this symbolism of "progress" and "grandeur" by linking the bloody nationalism of Agincourt to an obscured but bloodier imperialism of the nineteenth century. To the detriment of the modern-day spectacle, Henry V's procession, in Twain's description, is forthright about the cost in French lives and prisoners, whereas Victoria's Jubilee represses the human cost of the empire. More explicitly, Twain notes that the real creators of the "progress" and "accumulation" on display in 1897 are absent: "the capitalist, the manufacturer, the merchant, and the workingmen were not officially in the procession to get their large share of the resulting glory." And, most pointedly, current large contributors to the "imperial estate" are not represented: no manifestation exists, Twain reports, of Cecil Rhodes, his British South Africa Company, and his collaborator in imperial exploitation Dr. Leander Starr Jameson (210). The spectacle, then, while it still stands for the grandeur of England, obscures the real "history back of it"; expenditure, creation, production, and their human costs, are hidden, the spectacle operating as a fetish, an invocation of dominion and at the same time a distraction from its workings. This is "spectacle as amnesia" (in Michael Rogin's words), a performance of power involving a historical forgetting.[4] While it is not exactly meaningless show, in Twain's understanding of it there exists a disconnection between symbol and referent, or meaning and cause, with important political effect.

"The absence of the chief creators" of this magnificence and display, Twain nonetheless writes, "was perhaps not a serious disadvantage." Making an implicit comparison with the absent veterans in the Civil War march, Twain suggests that "one could supply the vacancies by imagination, and thus fill out the procession very effectively. One can enjoy a rainbow without necessarily forgetting the forces that made it" (210). In Twain's description, however, this spectacle does not at all invite such remembering, as did the vacant places for the Civil War dead. Attention is displaced instead onto beauties for the eye that are seemingly mute about their sources and causes; there exist no discernible gaps to mark the absences of imperialists, capitalists, and workers. The effect ultimately is to compromise Twain's distinction between symbol and show, for, if Victoria's Jubilee has a symbolic function, a "symbol" may then speak its meaning with a forked tongue, and if its participants provided a "show," showy spectacle may have a repressed history back of it. The story of "progress" in this essay, like the stories of progress in and between *The Prince and the Pauper* (1881) and *A Connecticut Yankee in King Arthur's Court* (1889), is subverted by a concomitant story about representation and its ruses. Twain splices a supposed rise from feudalism with a decay in the fidelity of symbolic cultural spectacle. The symbolic transparency of Henry V's procession is affirmed not only by contrast with Falstaff's lying, but also by contrast with Victoria's displacements. Victoria's Jubilee reveals a peculiarly modern structure (familiar to us from critiques of commodification and reification) in which the materials on display show no signs of the business or labor that produced them.

For Twain this theme of nineteenth-century decay and degeneration pertained not only to cultural symbols intended to stand for something else with some accuracy and reliability, but also to carnival, burlesque, parody, travesty. The dimensions of this view will become clearer in my discussion of his fiction; for now it will help to recall Twain's characterization of Mardi Gras in *Life on the Mississippi* (1883) as a deformed and deracinated festival, whose elements of religious meaning and of popular revelry, festivity, burlesque, and grotesquerie had been emptied out of it over time. As Twain put it, the "poor fantastic inventions and performances of the reveling rabble of the priest's day" as well as carnival's "religious feature" were "pretty well knocked out of it now." What remained was "Walter Scott Middle-age sham," a romanticization of knights and nobles by people of a class high above the rabble. At the back of the procession was a vestige of "giants, dwarfs, monstrosities, and other diverting grotesquerie—a startling and wonderful sort of show," but the heart of Mardi Gras now, he wrote, is "girly-girly romance," not "the funny and the grotesque." In short, the Mardi Gras of Twain's day provided neither a dramatization of religious belief (the release of sin and wantonness prior to the purification of Lent) nor an irreverent carnival of profanity, inversion, grotesquerie, and comedy. All that remained was a glorification, after the manner of Sir Walter Scott, of "the sillinesses and emptiness, sham grandeurs, sham gauds, and sham chivalries of a brainless and worthless long-vanished society."[5] *Both* transcendent public symbol and carnival irreverence have atrophied, the serious symbolism being transformed into a specious theater of southern aristocratic dominion, the grotesquerie made into "mere show, and meaningless."

This theme of decay in both spectacle and carnival appears as well in Twain's writing about the stage, here in elegies about the disappearance or degeneration of both "serious drama" and raucous burlesque. In "About Play-Acting," an essay published the year after "Queen Victoria's Jubilee," Twain laments an impoverishment in American theater as Shakespeare and tragedy have been replaced by vaudeville and variety.[6] After reproducing a couple of columns of theater advertisements from a New York newspaper—dominated by the vaudeville houses of F. F. Proctor, Tony Pastor, B. F. Keith, and Koster and Bial, along with ads for the Harlem Music Hall, Weber and Fields' Music Hall, and the Olympia Music Hall—Twain criticizes this "lightsome feast," this continuous diet of "mental sugar" (222). "Thirty years ago Edwin Booth played 'Hamlet' a hundred nights in New York," he writes, and in "the first half of this century tragedies and great tragedians were as common with us as farce and comedy." Now "light comedies and entertaining shows" have taken the place of "drama of depth and seriousness." Along with comedy and variety he would like to see "an occasional climb among the pomps of the intellectual snow-summits built by Shakespeare and those others" (224–25). Again he invokes a symbolic art that "stands for something," as opposed to a vaudeville that has neither depth nor raucous irreverence, both having been "knocked out of it."

But drama of depth and seriousness, like "pomps" and such symbolic processions as Victoria's Jubilee, became difficult to dissociate from the upper regions of cultural hierarchy and their interests. This association ultimately filled Twain's endorsement with ambivalence, as he discerned machinations of power in representations that otherwise passed as serious and "deep." In "About Play-Acting" this burden of doubt is temporarily missing, though its conditions are obvious—as Twain recommends that New York devote at least one theater to tragedy, presumably through the noblesse oblige of cultural guardians. "America devotes more time, labor, money, and attention to distributing literary and physical culture among the general public than does any other nation," he writes; "yet here you find her neglecting what is possibly the most effective of all the breeders and nurses and disseminators of high literary taste and lofty emotion— the tragic stage. To leave that powerful agency out is to haul the culture-wagon with a crippled team" (224). This affirmation of the cultural office of highbrow culture echoes Twain's advocacy in the early 1900s of the Children's Theatre of the New York Educational Alliance, a theater designed, as he put it, to "train and elevate" the immigrant children of the Lower East Side by showing them "pure and clean plays" (which, in this case, ranged from Shakespeare to a dramatization of *The Prince and the Pauper*). Writing about these working-class children, Twain makes more explicit his recognition of the influence of cultural authority in ostensibly serious and realistic repesentation.

Such theater is most effective, Twain wrote, when it *"builds with the facts of life,* and puts them before the child's very eyes, and vividly and intensely and convincingly displays them," so that for the spectators the play "is *real,* it is *actual life,* and its teachings are burnt into their hearts and minds as if by that tremendous and unrivaled trainer and teacher, *personal experience."* When the theater achieves this semblance of life, a spectator sits "fascinated, absorbed, entranced," and *"unconsciously"* receives "trainings that ennoble the pupil's character and conduct, *without his suspecting that he is being taught at all."* Tutoring through this subterfuge of realistic representation easily surpassed the more straightforward but less engaging pedagogies. "If we had forty theaters of this kind in this city of four millions, how they would educate and elevate!" Twain exclaimed. "It would make better citizens, honest citizens. One of the best gifts a millionaire could make would be a theater here and a theater there. It would make of you a real Republic, and bring about an educational level."[7]

Making a positive equation between disinterestedly realistic representation and a moral pedagogy was common enough, as Howells's doctrines of realism and his conception of the proper "truths of American life" make clear. In Twain's case, however, a sense of the exercise of cultural power in "realistic" representations, as we shall see, tinctures with distrust his affirmation of theater based on "the facts of life"—just as he qualified his affirmation of such "symbolic" spectacles with "history back of them." The ideal of a resonant or representative public symbol appeared more and more impossible to realize. Pessimistically, he also came to think that the weapons to wield against official, high-cultural illusions of reality—the weapons of burlesque, parody, and low-cultural play—had also been neutralized. I will focus on the dynamics of this in my discussion of *A Connecticut Yankee*. Pertinent to the problem, however, is Twain's nostalgia in 1906 for the minstrel show, which, after the 1870s, he wrote, "degenerated into a variety show and was nearly all variety show with a negro act or two thrown in incidentally." By the end of the century, "the real nigger show—the genuine nigger show, the extravagant nigger show—the show which to me had no peer" and which "made life a pleasure to me," had been "stone dead for thirty years."[8] Like drama of seriousness and depth, performances of extravagance and burlesque (as he here thought of minstrelsy) had been displaced by variety and vaudeville. An apparent cause, lurking offstage, seemed to Twain to be an entertainment business transformed by late-nineteenth-century capitalism and by what appeared to be a mass public.

Twain's concerns with symbol and show, sanctified meaning and burlesque, and "natural" signs and commercial ones interweave through *The Prince and the Pauper* and *A Connecticut Yankee*. Instead of simply grasping low culture as "show" and high culture as "symbol" naturally connected to its history, however, he demonstrates the deficiencies of high-cultural symbolic representation in a way that damages this separation of value. The effort to distinguish between, on the one hand, forthright representation in "serious," "symbolic" spectacles and, on the other, displacements and subterfuges, becomes a failed effort as theatricalizations of power and authority display themselves as ruses. Twain's doubts surface in *The Prince and the Pauper* despite its devotion to the legitimacy of genteelly "serious" literature; they are full-blown in *A Connecticut Yankee*. And in both of these books the fate of humor—travesty, burlesque, carnival—is grim, as it becomes in *The Prince and the Pauper* a companion rather than a subversion of official performances of power, and in *A Connecticut Yankee* a product in the same market as every other performance, not a source of critical irreverence. Although, as I shall demonstrate in the final chapter, Twain does not leave his consideration of performance at this impasse, he encumbers it with difficulties seemingly impossible to shake.

PAGEANTS AND CARNIVALS

The Prince and the Pauper is a story, on its face, of disorder reordered, of inversion righted, of misrepresentation revealed, and of misrecognition corrected. Its central subject, in other words, is the relationship between social order and representation. True, in its congruence between the return of order and the correction of misrecognition, its ambition *appears* to be to resolve the tension between "truthful," "realistic" representation and legitimate power—an ambition that seems to have alienated many twentieth-century critics. But the common dismissals of the book as clichéd, as melodramatic, or as an acquiescence to a genteel literature that forgot its collusion with cultural power overlook its self-conscious rehearsals of questions of representation, especially the spectacular, theatrical representation of social order. Far from a compliance with northern middle-class equations of truth, social order, and genteel representation, Twain's novel radically renders suspect the purpose and status of any public spectacle. Then, in accord with his anxiety about the degeneration of both public symbol and raucous burlesque, he also renders suspect the forces of inversion and disorder.

What Dwight Macdonald dismissed as "flaccid historical pageants" (the "ceremonials" Howells advised Twain to condense) exist in *The Prince and the Pauper* as examples of a kind of representation—as spectacular stagings of sovereignty, authority, and status.[9] "The River Pageant" is "showy" in its colors and uniforms, but Twain notes that it is carefully arranged by rank, categorized by hierarchy (esquires, judges, aldermen, ambassadors, nobles), with coats of arms, banners, and shields whose armorial bearings are all highly visible, the most prominent being those attendants dressed in the prince's liveries and embroidered with his blazon (107–8). The Coronation Day "Recognition Procession" too, while it has its dimensions of "show" in the flame jets, smoke, and explosions emitted at its starting point from the Tower of London, is a carefully ordered parade in which each has his place, a spectacular display of people ranged by birth, métier, and wealth: the king, the king's guard, the protector, nobles, vassals, the lord mayor, aldermen, officers and members of guilds, the artillery company, and so on (300). A Coronation Day historical pageant "representing the king's immediate progenitors" and "a bewildering succession of spectacular and symbolical tableaux, each of which typified and exalted some virtue, or talent, or merit, of the little king's" (302–3), declare a purpose more strongly symbolic than bewildering, and they crystallize the function of all this display: power and *vertu* are being dramatized, the origins and genealogy of authority are (apparently) being traced, and a rightful social order is (supposedly) getting clarified, in which the ideal identity of the king is expressed, and the identities of all others are defined in relation to it. The sheer excess of this pageantry should signal to us Twain's overt concern with questions of public symbolism.

Important, of course, for the integrity of such symbolism, the person whose identity these spectacles are meant to express is not there; the ground "back of" these symbols is absent. Behind the elaborate rankings of the River Pageant, designed to individuate, express, and secure the identity of the king, is Tom Canty, the impostor. No flow exists from divine or ideal authority to the king's, or from kingly authority through this symbolic hierarchy and the social order. Edward's conviction that he is "the very source of power in this broad realm" (281) is simply wrong; the structure of power carries on without concern for the existence or presence of its supposed origin. The Recognition Procession, the formal acknowledgment of the sovereign by his subjects, is a performance of *mis*recognition, unimpededly conferring kingly identity on Tom, not Edward. In sum, the ease with which Tom can take Edward's place and act as king, and the fact that Tom functions as king despite announcing his identity as a pauper, reveals the kingship as a function of costume and his audience's collective (and to some degree enforced) suspension of disbelief. *The Prince and the Pauper* underscores strongly the power of monarchical theater as the authenticator rather than the expression of kingship and power. The pageantry and spectacles constitute authority rather than express or objectify an essential social order, a fact that, while it is somewhat hidden away, begins to undo this ostensible story of temporary inversion and rightful reestablishment.

The rightful reestablishment of social order through the correction of misrepresentation, in fact, never securely takes place. For the moment in which the true king is to be spectacularly recognized and the misinterpretations of identity are to be clarified is a moment of uncertainty. As the lord protector says after quizzing Edward about kingly matters, his right answers "are not *proofs.*" What *is* taken as proof is the fact that Edward can remember where he put the Great Seal, which had been missing since he left the palace, a privileged memory, seemingly, because of the authenticating office of the seal. However, while Twain's interest in the reliability of indexical signs (as I argued in chapter 4) makes it highly significant that he chose the Great Seal as the authenticator of Edward's identity, the "proof" here is *not* a bodily impression or sign—not, in fact, even an impression of the seal; instead, Edward's memory of where it is verifies his kingship. Akin to determining the identities of the live Wilks brothers, in *Huckleberry Finn,* by asking them to remember the dead Wilks's tattoo, this proof of identity is even more pronouncedly cast adrift onto the uncertainties of memory and testimony. Edward's body fails to express his identity; authentication has to come from an external sign.

Then, in his double movement, as Twain undermines the grounding of serious symbolic spectacle in *The Prince and the Pauper,* he also neutralizes the power of carnival to undo the official order. There appears, at first, to be a counter-theater to official spectacle in the underworld Tom Canty emerges from. Offal Court—its name evoking pig entrails and waste—is a place of disorder, drunkenness, riot, brawling, and poverty (50–51). Its theater is rude and inversive, the apparent opposite of pageants of order and authority. It has Maypoles and fairs (53), Punch and Judy shows, monkeys "bravely dressed," and "plays" that resonate with those of Edwin Forrest and the Bowery boys—consisting predominantly of shouting and fighting "till all are slain" (62). Many of the rituals of the people of Offal Court, more pointedly, appear as subversions of hierarchy for the purpose of "festive" critique, worlds turned upside-down in order to contradict political norms, and not simply for the sake of disorderly inversion. The denizens react explicitly against the state spectacles of torture, burning witches and heretics, flogging people, placing them in stocks or on scaffolds, or impaling their heads as " 'object lessons' in English history" (134). Edward gazes upon a crowd of "gutter-scum," "wrinkled hags," and "loud, brazen, foul-mouthed" ruffians as they begin an "orgie" of drinking, "villainous" singing, and storytelling about abuses they have suffered at the hands of the authorities, burnings at the stake, ears cut off, skin branded. There are also moments of fighting back, as when one man claims to have killed a priest and is applauded. And there is mockery; for example, a derisive toast "to the merciful English law" after the litany of horrendous "punishments" (191–96).

The place of this apparent counter-theater in relation to the state's performances of power in spectacles of torture, however, is tellingly situated in the moment of what Mikhail Bakhtin calls the "primary carnivalistic act," the mock crowning of the slave, fool, or jester—a moment which, in this novel, does *not* lead to celebration of the relativity of social structure and authority.[10] When Edward, looking like a pauper and sounding insane, declares his royalty, he arouses some laughter and carnivalesque delight, but it is scant; instead of pleasure from the incongruity of his rags and his claims, he evokes jeers, abuse, kicks, and threats of a dunking in the horse pond (64–69, 126, 197). In the kindest response, one of the lead hooligans gives Edward permission to be a "king," but demands that he choose a different title, because, while these ruffians are indeed bad, they are not traitors to their monarch—after which they all shout, "Long live Edward, King of England." As an alternative, the "mangy rabble" crown Edward "Foo-foo the First, King of the Mooncalves," a title that elicits "hootings, cat-calls, and peals of laughter." Edward is "crowned with a tin basin, robed in a tattered blanket, throned upon a barrel, and sceptered with the tinker's soldering iron. Then all flung themselves upon their knees about him and sent up a chorus of ironical wailings and mocking supplications, whilst they swabbed their eyes with their soiled and ragged sleeves and aprons" (200–201). Mark Twain may use the typical trappings of the carnivalesque—the incomplete and grotesque body of a mooncalf, the prosaic basin and soldering iron—to carnivalize Edward's kingship. But the crowd, unaware of Edward's identity, does not.

In this episode, Twain has not provided us with a popular negative critique of the state or with a collective demystification of power. The crowning of "Foo-foo" hardly works as a conscious uncrowning of de jure authority. Instead, it is derision of a fool who, in the crowd's understanding, has crossed the boundary of proper behavior by claiming to be king. Given that the Offal Court's communal sense of the impropriety of official punishments, their cruelty and excessiveness, is immediately grasped by Edward, it appears that the crowd's mockery and railing against "merciful English law" is also a reaction against official deviation from accepted standards. Even if Twain depicts the people of Offal Court as lowlife, then, their riotousness is directed against deviations from social and civic norms. Not an exposure of the impostures of power, not truly an attack on the status quo, not really a licensed rebellion for the purpose of blowing off steam, their carnival finally has a conservative force, censuring the excesses and improprieties of both the outcast and the state.

Indeed, in Twain's anatomy of them, carnival and order have affiliations; ceremonies and riots, in *The Prince and the Pauper,* appear to be complementary. On Edward's birthday, "everybody took a holiday, and high and low, rich and poor, feasted and danced, and sang, and got very mellow." In complementarity rather than opposition, there were pageants and banners by day and bonfires and "troops of revelers" by night (47). The display of order, rank, and authority in the River Pageant is accompanied by a chaos of people "massed together on the river frontage," dancing, shouting, drinking, and lighting fireworks. And this "swarming hive of humanity" is busy drinking to the Prince of Wales (120); an undifferentiated mass standing in contrast to the fine discriminations and individualizations of the state's theatricalized power, it nonetheless exists as support of authority. The "rabble" is similarly full of revelry, drink, and patriotism in anticipation of the coronation (294).

In *The Prince and the Pauper,* then, the theater of public, communal symbols is rendered groundless, a construction of performance rather than expression, at the same time that mumming and blethering, carnival and street theater, are stripped of their power of inversive critique. The radical attack in this novel comes not from the plebeian culture found there but from Twain's depiction of a crisis in representation. What suffers damage in this novel, though somewhat covertly, is the assumption that there could be a refuge from mummery, lying, and disorder, that there exists a pole opposite that of the con games and dissimulations of Offal Court. The story in which the truth is obscured—by the typically carnivalesque practices of switching identities, mimicking the insignia of rank, adopting the clothing and manners of another social status—comes to a dubious end. The story in which authority is (accidentally) dethroned (again through typical carnivalesque practices of uncrowning, of bringing the high down low) lacks the proper security of the typical ending in which rightful order is resecured. But if there is no reliable recertification of the symbolic-social order, if transcendent symbols are repudiated as its guarantees, nonetheless only the underwriting and not the efficiency of this order is damaged. The theater of power, without its capacity of expression, upholds itself. And its difference from inversive counter-theater begins to disappear. Neither is grounded in "expression"; both involve posing and mumming. And both can be enlisted in the purpose of sustaining the structure of authority. This reevaluation of both serious public symbolism and irreverent, inversive theater sets the terms for *A Connecticut Yankee in King Arthur's Court*.

MARKET AND THEATER

A Connecticut Yankee launches a critique of representations that legitimize authority, extending the undermining in *The Prince and the Pauper* of the transcendent connection between the divine and the monarchical that identifies kingly power as a transparent expression of holy power. But it does this partly through Hank Morgan's market revolution which, while it profanes the transparency of sacred symbolism, institutes a new dynamic of oppositions—hearth and marketplace, private and public, mediumship and theatricality, automatism and effect—that establishes new bases for transparency. If, as I argued in the previous chapter, the novel eventually privileges unconscious mediumship and intimate revelation as optimum conditions for representation, this is possible only through contrast to Hank's self-conscious theatricality and marketplace publicity; Hank introduces this pairing to Arthurian England, a pairing in which mystification and demystification feed off each other. But in replacing divinely guaranteed expression with expression secured by privacy, unconsciousness, and automatism, he renders problematic any possibility of "authentic" public representation.

With Hank's set of nineteenth-century assumptions in place, Twain turns to the problem of public art. Much of the energy of the novel is devoted to demonstrating the ways in which market-mindedness and mechanical "effects" seem to ruin both serious representation and irreverent burlesque. If Hank's mockery undermines the legitimacy of Arthurian spectacles—through a kind of amalgamation of early modern marketplace profanity and joking and nineteenth-century burlesque—its threat is neutralized as it becomes part of Hank's capitalist regime and a commodity in his display. If serious expression becomes possible by placing it in the private sphere, seemingly divorced from the duplicitous theater of kings, knights, wizards, and other figures of power, its presentation in public becomes a contradiction. If the novel momentarily credits Hank with an attractive automatism, because he embodies performance as direct and machinelike efficiency and self-sufficiency, it transvalues this mechanism into the producer of "effects," fetishized signs seemingly unconnected to their causes. Yet, in a typically Twainian maneuver, the grounds of this critique are brought under scrutiny and their distinctions finally confounded, as the secret is turned into profitable display, and as truthful exposure turns into spectacular evasion.

Part of Twain's novel, then, is an evaluation of the effect of capitalism on representation. Twain uses Hank Morgan, the zealot of contracts and theater, profits and performance, to test an equation between theatricality and commodification. *A Connecticut Yankee* outlines a critique of spectacle as a dissociation of signs from referents and of signifiers from meaning which, partly because this dissociation resembles that between Hank's commodities and his industries, lays the blame on Hanks' late-nineteenth-century capitalism. In a way that anticipates one of our critical traditions—of Georg Lukács, Theodor Adorno, Guy Debord, Jean Baudrillard, and others—Twain arrives at a correspondence between what we might call a fetishization of both performative "effects" and produced commodities. The treatment here of effects and commodities, dissociations and fetishizations, however, is part of Twain's more general concern about representation in performance and spectacle, about the workings, in the service of power, of reemphasis, displacement, shiftings of foreground and background, and interruptions of circuits of representation.

In a pessimistic version of political theater and performance, Twain begins with corrupted representations in *A Connecticut Yankee* and further corrupts them, taking performances whose truth is already compromised by the interests of power and compounding this lack of fidelity through commodification. Performances and spectacles in Arthurian England are already "lies" that serve to bolster and sustain authority and its adulation. There is nothing especially peculiar about this to Hank Morgan, except that in Camelot everyone, including the performers, believes in the lies—a manifestation of the novel's begrudging nostalgia for a time of faith rather than skepticism, at the same time that it is a diagnosis of the Arthurian system of performance, power, deception, and belief. Merlin's magic, to Hank's eyes obviously fake, is nonetheless believed not only by the people but by Merlin as well (255). Knights tell outlandish stories about their exploits, and everyone listens trustingly to their performances, thereby affirming their position and privilege. Hank's repeated refrain is that the Arthurians are "a child-like and innocent lot; telling lies of the stateliest pattern with a most gentle and winning naivety, and ready and willing to listen to anybody else's lie, and believe it, too" (66). The public theater of untruths, such as Sir Kay's and Merlin's, and the unshakeable belief in it are indispensable for sustaining the performers' eminence; they work in what we might call a stunningly smooth operation of hegemony, a seamless action of consensus reality, unhindered by any existent notions of demystification.

Hank introduces subversions into this system of representation, belief, and social order—subversions that flow from his thoroughgoing capitalism, competitiveness, and marketplace suspicion. He concludes that, since everyone so firmly believed and feared Merlin's magic, "certainly a superior man like me ought to be shrewd enough to contrive some way to take advantage of such a state of things" (84), an entrepreneurial ambition imbued with the intent to dissimulate. Hank, of course, epitomizes a market-mindedness in which the profitability of misrepresentation is taken for granted and the admonition of *caveat emptor* is assumed as a matter of course. As he thinks, and the Arthurians do not, unsuspiciously believing in other people's tales and performances just "isn't business." His way of getting "down to business" before contracting to go adventuring with Alisande is precisely to disbelieve her, to interrogate her tale telling, to ask for "proofs that you are trustworthy and truthful" (136). For Hank, storytelling and performance quite literally are transactions that, like any business dealing, sensibly require suspicion from the consumer, because they also invite counterfeits from the teller. He reinterprets this world of trust in terms of the impersonal, devious, and suspicious representations of marketplace exchange. As he dismantles through suspicion and demystification the Arthurian system of oppressive belief, he lays the groundwork for the reign of doubt and conscious misrepresentation.

Hank's market regime, as Twain presents it, has a corrosive effect not only because it adds solicitation, commercial deceit, and suspicion to the public performances of power, but also because, as Hank explains in his backstage narrative, he quite consciously replaces the conception of symbols of power as expressions of sacred authority with a conception of all spectacles as theatrical/commercial "effects" unrelated to any concern for fidelity in representation. For example, his characterization of the royal touch for scrofula—"the king's-evil business"—commercializes this spectacular event in a way that nullifies the king as a medium and the healing as a channeling and issue of holy power. A theatrical ritual that affirmed the sacredness of the monarchy and secured the king as God's conduit and representative, assuring a continuity between God and king, providential order and earthly order, is transformed in Hank's understanding into a matter of stage and politics—a "one-night stand" that had an effect "as good as a tableau; in fact it had all the look of being gotten up for that, though it wasn't" (298–300). The king's representation of holiness is, in Hank's conception, merely an image for the glorification of power. Similarly, Hank's explosion of Merlin's tower, an act, he says, that "solidified my power" (108), he portrays to the people as a mediumistic channeling, accomplished, through Hank, "by fires from heaven" (102). But, of course, that circuit does not exist; as Hank explains to his readers, the explosion is caused instead by mass-produced fireworks whose real cause is hidden. In a double double-cross, Hank invokes divine expressiveness in order to bamboozle the Arthurians into believing in spectacles corrupted by both the will to dominate and the effects of the market.

Twain uses an ungroundedness, a release into the instability or fluidity of exchange, to characterize Hank's theater and, more generally, his system of value. He clarifies the point during the dinner Hank has with the provincial artisans, which draws sharp contrasts between values fixed through authority and the formlessness that follows Hank's introduction of market values into sixth-century England. As Hank explains, the artisans who had gathered for dinner at the house of Marco, the charcoal burner, "had the 'protection' system in full force" (369); more generally, central authority rather than decentered market demand regulates their economy. The magistrate, for example, sets workers' wages (376) and governs the length of a worker's employment (377)—in order to exploit the workers and keep the market in check. Back at Camelot, on the other hand, the Arthurians under Hank's direction "were working along down toward free trade" (369), toward marketing practices relieved of such order and constraint. When Hank tries to burst the artisans' self-satisfaction about having wages that are twice those in free-market Camelot by demonstrating that their cost of living is more than double, they "didn't grasp the situation at all" (371). Strangers to relative value, they cling to the fact that, judged by an absolute standard, their wages are higher, despite Hank's protest that "your wages are merely higher than ours in *name,* not in *fact*" (371). This seeming dissociation between names and facts is beyond the grasp of these men, and terrifying too; confounded by the fluctuations of liquidity and exchangeability in Hank's new market, they revert to their "set" values as a point of reference, and to the authority that does the setting as their solid ground.[11] But Hank has released values fixed by authority and tradition into the changeable arena of market, in much the same way that he uproots theatrical representation from its security in authority and (the Arthurians believe) in reference by turning his "effects" into floating consumables.[12]

More directly pertinent to Hank's actual performances, the threat of this commodified world of labile exchange resounds in the artisan banqueters' uncertainty about Hank's identity. Accustomed to a world in which signs of identity and status have a clarity and unequivocality, partly because there is such limited social mobility, partly because the possessions that signify high status are simply unavailable, Marco and his friends are stunned by the metamorphoses of Hank. Traveling in disguise, he looks like a humble farmer, below their station; yet in the dinner that he finances, the expenditure astounds his audience. Hank introduces the nineteenth-century availability of commodities into a land where scarcity insures identity, confounding a reliability in signs of status that rests on their unequal distribution. And each unveiling of a purchase is an "effect," a surprise without apparent explanation. As Hank says, "I don't know that I ever put a situation together better, or got happier spectacular effects out of the materials available" (365). A stranger, a traveler who cannot be reliably categorized by traditional frames of class, rank, and family, Hank represents a fluidity in the conventional signals of social identity that rivals the liquidity of his free market, and a mystery in his theatrical effects that rivals the mystery of commodities.[13]

The uncertainty in Hank's identity is heightened in the rest of the novel by his readiness to float his personae on a volatile market. This is apparent partly in his disposition to assume totally fabricated "attitudes" whenever he is in the public eye and, after gauging market and audience demands, to assume a new theatrical persona for each new contract and each new performance (which usually amount to the same thing). Hank's public self exists through his viewers' expenditure of attention. His sense of this identity as a market effect is underscored by his equation of reputation and investment when he declares that the publicly humiliated and discredited Merlin's "stock was flat" (105, 439). Always concerned to keep this salable self up, to maintain his "professional reputation" (103), he is forced to reflect on "how much reputation was worth" when "a new magician," a "celebrity from Asia," easily steals the attention and admiration of the court; "a man can keep his trade-mark current in such a country," the competitive Hank concludes, "but he can't sit around and do it; he has got to be on deck and attending to business, right along" (282). He has inaugurated an order and introduced an interpretive framework in which reputation maintenance is an economic business, social identity fluctuating like commodity value according to advertising, demand, and marketing.

Values and selves determined by transactions, exchange value replacing use value—the world Hank introduces operates (in Georg Lukács's famous formulation) according to "the structure of commodity-relations."[14] This extends to the fetishization and reification of Hank's commodities, processes that Twain exaggeratedly represents. The entire productive base, Hank's "system and machinery," his industries and factories, are hidden away backstage, in "quiet nooks and corners," moving "smoothly and privately along undisturbed in their obscure country retreats" (126–27). Hank has carefully "fenced away from the public view" what he calls "the civilization of the nineteenth century," but which more specifically is a system of "vast factories" (128–29). The result, of course, is that the Arthurians see every one of his commodities as something existing completely autonomously, a fantastic object appearing magically out of nowhere, with no trace on it of the means of its production, independent of the labor that fashioned it, with no available social explanation for its manufacture—with all the features, in other words, of Marx's fetishized commodities. As in the phantasmagoria of Queen Victoria's Jubilee, to refer to Twain's own model of the spectacle, there are no signs of the businessman, imperialist, and workers that enable these glorious things. They are quite consciously and explicitly hidden away.

Like the Jubilee, Hank's spectacles, Twain makes clear, have the same structure as his commodities. Under his regime, that is, signs too have become fetishized; their referents, like the indexical traces in commodities of production, have been obliterated. The advertising displays in *A Connecticut Yankee* serve perhaps as the clearest examples. For while such slogans as "Use Peterson's Prophylactic Tooth-Brush—All the Go" or *"Try Noyoudont"* (226–27) effectively echo late-nineteenth-century advertising conventions and codes, in a society which knows nothing of the codes—and moreover knows nothing of toothbrushes and toothpaste—they are meaningless, signs without referents (and, indeed, signifiers without signifieds). As if to make sure readers get this point, Hank advertises stove polish, though, he says, "There were no stoves yet, and so there could be nothing serious about stove-polish" (227). Explicitly, even heavy-handedly, Twain links the suppression of all signs of commodity production and the disappearance of reference itself in the (seemingly never "serious") spectacles and messages of mass culture.

By conjoining the "backstage" areas of both his industry and his spectacles and hiding the causes of both his products and his signs, by theatricalizing his commodities and commodifying his theater, Hank explicitly joins capitalism and derailed representation under the rubric of "effect." The double language of theater and commodification is perhaps most evident in the holy fountain miracle, which Hank thinks of as both "a matter of business" (256) and theater ("doors open at 10.30, performance to begin at 11.25 sharp," he announces [266]). He treats his theatrical effects as if they were promotions or merchandise. He wants, in this miracle, to make all the "properties impressive to the public eye" and to "get in every detail that will count"; the ambiguity in the term *property* and the language of counting suit the effects of Hank's theater, for he knows "the value of these things" in the theatrical market, and he is intent on playing his "effects for all they are worth." He is frankly in the business of selling something, and here his goods are signs, symbols, theatrical effects, and "style." "You can't throw too much style into a miracle," he declares. "It costs trouble, and work, and sometimes money; but it pays in the end" (265). Style, work, and money are all abstracted here to the level of exchange value.

This spectacle—of returning water to the holy fountain—is pointedly without "authentic" referents. The leak in the well is repaired before the performance, and the display of water and fire has no apparent connection to its real causes: a water pump, fireworks, the clandestine efforts of Hank's "experts," and Hank's hidden-away industry. And significance, as well as reference, is beside the point in this theatrical market.[15] After his "solemn stage-wait" (again for "effect") Hank presents a whole series of such theatrical effects: "a noble Latin chant"; an "attitude" with his face uplifted; colored fires of blue, red, green, and purple; his "grand exhibition of extra posturing and gesturing"; his five "words"—stunning, "big" ones, but nonsensical to his audience; and the final gushing of water from the fountain (267–68). None of these, as Twain presents them, has a generally discernible meaning. But they clearly operate in their own differential system, notable simply because they are more or less stupendous than the preceding or succeeding effects. "Show," as Twain has it in this scene, is separated from "symbol" precisely because marketplace exchange has stepped in to decree that attention-value depends simply upon outdoing the previous effect.[16]

The corrosive influence of the market on performance, as Twain's main line of inquiry works it out, ruins practices of representation that Hank Morgan presents as positive alternatives to Arthurian misrepresentation. James Cox and Walter Benn Michaels have argued that Hank Morgan is like a machine: there is a mechanical consistency between his actions and his character (Cox), and he embodies a nonsocial inflexibility and individuality (Michaels).[17] Indeed, I would argue, Twain invokes his conception of automatism as a guarantee of expression, presenting it this time in the guise of an efficient mechanism. With it comes the idea of mechanism not only as nonsocial, but (relatedly) as nontheatrical—mechanical in operation, and therefore oblivious to audience expectation. Hank's affection for telegraphs and telephones, after all, ought to suggest his kinship with these automatic representation machines. But, of course, he keeps these machines hidden, and transforms the communications they convey into spectacular, "magical" effects, thereby violating the mechanism and immediacy of their transmissions. It is only after Hank himself is transformed into a medium (as argued in the previous chapter), and his fondness for intimate domesticity seems to overpower his fondness for theater and market, that his own expressions begin to appear as nontheatrical automatisms. Before that, it is only by paradoxically taking Hank as *essentially* theatrical (Cox's strategy, and certainly a perversely Twainian doubling at work in this novel) that we can credit his "effects" with automatism. In this dimension of Twain's depiction of it, Hank's market turns efficiency into effect and productivism into product, thereby replacing the promise automatism held for representation with yet another flourish, disjoining cause and effect, referent and sign.

As in *The Prince and the Pauper,* Twain here calls into question not only serious representation but also carnival and joking. In *A Connecticut Yankee,* commodification foils not only public symbolism, but also inversive burlesque. The fate of humor under Hank's capitalism is to be transformed from irreverence into novelty, from burlesque into commodity, from play into effect. Early in the novel we know that Hank thinks of jokes as needing a proper market. He scorns Sir Dinadan's looking for "a fresh market for his jokes" (122), but decides to save his own quip—that such jokes can be classified by geological periods—for rerelease after the invention of geology, when the "market" will be "ripe." Ultimately, as joke effects become the same as marketable effects, the irreverence of humor finds itself, along with state spectacle, on the same continuum of consumable novelties.

The theatrical burlesque that Twain knew from the 1850s and 1860s was one of the frames for Hank's theater, as well as for Twain's novel. The familiar tactic of incongruously invading a scene from Sir Walter Scott, or Shakespeare, or Longfellow with prosaic people and modern-day details and products was well-known from hundreds of such burlesques, some of which, in fact, transplanted stage Yankees into pretentious European contexts or the middle ages.[18] Among Twain's many burlesques, the one most pertinent in this context is his *Burlesque Hamlet* (1881), in which the book salesman Basil Stockmar, a pragmatist equally interested in advertising, effects, and plain speaking, roams through Shakespeare's Denmark.[19] In that burlesque and in *A Connecticut Yankee,* Twain uses marketplace irreverence—the alignment Bakhtin saw between the profanities and cries of hawkers or barkers and streetfair abuse and mockery—to defame and deflate high symbolism. To some extent, that is, Twain celebrates nineteenth-century capitalism as an inheritor of the traditional marketplace joking directed at the church, high culture, and hierarchized society.[20] In a way historically more specific, Hank's factories and advertising campaigns represent (at least to him) a progressive attack on feudal powers: the freedom of his market foils the tyranny of king and church, and the playfulness of his advertising functions as car-nivalesque and burlesque undermining of "knight-errantry."

But Twain conflates burlesque and business, carnival and market, finally to bring ominous results. True, Hank's outfitting knights with advertising placards (for example, "Persimmons's Soap—All the Prime-Donne Use It") makes them look ludicrous (185). Having Sir Ozana le Cure Hardy travel about "all in armor except for a stove-pipe hat" (as part of Hank's promotional campaign for plug hats) makes him "as ridiculous a spectacle as one might want to see" and furthers Hank's project of making knighthood appear "grotesque and absurd" (246–47). At the same time, however, Hank's mocking advertisements appear to epitomize the process by which market-place burlesque and circus-style irreverence become metamor-phosed by commerciality, their undermining burlesque power fi-nally appearing indistinguishable from other consumables. Twain subsumes the fragmentation and play of burlesque, that is, within the equally phantasmagoric and fragmented landscape of new products.

As the final element in Twain's onslaught on commercial the-ater—necessary to mention before attending to his undermining of this critique—the audiences imagined in *A Connecticut Yankee* suit these transformations that Hank Morgan accomplishes. That is, un-ruly audiences, audiences of carnival and burlesque, are remade into mass audiences, compressed into a single reactive organism, as if they were the logical extensions of Hank's "effects," efficiently de-prived of even the possibility of responding in any way but the iden-tical. Hank's "grand attitude" at the eclipse spectacle sends a "shud-der" through "the mass like a wave" (93–94). The explosion of Merlin's tower results in "a thousand acres of human beings grovel-ing on the ground in a general collapse of consternation" (105). At the holy fountain miracle, the crowd unanimously hushes at Hank's be-ginning "attitude" and moans together at the first effects while vari-ous sections "collapsed like platoons"; at the last effect a "mighty groan of terror" issues "from the massed people" (269). Hank con-ceives of and describes his audiences in a way that complements his theatricality; his sense of them as a mass works hand in hand with his own nineteenth-century showmanship.

While this "massing" of people ultimately has the result of trans-forming spectators into elements of a servomechanism, themselves carefully calibrated effects of effects, it initially looks like part of Hank's undoing of Arthurian hegemony. As in *The Prince and the Pau-*

per but even more repellently, the carnivalesque in *A Connecticut Yan-kee* erupts in service of the state's cruelties, and Hank's moderniza-tion aims to alter this. His scorn for Arthurian crowds is turned against the unruly audiences of spectacular punishments. For exam-ple, as punishment for negligible offenses against nobles, Hank notes, commoners are dismembered by being pulled apart by horses, and "all the world came to see the show, and crack jokes, and have a good time" (209). Or, later, a mother with a baby at her breast is carted to the gallows for stealing in order to save her child from star-vation, and the crowd runs alongside her, "hooting, shouting pro-fane and ribald remarks, singing snatches of foul song, skipping, dancing—a very holiday of hellions, a sickening sight" (401). These are Arthurian audiences, supporting power by their consent and ac-tivity. Hank, it appears, at first brings truly irreverent burlesque to England, an apt replacement for Arthurian carnival as conservative cruelty. But the logic of the mass market and its effects transforms both humor and carnival crowds.

The change from rambunctious mob to pliant mass is drawn sharply when Hank and the king are saved from hanging. On the way to their execution, they are surrounded by a tremendous audi-ence and "were being made a holiday spectacle." When Arthur (like Edward) proclaims himself monarch, the crowd, more unruly here than in *The Prince and the Pauper*, lets out "a vast roar of laughter," then wants more entertainment, and "tried to provoke him to it by cat-calls, jeers, and shouts" (422–23). But after Hank and Arthur are rescued by the five hundred knights on bicycles, Hank thunders to the crowd: "On your knees, every rascal of you, and salute the king! Who fails shall sup in hell tonight!" As he explains, "I always use that high style when I'm climaxing an effect." This effect, "one of the gaudiest I ever instigated," gets the audience on their knees, with no more sounds of "deriding and insulting" (426). Although Hank speaks on behalf of the king, the spectacular effects of bicycles and attitudinizing, industrial effects and theatrical effects, are his own, products of modernity that render the people a modernly astonished and pliant mass. While Hank obliterates rambunctious popular col-lusion with tyranny, he introduces a new acquiescence of passive spectatorship.

Again, Hank's attack on the elements of Arthurian order are trans-formed into means for establishing his modern order. His transfor-mation of folk cruelties into disciplined spectatorship is part of a more general process that obliterates all aspects of carnival. *Before* Hank takes charge of the tournaments, for example, the Arthurian crowd is a "gaudy and gorgeous" one, full of "high animal spirits" and "innocent indecencies of language," with undisciplined and riotous inclinations to "sing, gamble, dance, carouse" (109). When he enters the lists and guns down his adversaries, his observers are "stupefied with astonishment" (438). The culmination of this, of course, is the Battle of the Sand Belt, which provides the most gruesome caricature of the process by which Hank manufactures theatrical effects that constitute his spectators as stunned masses; for the awesomely violent effects of this "performance," as Clarence describes it (469), transform the "swarming host" into a truly undifferentiated mass, which "did not exist as individuals, but merely as homogeneous protoplasm, with alloys of iron and buttons" (478).

My point is that the audiences Hank encounters belie his self-justifying versions of them as "rabbits" (109), "herds," or "sheep" (160) that he aims to turn into "men" (203). They may be apt to get "lost in reverent wonder" (259) or be rapt in "childish wonder and faith" (278) before a holy spectacle—that is, a "symbolic" spectacle. But this, like their predisposition to be unruly in their persecution of deviants, suits Twain's conception of public theater *before* its modern alterations. Hank introduces something new—spectacles that are "show" instead of "symbol," yet consolidate power by constituting their audiences as compliant masses. He makes entertainments for audiences only a late-nineteenth-century impresario could conceive.[21]

Having described Hank's theater as reified spectacle disjoined from its causes and referents, constituting a passive and totally mystified mass of onlookers, I must return to the crucial fact that Hank also partakes of the opposite of this theater—first in his insistence on narrating and describing in his manuscript all his backstage dealings, later in his unveiling for all of Arthurian England the modern civilization he had kept under wraps. The narration of his backstage dealings seems of course to come from the transformed Hank, the medium rather than an effectmeister, the narrator who sits cozily by the fire and talks easily, sleepily, and with "candid simplicity," the intimate teller of a confidential tale rather than the theatrical performer. But the distinctions on which the reliability of this backstage narration rests—between private revelation and public theatricality, a false front and an undisguised behind, a tale by the hearth and a spectacle in the street—are called into question, most pointedly by Hank's revelation to all of England, late in the novel, of his hidden industry and civilization.

When Hank "exposed" his industries "to an astonished world," this disclosure of the truth works as a displacement of attention; he bares all on the day after he spectacularly killed ten knights in the tournament (442), and the revelation turns eyes away from this brutality, exemplifying Hank's ability to "get up a diversion" (382). In connection with this, one thinks of the pilgrims who, watching the spectacle of slaves being whipped, comment on "the expert way in which the whip was handled," ignoring "anything else in the exhibition that invited comment" (245). Hank's moments of "truthful" exposure reframe his displays of backstage and covert operations as another kind of fetishization, not as frank unmaskings. Instead of focusing on commodities that obscure the industrial superstructure, attention is focused on inner workings in order to divert attention from the crass manipulations and outright brutalities of Hank's theater. A grasp of these dynamics of diversion and displacement forces a reinterpretation of Hank's reified spectacles, for the oppositions between backstage and display, secrecy and celebrity, or truthful private revelation and false public persona lose their distinctness in this shifting terrain of refocalization and reemphasis. The effect most especially is to discount the sanctity of the private, secret, and intimate. Backstage narration can serve to hide something, and confidential statements can lose their truth value. All of Hank's confidential chat may begin to suit this pattern, in which his focus on the preparations and operations of his spectacles serves as an effective means of obliterating (not only for his readers, but for himself) his deception, domination, and pacification of his audiences.

The strategy reaches its culmination in the Battle of the Sand Belt, a massacre which, while Hank darkly (and ironically?) calls it an "entertainment," is at least somewhat displaced from our attention and from Hank's by his devotion to secret wires, wire fences, his dynamo and its electrical connections, Gatling guns, dynamite deposits, and glass-cylinder dynamite torpedoes (466–68). For Hank, at least, if not for Twain or us, turning the background into the foreground, transforming covert actions into spectacle, serves as a reemphasis, a strategy of altering and refocusing attention, that absolves the performance of murder. This is part, finally, of Twain's examination of the machinations of theatricalizing and spectacularizing. Hank's effects and displays are operations that refocalize and, in Twain's analysis, act as hidings and mystifications, disavowals and forgettings. A derailing of criticism, his ushering readers into his backstage, and into his confidence, aims to forestall judgment, so that exposure is tantamount to evasion.[22]

The intimation here is one profoundly pessimistic about the possibilities of representation. Having, in the course of his inquiry, modeled the corruption of symbolic expression by power, and having then recaptured sincere and intimate expression by contrast to Hank Morgan–like public theatricality, Twain now locates revelations of the secret on the continuum of veilings, diversions, and dodges. Disclosures entail concealments. The transparency presumably rooted in privacy, intimacy, and unselfconsciousness loses its security.

In his curtain speech at the opening of the play *The Gilded Age,* Twain declared, "I wanted to have some fine situations and spectacular effects in this piece," including "a volcano in a state of eruption, with fire and smoke and earthquakes, and a great tossing river of blood-red lava," with the hero "booming down that red-hot river in a cast iron canoe." But the theater manager, Twain complained, told him that there were no volcanoes in Missouri and that "the hero would burn up." To which Twain claimed to have replied, "Put him in a patent fireproof safe and let him slide—all the more thrilling—and paint on it, 'This safe is from Herring's establishment,' " and use the advertising fee to pay for the volcano. The conjunction of spectacular theatrical effect and advertisement, of a commodity to buy and a hyperrealism untrue to the state of Missouri, strikingly foreshadows the equation of fetishized effects and fetishized commodities in *A Connecticut Yankee.* Equally premonitory—of Hank's Sand Belt theater—is the promise Twain makes to his audience for revision of the play, a promise that acknowledges the demand for increasingly stunning effects: "I am killing only one man in this tragedy now, and that is bad, for nothing helps out a play like bloodshed. But in a few days I propose to introduce smallpox into the last act. And if that don't work I shall close with a general massacre."[23]

In this speech, Twain adopts the role he would later flesh out in Hank Morgan, as well as the humorous and critical perspective he would elaborate in *A Connecticut Yankee* on marketing, entertainment merchandise, and the irrelevance of their requirements to accuracy in representation. He grasps this combination as *his* authorial problem: the impulse toward salable theatrical effect, the guilty conscience about the resulting infidelity to reality, and the counterstream of humor that spotlights and mocks this theatricality. But this very humor in his curtain speech, the means for rectifying theatrical excess, was of course played for all it was worth, and came to appear as much an effect as its targets. The problem this raised—not only that what looked like symbol could be "sham grandeur," and what looked like truthful revelation could be laid to "effect," but also that what looked like irreverent humor could be what it attacked—reappeared and underwent a more sophisticated analysis in Twain's last novels.

7

Melodrama, Transvestism, Phantasm
(Un)fixing the Theatrical Sign

It is easy to think of Mark Twain's last, major fictions as retreats from performance, its contexts, its publics, its politics. It has proven easy, that is, to characterize *Personal Recollections of Joan of Arc* (1896) as a sentimental escape to medieval idyll, or at least to the triumph of an idealized feminine purity, unbeset by the corrosive presence of, say, a modern-day Hank Morgan. And a long-standing critical tradition has understood *The Mysterious Stranger Manuscripts* (1897–1908) as a despairing and pessimistic withdrawal into the self, an about-face into dream and solipsism. After all, Twain insisted that he wrote *Joan of Arc* "for love," not for marketplace lucre,[1] and his decision to publish the book without his name on it can be taken as a repudiation of his humorous, theatrical, and salable self. His abstention from publishing any of the writing on his mysterious stranger, along with his declaration to Howells that he aimed to compose it as "a book which should take account of no one's feelings . . . a book which should say my say, right out of my heart, in the plainest language and without a limitation of any sort," might suggest a project inattentive to audience or effect, unselfconscious, flowingly free from concerns about rendition.[2]

This, needless to say, is not my understanding of these writings. For the recoils from audience, marketability, and theatricality are the symptoms of Twain's engagement with questions of performance. This late fiction, in fact, helpfully brings together the concerns I have thus far laid out, most especially the issues of mediumship and spectacle, but also those of the private and the public, idea and materialized effect, essence and act, realism and theatricality, feminine transparency and masculine posing, serious representation and carnival. The texts will serve here partly as recapitulations, partly as the far reaches of Twain's explorations of these matters. They replay his efforts to secure the reliability of expression in performance at the same time that they resurrect his doubts about that possibility. They once again displace onto the question of representation in performance larger anxieties about instabilities and contradictions in categories of gender and in public expression. And in the main characters of these stories Twain tries to "solve" these problems.

Joan of Arc is an attempt to reimagine the possibility of sincerity in public, an effort framed in Twain's most basic terms by focusing on a spiritual medium who becomes a spectacle; on an often entranced, perhaps "hysterical" female body whose unconsciousness is meant to certify for everyone the authenticity of her expression; on a mesmerized woman exposed to the public gaze.[3] An endeavor to test, through a hearth-loving young woman who dresses in men's clothes, whether feminine expressive authority can come onto the national stage without being discredited, it also strives to resecure reliable representation, and plenitude and purity in the expressive sign, in a way crucial for the novel's author. The promise of this, as well as the failure built into its terms, is figured in Joan's transvestism. *The Mysterious Stranger Manuscripts* situates a boyish, minstrel-loving, mimicking, wildly theatrical show-off within a monist mind and enables his most stunning "effects" through a genuine, mesmericlike mediumship. Akin to the deadpan style's process of enveloping burlesque effects within the continuities of a consciousness, these envelopments of theater and effect solve problems simultaneously of representation and cultural division. Almost a mirror-image of his collapsing processes of representation into material circuits, Twain's idealist monism more effectively undoes the distinctions between realism and theatricality, idea and "effective realization." In other words, both of these later efforts, in overlapping ways, are reconceptualizations of representation and performance, the one trying to bring mediumship and the expressive body into public visibility, the other collapsing theatricality into the interior. Twain works here with the same sort of terms—of the inside and the outside—that he did when, as he claimed in 1900, he had conceived of "a drama in the form of a dream," terms that could be reversed to enact a dream in the form of a drama.[4]

Joan of Arc is an example, at least in its broadest gestures, of melodrama as Peter Brooks has defined it: a narrative devoted to the triumph of virtue over dark designs bent on obscuring it and, most pertinently, a spectacularization of the pure, unambiguous image of this transcendent value in a setting (and in a historical period) where the signs of morality, and reference itself, have been put into doubt.[5] Twain's novel stages this drama at every level of its narrative. While the multiple mediation of the story, through the (fictional) translator and the less than fully trustworthy narrator, throws the available truth of Joan into doubt, the assertions of these men and the narrative direction of the story nonetheless tend to reaffirm melodramatic immediacy.[6] The "Translator's Preface" insists on the unequivocal meaning of Joan, on not only her virtue but also her truth and truthfulness "when lying was the common speech of men," on her stability and faith "when men believed in nothing and scoffed at all things"; it also stresses the eternally ideal nature of Joan's "character" and virtue, transcendent over all historical standards.[7] The narrator, Sieur Louis de Conte, similarly asserts "how clearly her character was defined, and how well it was known and established" (37). And the story insistently reenacts the public display and recognition of Joan's absoluteness, as her "deep earnestness and transparent sincerity" (72) repeatedly become spectacles for crowds—in the theater of royal audiences, processions, victory marches, trials, inquisitions.

   In its larger movements, again, *Joan of Arc* is a series of obscurings and melodramatic unveilings of the clarity and purity of Joan's meaning and identity—in, as Brooks describes the melodramatic, a "dramaturgy of virtue misprized and eventually recognized" (27). The machinations especially of the villainous Bishop Pierre Cauchon to "blacken" Joan's name during her trial—by suppressing evidence, twisting Joan's acts and words "from their right meaning" (342), retelling her character as "everything that she was *not* . . . every fact of her life distorted, perverted, reversed" (392–93)—are ultimately undone, partly because Joan's truth shines through for all to see, partly because the pope's court eventually "cleared her illustrious name from every spot and stain" (348, 460). As a redramatization of this unveiling, as yet another theatrical Twainian trial, the novel itself is both a manifestation of nineteenth-century anxiety over the loss of secure and transcendent meaning and an affirmation of the possibility of resurrecting it. Not only an instance of melodrama in general, but also part of the turn-of-the-century cult of Joan of Arc and a companion to the list of nineteenth-century plays about her, Twain's novel appropriated a figure, and a way of representing her, that had already been established as a hedge against effects of modernity.[8]

This sense of melodrama, as an endorsement of the pure and immediate sign—even though it arises from doubt and anxiety and is
embedded in possible narrative unreliability—gives Twain's novel a
capacity to assuage the distrust of signification, communal meaning,
and national theater that surfaced, especially, in *A Connecticut Yankee.* Joan herself is a clear agent for the relegitimation of a patriotic
state theater. At the same time that she, as a direct medium of heav-
enly revelation, rescues the possibility of representation, she rescues
monarchical authority as another kind of representation of the divine, and she stages a spectacular national theater whose signification of patriotism is seemingly free of the ruses in nineteenth-century
theaters of power. The melodramatic spectacularization of her virtue,
combined with the transparency of her female mediumship, sets the
conditions for reclaiming communal symbol. Whereas Hank Morgan
demolishes the idea that Arthur is God's representative, Joan is the
medium by which the dauphin's doubts about being the divinely
sanctioned heir are removed (113, 145). While Hank's spectacles are
effects drained of significance, separated from causes, distanced
from referents, and subversive of communal meaning, Joan's spectacles are free from theatricality, faithfully representing God, king,
country, and her own virtue.

As part of this relegitimation, the novel links the story lines of
Joan's apotheosis and the restitution of the throne; strong connections are drawn, that is, between the obscuring and revelation of Joan's
virtue and the recognition of properly divine kingly authority in the
dauphin, between the spectacles of Joan's transparent purity and the
king's coronation, between Joan's mediumship and the integrity of
national, public symbolism. The direct analogy drawn between a
priest's ordination by God's "appointed representative," which assures that his "authority can no longer be disputed or assailed," and
the king's anointment by a bishop, which removes all doubt of his
rightful authority (262), is implicitly triangulated with the moment
when "the authority and leadership" to save France are "vested in
[Joan] by the decree of God" (59). Similarly, just as Joan's character
and authority are obscured by Cauchon, the king's character and authority are clouded (283). Like Joan's virtue, then, kingly authority
also becomes the subject of melodramatic and spectacular unveiling,
and as the agent of this, Joan has a special grasp of the symbolic importance of the coronation as a public and dramatic recognition of

rightful power (261). She counts the coronation, a symbolic theater for "the people," among her major achievements. So entwined with the king's identity is Joan's identity as authenticator and visible aid for monarchical power, that after her name is blackened, she has to be publicly "rehabilitated" simply to legitimate the kingship (460).

Displaced onto this combination is Twain's contemporary and authorial concern—a redemption of public spectacle and national symbol through private, feminine mediumship. Instead of allowing entry onto the public stage to discredit Joan, he makes Joan the ideal and the guarantor of public drama free from theatricality. In effect, Twain brings together two pervasive meanings of Joan of Arc in the late nineteenth century: the nationalistic meaning she carried in France—where, especially after the 1878 defeats and in connection with the 1890s Dreyfus case, as Marina Warner writes, she became a political symbol of national values and unity;[9] and her romanticist meaning in American medievalism of the time, with its idealization of the middle ages as a prelapsarian era not yet fallen into dissociation, a period when (as Jackson Lears characterizes this belief) spontaneously immediate expression and "authentic experience" were supposedly still available.[10] Twain's concern, in this conjunction of mass culture and melodrama, is with the possibility that a mass national culture could share a "symbol," not just a showy spectacle.

In a strategy we might expect, Twain certifies Joan as a truthful medium and affirms her capacity for public sincerity partly by reducing her to an automatically functioning body. For example, de Conte (and Twain) may not be absolutely certain that "faces do really betray what is passing in men's minds" (366), but Joan's face and body are shown to us as quintessential (and feminine) self-expressers. She has all the characteristics of the undisciplined, automatically functioning body that, for Twain, certified authenticity. Called "the Bashful" because she was apt to blush even more quickly than the average "peasant girls," who are "bashful naturally" (30), she exemplifies that uncontrollable, bodily expression of emotion that epitomized self-revelation for Twain. Joan's body also registers Darwinian conceptions of natural expression—when her facial expression of distress (for France) is compared to the expression "in the face of a dumb animal that has received a mortal hurt" (33); or when, imprisoned, the "mute reproach" in her eyes is likened to "that veiled deep glow, that pathetic hurt dignity, that unsubdued and unsubduable spirit that burns and smolders in the eye of a caged eagle" (343). Mute but more expressive than words, as natural as an animal's, automatic, and feminine, Joan's bodily expressions of emotion help to certify her as transparent and true. When de Conte asserts that "fidelity to principle, fidelity to truth, fidelity to her word, all these were in her bone and in her flesh—they were parts of her" (404), he testifies to the reassuring link between somatic expression and semiotic legibility and reliability.

This bodily mediumship is aligned with Joan's function as channel for the divine. As a medium, of course, she is as unconscious as any automatism, fully absorbed, "in a trance," as de Conte says when he first spies on her communing with the Voices: "Her air was that of one who is lost in thought, steeped in dreams, and not conscious of herself or of the world" (55, 53). Similarly, when de Conte watches as she receives foretellings of the future, Joan echoes John F. Day in her unconscious mumblings and facial expressions. Predicting the military conscription of her male friends, there are "fleeting movements of her lips as if she might be occasionally saying parts of sentences to herself," while her face has "a dreamy and absent look in it"; she utters the fortunes, de Conte says, "as one who talks to himself aloud without knowing it, and none heard it but me" (45). Again, when she foresees and murmurs about the course of her campaign and her death—the premonition of the latter causing a "scarcely perceptible spasm" to flit across her face—only de Conte observes, and understands that she is "not conscious," "in a trance " (241). These combinations of entrancement and expression—uncontrolled spasms, mumblings, lip movements—underscore Twain's sense of mediumship as not only unconscious and passive, but also a physical circuit, a physiological or hysterical automatism. Her unconsciousness of audience, as with so many instances of secretly watched private emotion in Twain's fiction (when Tom Sawyer watches Aunt Polly weep over his supposed death, Huck watches Mary Jane weep over her dead uncle and over the selling of the slaves, and Huck watches Jim weep over the memory of his daughter), further guarantees the authenticity of Joan's expression.

An undercurrent nonetheless continually resurfaces in the midst of this effort to merge mediumship with public display, to imagine drama without theatricality and spectacle without dissociated effects. Predictably, Twain cannot sustain his treatment of Joan as the unequivocal vehicle for solving the problem of sincerity on the public stage. She instead becomes the occasion to explore and complicate—once again, but perhaps more pointedly than ever before—the oppositions that informed Twain's understanding of performance. The realistic and the theatrical, the private and the public, the spiritual and the fleshly, the divine and the human, and the feminine and the masculine all converge in *Joan of Arc*. And if melodrama involves display of the private, or the spectacular recognition of feminine virtue, then ultimately Twain takes melodrama in this novel as an oxymoronic ideal, as a problem of contradiction.

Joan's transvestism becomes a metaphor for the difficulties Twain raises, serving at once to define and distinguish the feminine and the masculine and to combine them, to promise a synthesis of the private and the public and to exemplify their division. Much as her feminine mediumship legitimizes her public theater, it sanctions her wearing armor and male attire; as she repeatedly says of her clothing, "I have done nothing but by command of God" (357). Her subordination and femininity are thereby, in turn, affirmed by her obedient transvestism. In this sense, a reciprocity exists in her between the private and the public, the feminine and the masculine, because the private sources of public display make the latter authentic, and because the masculine appearance in public is paradoxically an instance of feminine submission. But if, through this formulation, these terms are kept separate yet synthesized within Joan, they nonetheless have troublesomely irreconcilable dimensions in other instances. Before Joan is revealed as the military savior of France, the Paladin jokingly imagines her as an army captain, with "a steel helmet to blush behind and hide her embarrassment when she finds an army in front of her that she hasn't been introduced to" (34). Here the distinction between male armor and femininely blushing body becomes sharp, that between concealment and exposure, public prominence and shy withdrawal. Femininity and masculinity are returned to their "proper" spheres of public and private; transvestism joins them only to enable masculine masking to hide and protect blushing feminine transparency.

As Marjorie Garber has argued, transvestism often functions to register "cultural, social, or aesthetic dissonances" because "category crises" elsewhere in the culture, and the anxieties they produce, are displaced onto the cross-dresser.[11] Twain deposits Joan in the contradiction between an idealized public sincerity rooted in femininity and an idealized femininity properly excluded from the public sphere, and he makes her transvestism the figure of this cultural tension. As a counterpart of the doubleness in her transvestism, therefore, Joan in some instances resolves opposites, becomes a public spectacle of sincerity and truth, paraded about for all to admire; in others, feminine transparency reverts to the secret and hidden, publicity becoming incompatible with truthful exposure. As examples of the first, she repeatedly comes before imposing audiences—courts, judges, the king—and is "sincere and honest, and unmarred by timorous self-watching and constraint" (123), "unconscious" and "unaffected" (125), oblivious of massed spectators (107); at such moments she successfully transports the sincerity and lack of theatricality from the home to the public stage. Then again, she can exemplify secrecy as she preserves privacy for her mediumship and for herself. She keeps secret much of what her Voices say, from officials, interrogators, persecutors, even the king (123–24, 352). If, on the one hand, she can be quite lost in "thought, abstraction, dreams," and therefore prone to self-revelation, on the other hand, she is also apt to "cut a sentence in two and [change] the subject when apparently she was on the verge of a revelation of some sort" (48). Preserving the secrecy, hiding or obscuring the truth herself, becomes necessary to save—or to constitute—the integrity of the feminine, the intimate, the domestic. Twain thus repeatedly rehearses the collapsing and restitution of the terms the transvestite opposition invokes.

Melodramatic unveiling of truth and transparency, then, alternates with the careful preservation of secrecy, partly as a return to one of Twain's recurrent problems—that his nineteenth-century conception of public sincerity, based on a model rapidly falling apart, is deeply rooted in idealized femininity and domesticity, in the intimacy of the home.[12] Meshed with the problem that truthfulness and sincerity involve exposure of the intimate is the interweaving of the melodramatic pursuit of truth with voyeurism. Associating the unconscious feminine body with authenticity, of course, rested on this interweaving. And in *Joan of Arc* Twain repeats, again and again, versions of the conjunction between truth seeking and prurient prying into feminine privacy. In a configuration of instances that Twain condemns, the coerced exposure of the secrets from her Voices becomes linked to a violation of Joan's femininity, of a piece with "a dozen brutal common soldiers keeping guard night and day in the room where her cage was" (329). The eavesdropping violation of her confession to priest Nicolas Loyseleur (332–33, 367) and the inquisition's "profane . . . prying into matters which had proceeded from His hands under the awful seal of His secrecy" (344) merge with the theft of her clothes that forces her to return to her armor (441). While de Conte's ostensibly benign spectatorship is not condemned, his privileging of the melodramatically public recognition of Joan's pure feminine virtue is similarly related to his secret peeping on Joan's private moments. The narrator and the novel itself reproduce a combination of the pursuit of knowledge and voyeurism not unlike late-nineteenth-century researches into hysteria (a "disease" to which Joan's visions could be attributed), with their theatrical displays of unconscious and spasmodic female bodies.[13] De Conte's "personal recollections" conserve and expose secrecy partly in the service of melodrama, partly in the service of scopophilia.

The confusions that issue from Joan's public femininity—as admiration of virtue blends into voyeurism, and as preservation of her privacy and secrecy borders on the obscuring of her truth—point to a further problem of representation. To the extent that Joan is a clear and reliable sign, what is she a sign *of*? Do her unveilings expose saintly virtue or a sexual body? In some instances, the medium of her body clearly enough expresses divinity, as when a "new light in her eye" and "something wholly new and remarkable in her carriage and in the set of her head" appear after her Voices vest her with the authority to save France—a bodily expression made "as plainly as speech could have done it" (59). De Conte sees "a divine strange light kindling in her face" (363). Her face also has "a sweetness and serenity and purity that justly reflected her spiritual nature" (41), and in it there is "a deep, deep joy, a joy not of earth," for "she was not flesh, she was a spirit!" (270). In these cases, her body is a materialization and expression of the divine. However, perhaps because "she was a clay-made girl also—as human a girl as any in the world" (369), remembering communion with her Voices can elicit expression of a bodily ecstasy hard to distinguish from the erotic: on one occasion "a sudden deep glow shone in her eyes," her "breast heaved, and the color rose in her face"; on another, "her face lit up as with a flame, and she was like one in an ecstasy" (223).

In Joan, Twain engages the problem of the physical transmission of the divine, the channeling of the Logos, the source of meaning. In so doing, he forces the supposed clarity and reliability of Joan as a sign to confront his familiar doubts about expression through phys- ical mediums. When we learn, in addition, that Joan is "the spirit of France made flesh . . . our country embodied, our country made vis- ible flesh cast in a gracious form" (174), that she is "patriotism em- bodied, concreted, made flesh, and palpable to the touch and visible to the eye" (461), the less spiritual dimension of this problem comes to the fore—the materialization of an idea. And for Twain this process of expression continues to be problematic. The common nineteenth-century question of whether Joan acted as an instrument of a greater power or from her own inspiration is transformed by Twain into his concern with acting and identification.[14] The question becomes, that is, whether Joan's performance is a complete self- effacement and mediumistic submission to God's conception, or some kind of blend, an expression of herself nonetheless directed to the "realization" and embodiment of the divine. And, as with Twain's investigations of acting, the medium comes to interfere with the mes- sage. The automatisms of her fleshly body have an autonomy and ex- pressiveness that exceed her expression of the divine. The strength and certainty of her "character" impede the malleability of her medi- umship. The medium registers its own nature, and the referents of its surface signs become ambiguous. De Conte repeatedly insists that words fail him in conveying Joan to us (286); there is a "mysterious something," an "unwordable fascination" in Joan that everyone feels but cannot articulate except to say that she is "sent of God" (129). But finally for Twain, I would suggest, the possibly superior mediums of bodily expression and automatism are not unlike words, for they also fall short, obscuring while they reveal, expressing themselves as much as they express their divine referents.

Joan, then, is an uncertain sign in a melodrama. Her uncertainty derives partly from the function of her body as signifier of both the divine and itself. Imbricated with this, however, and adding to the uncertainty, is the contradictory demand that she be femininely se- cretive and publicly transparent, a demand that leads to both true ex- pression and protective subterfuge. And added to this is her trans- vestism, her gender uncertainty, her hybrid nature as androgyne, a person with a "hero-heart" and "a young girl's heart" (185), a "soft womanly voice" and a capacity to shout "Forward—march!" (225). As a result of these doublenesses, she embodies, on the one hand, Twain's medium-realist ideal, making her accounts of angels and voices "so life-like and real" (125) and dictating writings to de Conte which "flow" from her lips (133), "without effort and without preparation" (382) but with "unconscious eloquence" (106) that originates in "the heart, not the head" (125). On the other hand, she is an impeding medium, and "masculinely" capable of trickery and stratagem (e.g., 89–92, 320, 361), of catching and trapping her foes on the battlefield and in the courtroom, of misleading them by troop movements and by words.

Clearly enough, Twain—who claimed to be, like de Conte, Joan's amanuensis, simply transcribing what she had to say, never stopping to make up any of her story from *his* head—is finally also like Joan. That is, though distanced from Joan by the personae of the voyeur/amanuensis de Conte and the translator Jean François Alden, Twain nonetheless thought of himself as a medium for her voice as she was the medium of the Voices. Another mediumistic performance in public, Twain's writing was also a performance of cross-dressing and a locus for the conflicts that accompanied such transvestism. The book is theater that wants to deny its status as such, an act that aspires to serious public symbolism and resonance by insisting on its ingenuousness, a melodrama that wants to claim transparency of meaning by eschewing the market conditions that make it visible, as well as a reflection on the difficulties that accrue from these aspirations, a performance of the problems of performance. James Cox, in *The Fate of Humor,* writes that the main fact about the novel is that Twain tried to deny his identity as its author, that he published it without his name and revealed his authorship only later—a denial, for Cox, of Twain's own irreverence, irony, and play (252). I would argue, instead, that publishing it without his name crystallized his puzzle: it was to keep the novel from being associated with Twainian humorous kidding, but at the same time it obscured his "mediumship," which he wanted to emphasize; it preserved an origin in the private, the secret, at the same time that it concealed that quality and thereby foiled the aim of public sincerity. It rehearsed the difficulty of being both retiring and melodramatic, transparent and spectacular, "femininely" mediumistic and "masculinely" public.

There has been a tendency among critics of Mark Twain to read *Joan of Arc* and *The Mysterious Stranger Manuscripts* as antitheses of each other, and to take Joan as the opposite of Satan/44.[15] The justice of this is obvious: the one is mainly serious, the other seemingly ironic and playful; the dominant memory of Joan is that of the sentimental embodiment of pure womanhood, while the mysterious stranger is remembered as a bad boy. In the terms important for questions of performance, Joan, Twain frequently insists, shies away from the limelight and conspicuousness, evincing an affinity for the intimacy and transparency of the home. Forty-four declares, on the other hand, that "I love shows and spectacles, and stunning dramatics, and I love to astonish people, and show off, and be and do all the gaudy things a boy loves to be and do."[16] He revels in the "ghastly effects" of his spectacular eclipse (388), which he thinks "beat Barnum and Bailey hands down" (391). He is proud of his "effect" of "pathos" when, as part of his performance as a minstrel, he sings a mournfully nostalgic song that transports August to a southern log cabin (354–56). In the incarnations of Satan and 44, this mysterious stranger is always a virtuoso of mimicry and rendition, reveling in theatricality and insistently treating moments of convincing realism or expression in his magic theater as mere "entertainment."[17]

But, as I hope I have made clear, it was no accident that Twain chose a publicly performing woman rather than a retiring Victorian heroine for his melodrama of virtue and representation. And the obsession in *The Mysterious Stranger Manuscripts* with dreaming, somnambulism, trance, and telepathy is inextricable from the bad-boy antics of Satan and 44. The spectacles and effects of the "mysterious strangers" in these stories, that is, depend finally on mediumship and clairvoyance. And in the terms Mark Twain had been fashioning, this is tantamount to saying that theatricality here is rooted in transparency, that dissociated spectacle has been reencircled by the connections of communication and expression. The three manuscripts— "The Chronicle of Young Satan" (1897–1900), about Young Satan (also known as Philip Traum) and narrated by Theodor Fischer; "Schoolhouse Hill" (1898), about 44 and set in the St. Petersburg of Tom and Huck; and "No. 44, The Mysterious Stranger" (1902–8), narrated by August Feldner—are in fact devoted to mediating the disjunctions between mediumship and public performance, realism and spectacle, and therefore have a close kinship to *Joan of Arc*. The opposition in *Joan of Arc* between spirit and flesh becomes in *The Mysterious Stranger Manuscripts* an organizing obsession, and Twain handles it in a way that works a transvaluation of the idea that "effects" and "expressions" are "materializations," "realizations," or inadequate translations of spiritual or mental realities. The widespread inclination in Mark Twain studies to discount as a facile determinism the insistence in these writings that the human mind is merely a machine, or simply to fault Twain for the contradiction between this materialist determinism and the monist mind that emerges at the end, underestimates both Twain's engagement with these problems and their implications for his understanding of performance.[18]

Dreaming, dream selves, and dream sprites play such a prominent role in *The Mysterious Stranger Manuscripts* because of their intermediate status between body and mind; they serve much as somnambulists and people in trances did to focus mind-body issues in late-nineteenth-century psychology and psychic research. In "No. 44, The Mysterious Stranger," 44 at one point explains that dream selves "have no substance, they are only spirits," and therefore exist in contrast to the workaday self, which "can't get away from the flesh, and is clogged and hindered by it" (315). Later, however, he says that though dream selves differ from waking selves in being more imaginative, they are nonetheless "functioned by the brain and the nerves, and are physical and mortal" (342–43). The contradiction crystallizes the issue for Twain, as well as his confusion about it. It is the materialist explanation, however, that finally seems to carry the greater weight: Twain later suggests that the dream self "duplicates" have a kinship to the duplicates made by phonographs and cameras, which 44 brings back from the future—as if some kind of physical, mechanical, indexical process of registration fabricated the dream duplicate from the "original" human body and brain, and as if there existed between duplicate and waking self a material, mediumistic connection (364–65).[19] Forty-four reports, additionally, that in ancient times dream sprites carried messages with a "perfect verbal accuracy" that equaled the telephone and surpassed the telegraph—though communication via this medium fell into disuse as careless interpretation and indefinite messages spiraled toward incoherence (382–85). Despite Twain's vacillation on the substantiality of dream representations, then, in his most consistent sense they appear to have a kinship to mental telegraphy, existing in an electriclike medium and registered by automatic processes.

When we learn that both dream selves and waking selves have a physiological basis, however, we also learn of the existence of the soul, a third self that is free of "encumbering flesh," that is able "to exhibit forces, passions and emotions" without relying on their embodiment in the densities and impediments of matter (343). It is as if Twain's dissatisfaction with physical mediums of expression (and existence) has extended past bodies and words to include the faster and clearer mediums of mental telegraphy and dream communication, with their misfirings of wording and interpretation, so that the ultimately desirable means of communication is entirely free of the physical. Forty-four, who notes that "words cannot even convey *human* thought capably" (318), communes with August spirit to spirit, in the form—as August's "limited human mentality" experiences it—of "a single sudden flash as of lightning" (319). No medium carries the communication. No translation from conception to expression takes place.

Nonetheless, the spiritual forces exercised by Young Satan, 44, and August's soul have characteristics remarkably like those imagined for mesmeric, odylic, and electrobiologic currents—so that, almost like dream selves, they seem to have physical properties. In "The Chronicle," Satan has a powerful "influence" on everyone in his presence (65), evoking an "ecstasy that flowed along our veins" (50), a "tingling freshening-up sensation" (64), something that makes one's "blood leap" (74)—physiological responses to physical proximity like those from the exercise of animal magnetism. There is a similar "soul-refreshment" that "always charged the atmosphere" in 44's presence and "made you perceive that he was come, whether he was visible or not" (356); an emanation subject to the physical conditions of distance, this "life-giving" influence "invaded the air" only "when 44 was around." In much the same way that somnambulists in mesmeric doctrine were said to be more receptive to magnetically conveyed messages, it is the dream selves, especially, who feel 44's influence (380), and August is most attuned to it in his invisible soul-state, when he can sense that "a subtle influence blew upon my spirit from his" (403). Although ostensibly given a nonphysical basis, this force echoes the flowing of the ethereal fluid that "influence" originally named, and certainly evoked notions of human currents of electricity and magnetism. As with 44, whose *touch* puts people into states of somnambulism and trance (207–8), when August's invisible, substanceless soul self comes into contact with his love object, Marget (as she walks through him), his spirit influence acts upon her "hypnotically" and plunges her into "somnambulic sleep," causing her "absorbed, unconscious" dream self to take over—quite in the way, of course, that the mesmerist's touch and mesmeric fluid were supposed to induce trance and sleepwalking (342).[20]

In effect, Twain reproduces commonplace perplexities about the opposition between spirit and matter, mind and body, that riddled late-nineteenth-century culture, from popular belief through scientific esoterica. The pseudosciences Twain looked into—phrenology and phrenomagnetism, mesmerism, mind-cure, odylism, homeopathy—all displayed radical ambiguities over whether the vital force, imponderable fluid, or universal energy they discerned behind all phenomena had an essentially material or spiritual nature.[21] This was equally true of spiritualism, with its tendency to look for scientific explanations of spiritual phenomena.[22] Even the otherwise staunchly materialist kind of mental physiology that, I have suggested, informed Twain's thinking about thought transference and literary creation tended to preserve a place for spirit, mind, or God: William Carpenter ultimately thought that all phenomena originated in spirit, and that all natural forces could be manifestations of the mental force of God; and Thomas Laycock, in accord with the German philosophy he meshed with his physiology, posited a transcendent mind that manifested itself in nature.[23]

The confusions about the body-machine and mind, and about matter and spirit, that appear in Twain's *What is Man?* (1906) wed his thinking even more closely to the vexed deliberations over these matters in psychophysiology. Twain replays the emphasis William Carpenter and others had placed on reflex action and unconscious cerebration when his Old Man elaborates the idea that "the human being is merely a machine" (125) by asserting that the brain operates in an automatic, often unconscious way, processing information (128–30), playing chess, singing songs, or fashioning dreams quite on its own (178), flashing out wit without reflection (182), or playing the piano while one is consciously thinking of something else (210). But there is also an accord with Carpenter and some of the other mental physiologists in the Old Man's idea that one's *spirit* is the motivating force of the entire human machinery (155, 185, 202). Twain's Young Man rightly objects to his interlocutor's "elusive terminology." But the response to his objection exacerbates the confusion between spirit and matter, as the Old Man not only fragments human identity into body

and mind, a feeling "me" and an intellectual "me," a "moral territory" and a parcel of "cerebration," but also blurs the distinctions
among these fragments, arguing that "spirit" is affected by the body
(when it drinks alcohol, or cracks its skull, or sends nerve impulses)
(203). When the Old Man adds, finally, that there might also be a
"Soul," though nobody knows what that might be (206), the uncertainty about the selves arrayed along the border between spirit and
body equals that in the *Mysterious Stranger Manuscripts.*

The mysterious stranger stories, however, push further toward the
realm of spirit and soul in a way that seems to echo such works as
Phantasms of the Living, a book by the principal writers of the Society
for Psychical Research that Twain read in 1896.[24] This text, especially
in the sections contributed by F. W. H. Myers (who advised the
Clemenses on mediums to see in order to contact their dead daughter Susy), strives to accommodate the theories of mental physiology,
including Carpenter's "unconscious cerebration," as partial explanations of psychic phenomena at the same time that it suggests the limitations of materialist explanation.[25] Magnetism, electricity, heat, "vi-
bratory energy," "electro-biology," "brainwaves," and other physical
forces can serve only as analogies or metaphors for understanding
telepathic transmission, according to Myers and his coauthor Edmund Gurney, since no material basis for such communication has
been discovered (I, 111–13; II, 315). And, these writers are inclined to
believe, materialist explanations are likely to fall short, unable to account for telepathic communications. While studiously avoiding
statements about the ontological status of apparitions or the means by
which "thought-transference" operates, they pointedly call physical
and physiological explanations into question and imply the existence
of a spiritual realm.

In light of the interest Twain had in the Society for Psychical Research, it should be obvious that, despite the abuse he unleashed in
Christian Science (1907) on Mary Baker Eddy's writing and entrepre-
neurship, Eddy's ideas about the primacy of mind or spirit over matter resonated with Twain's thinking and bore upon the concerns of
The Mysterious Stranger Manuscripts. Eddy's attack in *Science and
Health* on mesmerism, animal magnetism, physiology, and the materialist versions of spiritualism and mind-cure has a striking kinship,
especially, to "No. 44."[26] Her declaration that spirit has no need for a
"material method for the transmission of messages," and that it

"needs no wires nor electricity in order to be omnipresent" (78), could have come from the mouth of Twain's mysterious stranger. And her foundational belief that mind is all, that it causes everything, that every effect is a mental phenomenon—though Twain mocks it in *Christian Science*—suits very well the ending of "No. 44" (written in 1908), when August learns that he is nothing "but a *thought*" ("no body, no blood, no bones"), that all the world is nothing but his dream, and that "miseries and maladies of mind and body" come from his imagination (186–87). The difference, of course, is that Eddy's "mind" is benign, whereas Twain's is unconscious, fabricating the perversities of a dreamer.

Although "No. 44" has commonalities with Christian Science, the collapsing in this story of the spirit-matter opposition into a monism of mind has a genealogy far more wide-ranging than Twain's interest in Eddy, and its implications ramify through Twain's long-standing, complex cluster of concerns about literary creation, mediumship, and performance. It derives, for example, not only from a preoccupation with divisions and connections between mind and body, but also from an uncertainty about distinguishing between what one may unconsciously imagine and what one may receive *ab extra*—that key investigative issue for late-nineteenth-century research into mediums, somnambulists, and the entranced. Twain's attention to this problem of whether the psychic economy is enclosed or permeated, and his resolution of it, bore upon his understanding of his own writing processes, his sense of his own passivity (or femininity) and control (or masculinity) in these processes, his worries about the disjunctions between representations and referents, and, finally, his misgivings about theatrical "effects" conceived as "realizations" or "materializations" of "ideas."

Behind his fulminations about the power, popularity, and hypocrisy of Mary Baker Eddy lay a number of earnest uncertainties that Christian Science crystallized for Twain. For example, he seems inclined to credit the ideas of Phineas Parkhurst Quimby, the mesmerist turned mind-curist who became Eddy's mentor and from whom Twain thought Eddy plagiarized.[27] Quimby's repudiation of the mesmerist idea that healing occurred through an equilibration of the flow of fluid or magnetism through the body, and his affirmation that suggestion and imagination accomplished cures, appealed to Twain—who repeatedly asserted in *Christian Science* that the patient's imagination was crucial for all apparently miraculous healing, from the king's evil to mind-cure, and that there is nothing fresh about this idea (231–33, 241, 257, 348). In contrast, Twain wrote, Eddy's Christian Science argues that "the Spirit of God (life and love) pervades the universe like an atmosphere," and that the inhalation of this "transforming air" or "divine fluid" (348) will clean and purify one's body. Human imaginations in Eddy's theory, Twain declared, are really not at work; the patient is merely recipient, and the healer's mind "performs no office but to convey that force to the patient"; it is "merely the wire which carries the electric fluid, so to speak, and delivers the message" (349). The distinction resonates in Twain's criticism of Eddy's claim to have written *Science and Health* under the inspiration of God. Was she, Twain asks, God's amanuensis, or telephone, or stenographer, or is she rightly the author? Were the ideas, and the language, hers or his? Did her imagination play a part, or was she simply a channel for the divine (284–85)?

This distinction between the work of "electric fluid" and the work of the imagination, or between messages from beyond and messages from the unconscious, resonates, of course, with the Twainian models for creativity that I discussed in chapter 5—the interpsychic model in which mesmeric force is sent to Twain from Dan De Quille, and the corresponding intrapsychic model of creative eruptions from Twain's interior. It should also recall Twain's letter to the Society for Psychical Research, in which he declared that he felt "like a mere amanuensis when I sit down to write," his "powerful impulses" coming from "somebody else," so that he felt "that that other person is supplying the thoughts to me, and that I am merely writing from dictation."[28] This uncertainty over where the ideas come from matches his uncertainty over whether "unconscious plagiarism" was the result of mental telegraphy or unmonitored remembering. And this fundamental question was at issue for investigators ranging from the Society for Psychical Research, which was inclined to credit telepathy, to mental physiologists, who were inclined to discredit it, to such researchers as Jean-Martin Charcot and Pierre Janet, who, Susan Gillman has argued, had a powerful effect on Twain's later writing[29] and who eventually attributed the effects of mediumship to imagination and suggestion.[30] Twain addresses, and provisionally works out, his uncertainties about the matter in "No. 44, The Mysterious Stranger."

As I argued in chapter 5, Twain had been ready, and apt, to internalize the model of mental telegraphy, transforming his sense that ideas came to him "as if" transmitted from someone else into a conception of his own unconscious automatisms. Mental telegraphs traveled the wires of his own nervous system; the twin communicants were within him. This conception, supported by much Victorian psychophysiology, seems to have brought two bonuses. First, the autogenesis of his automatic, bachelor-machine representations rescued him from feminization, from a simple self-conception as medium and amanuensis. Second, his representations apparently had physical causes, were indexical transmissions, with a naturalness that underwrote their fidelity to reality; the troublesome gap in representation between idea and expression, emotion and sign, was spanned by physical matter. If, in this conception, he collapsed "spirit" and "idea" into matter, in "No. 44, The Mysterious Stranger" the direction is reversed. Mental telegraphy has become an affair of pure spirit. Medium and source are once again conflated into one, but this time their unity is not "clogged" by flesh.

And many of the benefits are the same. At stake throughout *The Mysterious Stranger Manuscripts* had been questions of mediumship and gender, seminal "influence" and passive recipience. In a Svengali-Trilby sort of relationship, the "influence" of Young Satan, Theodor reports, made them all "love him" and want to "be his slaves, to do with as he would" (50). Importantly, the profound romantic-sexual effect Satan's influence has on Marget and on Theodor's sister Lilly (90, 101) (in accord with the sexual magic attributed to mesmerists) works on males, too, so that Seppi Wohlmeyer feels Satan's presence "as if he was a lover and had found his sweetheart which had been lost" (74). Theodor's sense that "intercourse with [Satan] had colored my mind, of course, he being a strong personality and I a weak one" (165) echoes August's experience with 44; the illuminating and invading flash of knowledge that August receives from 44, for example, resembles the powerful "mental telegraph" that Twain thought he received, while passive and recumbent, from Dan De Quille. And the eagerness August shows to be the "instrument" of the magician Balthasar's power (246), or to be "invaded" as a vehicle of divine salvation, underscores his predisposition to be a passive medium—a predisposition undoubtedly connected to his self-conception as a "girl-boy" and the intense shame he feels at being called "bottle-assed" (physically womanlike) (263). Mediumship in these stories, that is to say, reproduces common notions of a mesmerist's seminal force subduing and imbuing a femininely passive medium, although, in his familiar way, Twain makes "addle-headed feminine men" mediums as well.

Twain's reaction to such feminization propelled the transfigurations of mediumship in "No. 44." They begin with August's conscious reason for wanting to become an "instrument"; he hopes to ally himself with a greater power that will make him "conspicuous, and wondered at and talked about" (246) or that will give him glory. Submission, that is, leads to grandiosity with an effect different from Joan of Arc's mediumship, since it is the conspicuousness, not the submission, that is valued. Such circulation—and, finally, reversal—of the terms of dominance and submission is even more pointed in 44's playing the role of the medium even though he is the source of the power. He does this when, through his clairvoyance, he pretends that August telepathically prompts him in the completion of his composing room tasks (256–59). But 44's tendency to disguise his power as mediumship occurs most strikingly when he makes it seem as if all the miracles and enchantments he enacts flow from the "inspiration and command" of the magician Balthasar (295–97, 301). Forty-four conforms his miracles to Balthasar's commands—to the point of burning himself to death. He persuades everyone, as Doangivadam puts it, that "he isn't the *source*; whatever power he has, he gets from his master, the magician here" (295). But actually, under the guise of being an instrument and medium, 44 takes his pleasure in conspicuousness and performance.

While this may appear at first to be simply one of 44's inconsequential games, it actually presages the resolution Twain pushes his story toward. For just as 44, the apparent medium, is really the source of power, so August, the bottle-assed girl-boy, the character with the weak mind, the seemingly passive recipient of 44's influence and force, is actually the dreaming creator of the universe. His femininity is enclosed within a psychic economy that finally, cosmically, also initiates all power and force. In other words, as Twain's internalization of mental telegraphy finessed the specter of feminization, embracing as his own both seminal upwellings and passive reception, so this internalization of the universe secures an ultimate bachelor machine—except that, in this case, there is no "machine," no matter or flesh. This disembodied creativity neither fully is, nor needs, the femininely creative body.

The resolution also (imaginatively at least) solves the problem of representation. In "Chronicle of Young Satan," Satan explains that his mind "creates without materials; creates fluids, solids, colors—anything, everything—out of the airy nothing which is called Thought. A man imagines a silk thread, imagines a machine to make it, imagines a picture, then by weeks of labor embroiders it on a canvas with the thread. I *think* the whole thing, and in a moment it is before you—created" (114). Twain makes a sharp contrast here between the human labor of "realizing" an idea and Satan's instantaneous creation, and between the intervening mediums of earthly artistry and Satan's mediumless enactments. Satan's method is possible because for him there is no distinction between spirit and matter, and therefore no translation necessary between thought and realization or expression. The erasure of this distinction, I believe, lurks behind Satan's and 44's conflation of reality and theater, life and entertainment. For Satan there is no distinction between representation and the actual; the "show" he puts on so the boys can "be entertained," his "theatre" of human history, consisting of "fearful spectacles" of murders, massacres, and disasters, is not a representation, but the real thing (134–37). He can set a poem or a tale to music and in the performance make it "just as if you could see it" (93, 105), or tell stories and make everyone see and feel them, "as if we were on the spot and looking at them with our own eyes" (50), because there is no difference between the performance and the reality; there is no "as if." Forty-four, too, presents a "show" of the *real* past, not an illusion or representation of it (332). The gap between idea and representation is bridged because both are finally of the same order—thought, dream. "Materialization" and "realization" do not really happen, and the mistranslations that dog such processes disappear.

This is the sort of solution Twain toyed with in his last years, one that, through phantasm, remedied the conundrums that had bedeviled him throughout his career. By erasing the line that separated mind from body and idea from realization, he erased the divisions within performance between emotion and expression, conception and medium, character and actor, realism and effect. The social and cultural baggage that these questions of representation had always carried for Twain reappear, too, in *The Mysterious Stranger Manu-*

scripts, as 44's "vulgar" entertainments ruffle the polite sensibilities of August, or as the instabilities and turbulence of middle-class orderings of the public and the private, or the masculine and the feminine, resurface. The phantasmatic ending would annihilate these problems as well, conflating their oppositions, and the cultural tensions accompanying them, on the ground of Twain's metaphysical research. Never really comforted by such imaginary solutions, however, Twain was certainly stopped only by his death from returning to these difficulties of culture, representation, and performance and treating them in some new guise. His writings, fortunately, are multifarious enough to keep inviting and repaying our return not only to his texts, but to the record there of the difficulties we inherited from his time.

Notes

INTRODUCTION

1. See Bernard DeVoto's remarks on Twain's burlesque, extravaganza, improvisation, and manipulation in *Mark Twain's America* (Boston: Little, Brown, 1932), 312. Edgar Branch judges Twain's early writings to be "theatrical rather than dramatic" throughout *The Literary Apprenticeship of Mark Twain* (Urbana: University of Illinois Press, 1950), but see especially 21, 94–110. Henry Nash Smith traces moments when Twain frees himself from his "preoccupation with eloquence" and rhetorical effect, and renders experience "directly" by becoming absorbed in a scene or memory, but these are only moments of self-forgetting (*Mark Twain: The Development of a Writer* [Cambridge, Mass.: Belknap Press of Harvard University Press, 1962], 84–87). John C. Gerber, though he treats Twain's personae seriously, finally characterizes them as only "cleverly staged comic acts" ("Mark Twain's Use of the Comic Pose," *PMLA* 77 [1962]: 304). Warner Berthoff directs perhaps the most sustained criticism against Twain's "art of the performer," its "machinery" of manipulation and staging generally overpowering instances of "the free flow of perception" and "visionary truth and beauty"; see Berthoff's *The Ferment of Realism: American Literature 1884–1919* (New York: Free Press, 1965), 61–64. Dwight Macdonald, in "Mark Twain: An Unsentimental Journey," *The New Yorker* 36 (9 April 1960), writes that Twain's "actor's sensibility" produced a "coarse" writing attuned to idiom and delivery rather than "literary technique" (165, 177). And Guy Cardwell discounts Twain's burlesquing, caricaturing, striving for effects, mimicry, and "theatricalities" (*The Man Who Was Mark Twain: Images and Ideologies* [New Haven: Yale University Press, 1991], 45).

2. James M. Cox, *Mark Twain: The Fate of Humor* (Princeton: Princeton University Press, 1966). Constance Rourke, in *American Humor: A Study of the National Character* (New York: Harcourt, Brace, 1931), situates Twain among the entertainment figures of the backwoodsman, the Yankee, and the black-faced minstrel, and in an American tradition of comic display and masking that repudiates emotional expression.

3. *Mark Twain–Howells Letters: The Correspondence of Samuel L. Clemens and William Dean Howells, 1872–1910*, ed. Henry Nash Smith and William M. Gibson, 2 vols. (Cambridge, Mass.: Belknap Press of Harvard University Press, 1960), II, 780.

4. This is the argument made by Michael Davitt Bell, as part of his generally persuasive challenge to the coherence or distinctiveness of any general definition of American realism, in *The Problem of American Realism: Studies in the Cultural History of a Literary Idea* (Chicago: University of Chicago Press, 1993). See the chapter on Mark Twain for the specific argument that Twain is not a realist because he shows little concern for the social and moral responsibility that Howells thought defined a realist novelist (39–69).

5. Forrest G. Robinson, *In Bad Faith: The Dynamics of Deception in Mark Twain's America* (Cambridge, Mass.: Harvard University Press, 1986), and Susan Gillman, *Dark Twins: Imposture and Identity in Mark Twain's America* (Chicago: University of Chicago Press, 1989).

6. Franklin Rogers, *Mark Twain's Burlesque Patterns as Seen in the Novels and Narratives, 1855–1885* (Dallas: Southern Methodist University Press, 1960).

7. Lawrence Levine, *Highbrow/Lowbrow: The Emergence of Cultural Hierarchy in America* (Cambridge, Mass.: Harvard University Press, 1988). Levine does the most thorough job of recounting this history, but on the establishment of divisions between "high" and "low" theaters and repertoires, and between disciplined, bourgeois audiences and raucous music-hall ones, also see Garff B. Wilson, *A History of American Acting* (Bloomington: Indiana University Press, 1966), 107, 173; Claudia D. Johnson, "That Guilty Third Tier: Prostitution in Nineteenth-Century Theaters," *American Quarterly* 27 (December 1975): 575–84; and Lewis A. Erenberg, *Steppin' Out: New York Nightlife and the Transformation of American Culture, 1890–1930* (Chicago: University of Chicago Press, 1981), 14–23.

8. See Mark Twain, *The Adventures of Thomas Jefferson Snodgrass,* ed. Charles Honce (Chicago: Pascal Covici, 1928), 4–12, and idem, *Mark Twain's Travels with Mr. Brown,* ed. Franklin Walker and Ezra Dane (New York: Knopf, 1940), 223. On the stratification within nineteenth-century theaters, see David Grimsted, *Melodrama Unveiled: American Theatre and Culture, 1800–1850* (Chicago: University of Chicago Press, 1968), 53–55; Francis Hodge, *Yankee Theatre: The Image of America on the Stage, 1825–1850* (Austin: University of Texas Press, 1964), 21–23; and Robert C. Toll, *On With the Show* (New York: Oxford University Press, 1976), 6.

9. The expansion of the number of theaters during this period was phenomenal. Between 1864 and 1870, for example, there was a 67 percent increase in the number of theaters in the country, and an 85 percent increase nationally in gross ticket receipts—all accelerated by population growth and the westward expansion enabled by railroads (see Eugene K. Bristow and William R. Reardon, "Box Office, U.S.A., 1864–1870: Regional Profiles," *Theatre Survey* 8 [1967]: 124).

10. Mark Twain, *Mark Twain in Eruption: Hitherto Unpublished Pages about Men and Events,* ed. Bernard DeVoto (New York: Harper and Brothers, 1940), 255. See, for an elaboration of this point of view, Rodman Gilder, "Mark Twain Detested the Theatre," *Theatre Arts* 28 (1944): 109–16.

11. Alan Gribben, *Mark Twain's Library: A Reconstruction,* 2 vols. (Boston: G. K. Hall, 1980).

12. Mark Twain, *Mark Twain Speaking*, ed. Paul Fatout (Iowa City: University of Iowa Press, 1976), 338–39.

13. For the history of Twain's playwriting, see Thomas Schirer, *Mark Twain and the Theatre* (Nuremberg: Hans Carl, 1984). Schirer notes eleven plays that Twain attempted by himself, involvement in ten collaborations on plays, and translations of three plays from German into English (105).

14. Peter Brooks, *The Melodramatic Imagination: Balzac, Henry James, Melodrama and the Mode of Excess* (New Haven: Yale University Press, 1976); Nina Auerbach, *Private Theatricals: The Lives of the Victorians* (Cambridge, Mass.: Harvard University Press, 1990), and "Secret Performances: George Eliot and the Art of Acting," in *Romantic Imprisonment: Women and Other Glorified Outcasts* (New York: Columbia University Press, 1985), 253–67; Martin Meisel, *Realizations: Narrative, Pictorial, and Theatrical Arts in Nineteenth-Century England* (Princeton: Princeton University Press, 1983). On Dickens, Twain's theatrical British counterpart, see Robert Garis, *The Dickens Theatre: A Reassessment of the Novels* (London: Oxford University Press, 1965); William Axton, *Circle of Fire: Dickens' Vision and Style and the Popular Victorian Theater* (Lexington: University Press of Kentucky, 1966); and Edwin M. Eigner, *The Dickens Pantomime* (Berkeley and Los Angeles: University of California Press, 1989). Also pertinent to the relation between novels and theater are Gillian Beer, " 'Coming Wonders': Uses of Theatre in the Victorian Novel," in *English Drama: Forms and Development*, ed. Marie Axton and Raymond Williams (Cambridge: Cambridge University Press, 1977), 164–85, and Brenda Murphy, *American Realism and American Drama, 1880–1940* (Cambridge: Cambridge University Press, 1987), which argues for the influence of theories of literary realism on American drama.

15. John C. Gerber, Introduction, *The Adventures of Tom Sawyer; Tom Sawyer Abroad; Tom Sawyer, Detective* (Berkeley and Los Angeles: University of California Press, 1980), 9, 15; Lin Salamo, Introduction, *The Prince and the Pauper* (Berkeley and Los Angeles: University of California Press, 1979), 3–4.

16. The phrase is from Twain's denunciation of Rev. William A. Sabine for refusing to conduct the comedian George Holland's funeral service because Holland was an actor. The piece is devoted to the argument that theater teaches morals as effectively, even more effectively, than do ministers such as Sabine. See "The Indignity Put upon the Remains of George Holland by the Rev. Mr. Sabine," in *What Is Man? and Other Philosophical Writings*, ed. Paul Baender (Berkeley and Los Angeles: University of California Press, 1973), 52.

17. Albert Bigelow Paine, *Mark Twain: A Biography*, 3 vols. (New York: Chelsea House, 1980), II, 571.

18. William Dean Howells, "My Mark Twain," in *Literary Friends and Acquaintance*, ed. David F. Hiatt and Edwin H. Cady (Bloomington: Indiana University Press, 1968), 288.

19. William Dean Howells, "The Man of Letters as a Man of Business," *Scribner's* (October 1893): 444, and *Mark Twain's Letters*, arranged with comment by Albert Bigelow Paine, 2 vols. (New York: Harper and Brothers, 1917), II, 528.

20. *Early Tales and Sketches, Volume 1: 1851–1864*, ed. Edgar Marquess Branch and Robert H. Hirst (Berkeley and Los Angeles: University of California Press, 1979), 78–82.

21. For a concise and lucid statement of the difficulties in scholarship when we believe *both* that culture is socially constructed *and* that society is culturally constructed, see Robert F. Berkhofer, Jr., "A New Context for a New American Studies?" *American Quarterly* 41 (1989): 588–613. Berkhofer's (rightly) hesitant sense that scholars must contextualize reflexively, that they "must all textualize as they contextualize, poeticize as they politicize," is persuasive. Also helpful is Lynn Hunt, ed., *The New Cultural History* (Berkeley and Los Angeles: University of California Press, 1989), in whose first part historians grapple with the problems of conducting historical investigations of, and within, "discursive formations."

22. See Minnie M. Brashear, *Mark Twain: Son of Missouri* (Chapel Hill: University of North Carolina Press, 1934), 134, 141.

23. See Neil Harris, *Humbug: The Art of P. T. Barnum* (Chicago: University of Chicago Press, 1973).

24. See John F. Kasson, *Rudeness and Civility: Manners in Nineteenth-Century Urban America* (New York: Hill and Wang, 1990), especially chap. 7, "The Disciplining of Spectatorship." Also see Bruce A. McConachie, "Pacifying American Theatrical Audiences, 1820–1900," in *For Fun and Profit: The Transformation of Leisure into Consumption*, ed. Richard Butsch (Philadelphia: Temple University Press, 1990), 47–70.

25. According to Minnie M. Brashear, in 1847 the population of Hannibal was 3,500 (*Mark Twain: Son of Missouri*, 77). Elbert R. Bowen writes that, according to the Seventh Census, the population in 1850 was 2,020, excluding slaves (*Theatrical Entertainment in Rural Missouri before the Civil War* [Columbia: University of Missouri Press, 1959], 52).

26. *Mark Twain's Autobiography*, ed. Albert Bigelow Paine, 2 vols. (New York: Harper and Brothers, 1929), I, 120.

27. See Bowen, *Theatrical Entertainment*, 2–4, and Dixon Wecter, *Sam Clemens of Hannibal* (Boston: Houghton Mifflin, 1952), 111.

28. Bowen, *Theatrical Entertainment*, 123. Also see ibid., 71–82, and Wecter, *Sam Clemens of Hannibal*, 186.

29. *Mark Twain in Eruption*, 110.

30. On the bad reputation among "upright citizens" that showboats had during the 1840s through the 1870s, see Philip Graham, *Showboats: The History of an American Institution* (Austin: University of Texas Press, 1961), 7, 26–27, 35, 37, 52, 189.

31. Quoted in Wecter, *Sam Clemens of Hannibal*, 187.

32. See ibid., 155.

33. At the beginning of "Old Times on the Mississippi," Mark Twain recalled that circus performances always left all the boys in the town "burning to become clowns," and "the first negro minstrel show that came to our section left us all suffering to try that kind of life." In notes he made much later, as he tried to gather memories about Hannibal that could serve as literary material, he mentioned a comic minstrel routine known as the "Long Dog

Scratch" and singled out the circus and a "Nigger Show" (*Mark Twain's Hannibal, Huck and Tom*, ed. Walter Blair [Berkeley and Los Angeles: University of California Press, 1969], 34, 37).

34. Ibid., 51–52.

35. On Dan Rice, see especially Graham, *Showboats*, 34–39. Also see Harold Edward Briggs and Ernestine Bennett Briggs, "The Early Theatre in the Upper Mississippi Valley," *Mid-America* 31 (1949): 140; Joseph S. Schick, "Early Showboat and Circus in the Upper Valley," *Mid-America* 32 (1950): 222; Wecter, *Sam Clemens of Hannibal*, 192; Bowen, *Theatrical Entertainment*, 30.

36. Quoted in Bowen, *Theatrical Entertainment*, 29, and Wecter, *Sam Clemens of Hannibal*, 192.

37. On respectable and rowdy styles of male public behavior, especially among working-class males, see Susan G. Davis, *Parades and Power: Street Theatre in Nineteenth-Century Philadelphia* (Philadelphia: Temple University Press, 1986), 20–23, 151–53.

38. Clifford Geertz, "Deep Play: Notes on the Balinese Cockfight," in *The Interpretation of Cultures* (New York: Basic Books, 1973), 412–53.

1. ACTING LIKE A MAN

1. Berthoff, *The Ferment of Realism*, 62.

2. See Gillian Brown's argument in *Domestic Individualism: Imagining Self in Nineteenth-Century America* (Berkeley and Los Angeles: University of California Press, 1990) that the feminine interior in middle-class ideology—for men as well as for women—was the perceived guarantor of the integrity of the individual.

3. Peter N. Stearns, *Be a Man! Males in Modern Society* (New York: Holmes and Meier, 1979), 96–112; Peter G. Filene, *Him/Her/Self: Sex Roles in Modern America*, 2d ed. (Baltimore: Johns Hopkins University Press, 1986), 69–93; Clyde Griffen, "Reconstructing Masculinity from the Evangelical Revival to the Waning of Progressivism: A Speculative Synthesis," in *Meanings for Manhood: Constructions of Masculinity in Victorian America*, ed. Mark C. Carnes and Clyde Griffen (Chicago: University of Chicago Press, 1990), 183–205. Also, John Higham's well-known account, "The Reorientation of American Culture in the 1890's," while preoccupied with "a farreaching reaction against the constrictions of a routinized society," reveals how profoundly concerned with masculinity were the late-nineteenth-century demands for a "strenuous life" of "muscular spirit," prowess, "vital force," and virility that could replace not only the enervations supposedly caused by mechanization, but also those attributed to effeminacy, overcivilization, and parlor domesticity (*Writing American History: Essays on Modern Scholarship* [Bloomington: Indiana University Press, 1970], 73–102).

4. See, especially, Elliott J. Gorn, *The Manly Art: Bare-Knuckle Prize Fighting in America* (Ithaca: Cornell University Press, 1986), and Erenberg, *Steppin' Out*, for the argument that working-class styles became models of leisure and pleasure for the dominant culture.

5. Elaine Showalter, *Sexual Anarchy: Gender and Culture at the Fin de Siècle* (New York: Viking, 1990), especially 3–14.

6. John Lauber, *The Making of Mark Twain: A Biography* (New York: Farrar, Straus and Giroux, 1985), 51.

7. Carroll Smith-Rosenberg, "Sex as Symbol in Victorian America," *Prospects: An Annual of American Cultural Studies* 5 (1980): 55–59. On the changes in apprenticeship in the printing trade, see Ava Baron, "Acquiring Manly Competence: The Demise of Apprenticeship and the Remasculinization of Printers' Work," in *Meanings for Manhood,* ed. Carnes and Griffen, 152–63. On the general change for workingmen from the apprentice system to wage labor, see Sean Wilentz, *Chants Democratic: New York City and the Rise of the American Working Class, 1788–1850* (New York: Oxford University Press, 1984), especially 107–42.

8. *Mark Twain's Travels with Mr. Brown,* 84. George C. D. Odell in *Annals of the New York Stage,* 15 vols. (New York: Columbia University Press, 1927–49), VI, 258, 329, notes that in 1853 Mademoiselle Couret's model artists were performing at George Len's Franklin Museum; this may have been the show Clemens saw.

9. *Mark Twain's Letters in the Muscatine Journal,* ed. Edgar M. Branch (Chicago: The Mark Twain Association of America, 1942), 13.

10. For general accounts of gender-segregated leisure in the middle and later nineteenth century, see Kathy Peiss, *Cheap Amusements: Working Women and Leisure in Turn-of-the-Century New York* (Philadelphia: Temple University Press, 1986), especially 16–21, 56–57, and idem, "Commercial Leisure and the 'Woman Question,' " in *For Fun and Profit,* ed. Butsch, 106–9. Peiss helpfully stresses the ways in which commercial leisure—theaters, saloons, billiard halls, music halls, dance houses, arcades, etc.—expressed and shaped male culture and an ethos of rowdiness. Mary P. Ryan, too, discusses public domains as masculine (including parades, street festivals, cafés, restaurants, mechanics' institutes, etc.), with a new segregation of men and women occurring in the 1840s; see Ryan, *Women in Public: Between Banners and Ballots, 1825–1880* (Baltimore: Johns Hopkins University Press, 1990). Robert C. Allen, in *Horrible Prettiness: Burlesque and American Culture* (Chapel Hill: University of North Carolina Press, 1991), 64–66, rightly observes that leisure spots reinforced solidarities of gender, class, and race.

11. See Arthur Herman Wilson, *A History of the Philadelphia Theatre, 1853–1855* (Philadelphia: University of Pennsylvania Press, 1935), 37, 47–48.

12. Although Jon M. Kingsdale focuses on later, turn-of-the-century saloons, see his "The 'Poor Man's Club': Social Functions of the Urban Working-Class Saloon," *American Quarterly* 25 (1973): 472–89. Also pertinent is Roy Rosenzweig, *Eight Hours for What We Will: Workers and Leisure in an Industrial City, 1870–1920* (Cambridge: Cambridge University Press, 1983), on the "alternative culture" of saloons as a preserve of male sociability, an escape from middle-class culture and crowded tenements, and a place for singing, storytelling, prizefighting, and gambling (see especially 45–58).

13. Henry Ward Beecher, *Lectures to Young Men on Various Important Subjects,* new ed. (New York: J. B. Ford, 1873), 163, 185. This edition adds four newer lectures to the original seven lectures of the 1844 edition.

14. William Knight Northall, *Before and Behind the Curtain; or Fifteen Years' Observation among the Theatres of New York* (New York: W. F. Burgess, 1851), 7.

15. Quoted in Grimsted, *Melodrama Unveiled,* 25.

16. Richard Moody, *The Astor Place Riot* (Bloomington: Indiana University Press, 1958).

17. For Clemens's remarks on Forrest's New York performance, see *Mark Twain's Letters, Volume 1: 1853–1866,* ed. Edgar Marquess Branch, Michael B. Frank, and Kenneth M. Sanderson (Berkeley and Los Angeles: University of California Press, 1987), 16. In this letter Clemens also says he regrets having missed the actor in *Damon and Pythias* in New York, and he notes that Forrest will appear in Philadelphia "on Monday night." Forrest opened at the Walnut Street Theatre in Philadelphia on Monday, October 10 (Wilson, *A History of the Philadelphia Theatre,* 689). The next existing letter from Clemens, dated October 26, came from Philadelphia, in which he told his family that his work schedule was flexible enough to allow him to stay at the theater until midnight (*Mark Twain's Letters, Volume 1,* 19). Sometime in January 1854, Clemens moved to Washington, and, in a letter to his brother Orion's newspaper, he wrote that he had seen Forrest play Othello at the National Theatre on February 17 (ibid., 42–43).

18. On the Bowery b'hoy subculture, see Wilentz, *Chants Democratic,* 257–71, and Christine Stansell, *City of Women: Sex and Class in New York, 1789–1860* (New York: Knopf, 1986), 89–101. Also see John Dizikes, *Sportsmen and Gamesmen* (Boston: Houghton Mifflin, 1981), 193–225; Allen, *Horrible Prettiness,* 65–66; and Eric Lott, *Love and Theft: Blackface Minstrelsy and the American Working Class* (New York: Oxford University Press, 1993), 72–73, 81–84.

19. *The Adventures of Thomas Jefferson Snodgrass,* 3–15.

20. Herbert G. Gutman's influential overview of the persistence of preindustrial traditions among urban working people appears in *Work, Culture, and Society in Industrializing America: Essays in American Working-Class and Social History* (New York: Knopf, 1976), 3–78. Bruce Laurie, *Working People of Philadelphia, 1800–1850* (Philadelphia: Temple University Press, 1980), discusses the multiple cultures among the urban working class, and Wilentz, in *Chants Democratic,* properly notes the reductiveness of dividing people into exclusive categories, such as abstemious and respectable trade unionists and Bowery roisterers (270). Both tendencies could exist, of course, in a culture and in a person.

21. Carroll Smith-Rosenberg, "Davy Crockett as Trickster: Pornography, Liminality, and Symbolic Inversion in Victorian America," in *Disorderly Conduct: Visions of Gender in Victorian America* (New York: Oxford University Press, 1985), 90–108.

22. Jerrold Seigel, *Bohemian Paris: Culture, Politics, and the Boundaries of Bourgeois Life, 1830–1930* (New York: Viking Penguin, 1986).

23. *Early Tales and Sketches, Volume 1,* 251–52.

24. *Mark Twain's Travels with Mr. Brown,* 270–74.

25. Mark Twain's own list of the spectacles of Virginia City includes "theaters, 'hurdy-gurdy houses,' wide-open gambling places, political pow-wows, civic processions, street fights, murders, inquests, riots," and so on (*Roughing It* [Berkeley and Los Angeles: University of California Press, 1972], 274).

26. Dizikes, *Sportsmen and Gamesmen,* 193.

27. On theaters and entertainment in Virginia City, see Margaret G. Watson, *Silver Theatre, Amusements of the Mining Frontier in Early Nevada, 1850–1864* (Glendale, Calif.: Arthur H. Clark, 1964), 129–31, 159, and Paul Fatout, *Mark Twain in Virginia City* (Bloomington: Indiana University Press, 1964), 52, 57, 72–75. On Virginia City as a "mecca" for prizefighting, see Gorn, *The Manly Art,* 163–65.

28. See the Introduction to *Mark Twain of the "Enterprise": Newspaper Articles and Other Documents 1862–1864,* ed. Henry Nash Smith and Frederick Anderson (Berkeley and Los Angeles: University of California Press, 1957), 5. Also see Schirer, *Mark Twain and the Theatre,* 12–14.

29. On Clemens's friendship with Doten, see Paul Fatout, "Mark Twain's Nom de Plume," in *Mark Twain: A Profile,* ed. Justin Kaplan (New York: Hill and Wang, 1967), 162–65. On Alf Doten, his friendship with Twain's roommate Dan De Quille (William Wright), and their cruising, see Marion S. Goldman, *Gold Diggers and Silver Miners: Prostitution and Social Life on the Comstock Lode* (Ann Arbor: University of Michigan Press, 1981), 97, 111–12. Goldman also provides the best account of the vice districts in Virginia City.

30. Fatout, *Mark Twain in Virginia City,* 37.

31. Clemens carried on feuds with Clement T. Rice (whom he called the Unreliable) and Adair Wilson (whom he called the Unimportant) of the Virginia City *Union;* Charlie Parker (the Obese) of the Virginia City *Evening Bulletin;* William Wright (Dan De Quille), his companion on the *Enterprise;* and Albert S. Evans (Fitz Smythe) of the *Alta California.* See, as a good example, the series of attacks on Fitz Smythe, in *Early Tales and Sketches, Volume 2: 1864–1865,* ed. Edgar Marquess Branch and Robert H. Hirst (Berkeley and Los Angeles: University of California Press, 1981), 329–58. Edgar Branch, in *The Literary Apprenticeship of Mark Twain,* provides a good account of this feuding.

32. Mary Ryan, *Cradle of the Middle Class: The Family in Oneida County, New York, 1790–1865* (Cambridge: Cambridge University Press, 1981).

33. Nancy Armstrong, *Desire and Domestic Fiction: A Political History of the Novel* (New York: Oxford University Press, 1987).

34. "Burlesque *Il Trovatore,*" in *Mark Twain's Satires and Burlesques,* ed. Franklin R. Rogers (Berkeley and Los Angeles: University of California Press, 1968), 19–24.

35. Fatout, *Mark Twain in Virginia City,* 80.

36. *Clemens of the "Call": Mark Twain in San Francisco,* ed. Edgar M. Branch (Berkeley and Los Angeles: University of California Press, 1969), 97, and *Early Tales and Sketches, Volume 2,* 172.

37. Ann Douglas, *The Feminization of American Culture* (New York: Avon, 1978); see especially 308–9 and the discussion of Melville in chap. 9. For critiques and historicizations of the association between mass culture and the feminine, see Andreas Huyssen, "Mass Culture as Woman: Modernism's Other," in *Studies in Entertainment: Critical Approaches to Mass Culture,* ed. Tania Modleski (Bloomington: Indiana University Press, 1986), 188–207, and Tania Modleski, "Femininity as Mas[s]querade: A Feminist Approach to Mass Culture," in *High Theory/Low Culture: Analysing Popular Television and Film,* ed. Colin MacCabe (New York: St. Martin's Press, 1986), 37–52.

38. *Early Tales and Sketches, Volume 2,* 235.

39. *Early Tales and Sketches, Volume 1,* 155–59, 320–26.

40. See *Contributions to "The Galaxy" 1868–1871,* ed. Bruce R. McElderry, Jr. (Gainesville, Fla.: Scholars' Facsimiles and Reprints, 1961), 47–50, for Mark Twain's comments, in retrospect, about these hoaxes.

41. *The Washoe Giant in San Francisco,* ed. Franklin Walker (San Francisco: George Fields, 1938), 58–60. Friedrich Halm was the pseudonym of Baron Eligius Franz Joseph von Münch-Bellinghausen. Originally *Der Sohn der Wildniss, Ingomar* was translated into English by William H. Charlton.

42. This is the argument made by Eve Kosofsky Sedgwick throughout *Between Men: English Literature and Male Homosocial Desire* (New York: Columbia University Press, 1985), but see, for example, 25–26.

43. See Claudia D. Johnson, "Burlesques of Shakespeare: The Democratic American's 'Light Artillery,' " *Theatre Survey* 21 (1980): 49–62. Ever since the Olympic and Chambers Street theaters in New York specialized in burlesques in the 1830s and 1840s and lowered their prices, burlesque was associated with audiences of Bowery b'hoys, mechanics, newsboys, and apprentices. See David Rinear, "Burlesque Comes to New York: William Mitchell's First Season at the Olympic," *Nineteenth-Century Theatre Research* 2 (1974): 23–34, and George Kummer, "The Americanization of Burlesque, 1840–1860," in *Popular Literature in America:A Symposium in Honor of Lyon N. Richardson,* ed. James C. Austin and Donald A. Koch (Bowling Green, Ohio: Bowling Green University Popular Press, 1972), 146–54.

The literary critics who have attended most closely to Mark Twain's burlesques—such as Walter Blair, Franklin Rogers, and David E. E. Sloane—have insistently stressed their belletrism. Seemingly anxious to dissociate Clemens from low burlesque, and from its vulgar, roughneck culture, they connect his burlesquing to a tradition that devolves from the burlesques printed in *Vanity Fair*—the New York, bohemian, literary magazine—and that is connected to British and Irish literary burlesque, such as Dickens's *Pickwick Papers* and Thackeray's burlesque novels (Walter Blair, "Burlesques in Nineteenth-Century American Humor," *American Literature* 2 [1930]: 236–37, 246; Rogers, *Mark Twain's Burlesque Patterns,* 12–17; David E. E. Sloane, *Mark Twain as a Literary Comedian* [Baton Rouge: Louisiana State University Press, 1979], 4–7, 58). It is true that Twain sought out the bohemian literati of Virginia City and San Francisco and wrote burlesque novels in the style of Bret Harte, Charles Webb, and Orpheus C. Kerr. But Constance Rourke, Bernard

DeVoto, and Edgar Branch were right to invoke a widespread "spirit" of burlesque in the theater, newspapers, and comic periodicals as the context for Twain's writing (Rourke, *American Humor*, 101–2, 169; DeVoto, *Mark Twain's America*, 165; Branch, *The Literary Apprenticeship of Mark Twain*, 83). Lawrence W. Levine's recent tracing in *Highbrow/Lowbrow* of the changing cultural place of nineteenth-century burlesque—its displacement from a more or less common, national culture that embraced both Shakespeare and Shakespeare travesty on the same bill, and its marginalization in working-class theaters and minstrel houses as the geography of entertainments came to match new hierarchies of taste—furnishes a most helpful account of the dynamic of cultural hierarchy and antagonism in which we should understand Mark Twain's burlesques.

If his burlesques had an ingredient of belletrism, it belonged to the bohemianism that also romanticized the burlesque shows of the rowdy b'hoys. And both literary elitism and working-class irreverence were opposed to the bourgeois Victorian home and its proprieties and amusements. The burlesque *novels*, I would suggest, had as much to do with an attack on the form that represented the privatized and emotional subjectivity of the middle-class hearth as they had to do with aspirations to literariness. And the burlesquers of novels were as much a part of the tradition of rowdy theatrical burlesques as they were of belles lettres. Twain's bohemian mentor, Charles Henry Webb, made his name—and a substantial income, according to Twain—with a burlesque of Dion Boucicault's *Arrah-na-Pogue*, not with his writing for the *Californian*. (On Webb's *Arrah-no-Poke, or Arrah of the Gold Pomme de Terre*, see Ettore Rella, *A History of Burlesque*, vol. 14 of *The San Francisco Theatre Research Monographs: A Monograph History of the San Francisco Stage and Its People from 1849 to the Present Day*, ed. Lawrence Estavan [San Francisco: Work Projects Administration, 1938–42], 65–68. Twain's notice of the burlesque appears in *Early Tales and Sketches, Volume 2*, 380–84.) Twain's friend Artemus Ward (Charles Farrar Browne), a bohemian and dandy and former contributor to *Vanity Fair*, wrote burlesques of *The Octoroon*, *Arrah-na-Pogue*, *Othello*, and other plays in the burlesque-hall spirit (*The Complete Works of Artemus Ward* [1898; rpt. New York: Burt Franklin, 1970], 45–50, 417–21). When Artemus Ward put on his show in Virginia City in 1863, after having gotten drunk with Mark Twain and the *Enterprise* staff, he blackened his face and gave an unscheduled performance with a minstrel troupe at the Niagara Music Hall, delivering a nonsensical burlesque oration typical of minstrelsy (Watson, *Silver Theatre*, 231). Such a performance, more than literariness, set the conditions for Twain's burlesques.

44. See Rella, *A History of Burlesque*, 66.

45. Twain's burlesque review appears in *Early Tales and Sketches, Volume 2*, 79–85.

46. *Mark Twain in Eruption*, 255.

47. On caricaturing monologuists, minstrels, and female performers in Virginia City during Mark Twain's stay there, see Watson, *Silver Theatre*. Often the same performers, and at least the same kinds of performers, were fea-

tured in the melodeons, minstrel halls, and taverns of San Francisco; see Edmond M. Gagey, *The San Francisco Stage* (New York: Columbia University Press, 1950), and *The San Francisco Theatre Research Monographs*, ed. Estavan, especially vol. 1, *Introduction to the Series;* vol. 13, *Minstrelsy;* and vol. 14, *A History of Burlesque.* For information about the melodeons, saloons, and burlesque houses in Virginia City's bawdy district, see Goldman, *Gold Diggers and Silver Miners.*

48. Susan G. Davis gives an account of the circulation of "styles, dramatic techniques, devices and symbols" between street theater and the stage in her study *Parades and Power,* 15–16, 95–96, 102. David Roediger, too, in *The Wages of Whiteness: Race and the Making of the American Working Class* (London: Verso, 1991), writes of blackface on both stage and street (104–5).

49. *Early Tales and Sketches, Volume 2,* 449. An informative study of the African-American community in San Francisco during these years is Douglas Henry Daniels, *Pioneer Urbanites: A Social and Cultural History of Black San Francisco* (Philadelphia: Temple University Press, 1980); for a discussion of dances and festivities, including the one Twain reported on, see 146–47. Also see Eric J. Sundquist, *To Wake the Nations: Race in the Making of American Literature* (Cambridge, Mass.: Belknap Press of Harvard University Press, 1993), 271–94, on the ways African-American cakewalks could combine minstrel conventions and their mockery, stereotypical buffoonery and parody of white manners.

50. My argument is at odds, obviously, with Guy Cardwell's assertion that, until about 1867, Twain was quite simply and crudely a white racist, invariably portraying blacks as ignorant, childlike, vulgar, inferior, etc.; see Cardwell, *The Man Who Was Mark Twain,* 109, 167–70, 180–200. I hope to complicate Twain's treatment of race in a way that will bypass the familiar argument over whether or not he was a minstrel-loving white supremacist, an argument whose tendency toward absolutism neglects the complexities in both minstrelsy and Twain's writing.

51. Homi Bhabha, "Of Mimicry and Man: The Ambivalence of Colonial Discourse," *October* 28 (1984): 125–34, is useful on this issue, because the author argues that white racist caricatures and mimicry have "identity-effects" that "are always crucially *split.*" There exists a menacing excess in such mimicries, partly because they are designed *not* to get representation quite right, and thereby always leave a dimension of the mimicked unfixed, unknown, ungrasped.

52. Eric Lott, in *Love and Theft,* provides an especially cogent and helpful examination of the ambivalences white audiences invested in the minstrel image. But also see Nathan Irvin Huggins, *Harlem Renaissance* (New York: Oxford University Press, 1971), 244–301; Berndt Ostendorf, "Minstrelsy: Imitation, Parody and Travesty in Black-White Interaction Rituals 1830–1920," in *Black Literature in White America* (Totowa, N.J.: Barnes and Noble, 1982), 65–94; Roediger, *The Wages of Whiteness,* especially 95–131; and Michael Rogin, "Blackface, White Noise: The Jewish Jazz Singer Finds His Voice," *Critical Inquiry* 18 (1992): 417–53.

53. *Mark Twain in Eruption,* 111. On minstrelsy in Hannibal, see Bowen, *Theatrical Entertainment,* 41, and Brashear, *Mark Twain: Son of Missouri,* 142.

54. *Early Tales and Sketches, Volume 2,* 233.

55. See Twain's extended description and discussion of minstrelsy in *Mark Twain in Eruption,* 111–14.

56. Quoted in the entry for Adelaide Sartoris in Gribben, *Mark Twain's Library,* II, 604.

57. Relevant to my argument is Shelley Fisher Fishkin's *Was Huck Black? Mark Twain and African-American Voices* (New York: Oxford University Press, 1993), not only in the author's general point that Twain's imagination was pervasively shaped by a multiracial community, but also in the more particular point that he was familiar with and adopted "signifying" practices for social satire (see especially 53–76). Fishkin, however, is more concerned with characterizing Twain as an embodiment of "multiculturalism," with demonstrating the influences of particular African Americans on his creation of Huck, and with deciding the (impossible?) question of when he drew on African-American culture and when he drew on minstrelsy, than she is with my concerns—assessing the complex ends to which elements attributable to African-American culture are put, and how such cultural borrowings work within a field of cultural conflicts.

58. Henry Louis Gates, Jr., *The Signifying Monkey: A Theory of African-American Literary Criticism* (New York: Oxford University Press, 1988), 46–53, 78, 85. But also see Houston A. Baker, Jr.'s, argument that, even if minstrel nonsense has ludic elements, it was nonetheless primarily a white creation of African Americans as brutish *"mis-speakers,"* a creation that African-American writers had to reinhabit, rework, re-sound, master—or deny, replacing it with "authentic" African-American sounds (*Modernism and the Harlem Renaissance* [Chicago: University of Chicago Press, 1987], 17–24, 56).

59. These arguments are made persuasively by William J. Mahar, "Black English in Early Blackface Minstrelsy: A New Interpretation of the Sources of Minstrel Show Dialect," *American Quarterly* 37 (summer 1985): 260–85.

60. For Twain's remarks on Birch, see "The Lick House Ball," *Early Tales and Sketches, Volume 1,* 316.

61. For considerations of such features in African-American language—talking without getting to the point, puns, boasting, put-ons, mimicries, etc.—see Geneva Smitherman, *Talkin and Testifyin: The Language of Black America* (Detroit: Wayne State University Press, 1977), e.g., 79–83, 94–100, 142–63, and Claudia Mitchell-Kernan, "Signifying, Loud-Talking, and Marking," in *Rappin' and Stylin' Out: Communication in Urban Black America,* ed. Thomas Kochman (Urbana: University of Illinois Press, 1972), 315–35.

62. *"Ah Sin," a Dramatic Work by Mark Twain and Bret Harte,* ed. Frederick Anderson (San Francisco: Book Club of California, 1961).

63. Robert C. Toll, *Blacking Up: The Minstrel Show in Nineteenth-Century America* (New York: Oxford University Press, 1974), 169–70. On similar stage

representations of the Chinese in the United States in the second half of the nineteenth century, many of them patterned on Harte's "heathen Chinee," see Stuart W. Hyde, "The Chinese Stereotype in American Melodrama," *California Historical Society Quarterly* 34 (1955): 357–67, and William Purviance Fenn, *Ah Sin and His Brethren in American Literature* (Beijing: College of Chinese Studies, 1933), 75, 100–101.

64. There were of course general, though never consistent, tendencies among whites to conflate images of African Americans and Chinese into a vague Other; see Dan Cardwell, "The Negroization of the Chinese Stereotype in California," *Southern California Quarterly* 53 (1971): 123–32; Ronald Takaki, *Iron Cages: Race and Culture in Nineteenth-Century America* (New York: Oxford University Press, 1990), 216–19; Stuart C. Miller, *The Unwelcome Immigrant: The American Image of the Chinese, 1785–1882* (Berkeley and Los Angeles: University of California Press, 1969), 7, 155; and Alexander Saxton, *The Indispensable Enemy: Labor and the Anti-Chinese Movement in California* (Berkeley and Los Angeles: University of California Press, 1971), 260.

65. Toni Morrison's *Playing in the Dark: Whiteness and the Literary Imagination* (Cambridge, Mass.: Harvard University Press, 1992) is indispensable for an understanding of this sort of displacement—for an understanding, that is, of the ways in which white authors have constructed race metaphorically and allegorically, using it as a vehicle for articulating *other* cultural and social problems—of class, gender, identity, etc. Also see the critique by bell hooks of blackness as a metaphor in the white imagination in "Eating the Other," in *Black Looks: Race and Representation* (Boston: South End Press, 1992), 21–40.

66. See Dizikes, *Sportsmen and Gamesmen*, 227–32, for an account of Menken and the bohemian, sporting, theatrical subculture she knew.

67. For examples of the jokes, see Fatout, *Mark Twain in Virginia City*, 157, and Branch, *The Literary Apprenticeship of Mark Twain*, 288 n. 98. For Goodman's defense of Menken, see Fatout, *Mark Twain in Virginia City*, 163–64.

68. Menken was attacked especially by the Virginia City *Union*; see Watson, *Silver Theatre*, 259, and Fatout, *Mark Twain in Virginia City*, 157, 163.

69. Fatout, *Mark Twain in Virginia City*, 162–63.

70. "The Menken—Written Especially for Gentlemen," in *Mark Twain of the "Enterprise,"* 78–79.

71. The San Francisco burlesques of Menken and *Mazeppa* are noted in Gagey, *The San Francisco Stage*, 91, and Rella, *A History of Burlesque*, 62–63, 213. For the Virginia City burlesques, see Watson, *Silver Theatre*, 251, 258–59, 311. Also see Twain's review of another *Mazeppa*, starring Emily Jordan, in *Clemens of the "Call,"* 94–95. And see *Early Tales and Sketches, Volume 2*, 521.

72. *The Washoe Giant in San Francisco*, 102–3.

73. Mary Russo, "Female Grotesques: Carnival and Theory," in *Feminist Studies/Critical Studies*, ed. Teresa de Lauretis (Bloomington: Indiana University Press, 1986), 222.

74. *Mark Twain's Travels with Mr. Brown*, 84.

75. Peter Stallybrass and Allon White, *The Politics and Poetics of Trans-gression* (Ithaca: Cornell University Press, 1986), 188, 200.

2. "FUNNY PERSONATIONS"

1. "A Notable Dinner," Hartford *Courant*, October 13, 1890, p. 2.

2. Paul Baender, "The Jumping Frog as a Comedian's First Virtue," *Philological Quarterly* 60 (1963): 194. Critics, of course, have written about the deadpan style, but usually as a kind of archetype in American literature of the "wise fool"—a figure given little historical specificity, usually treated in a broad sweep of American humor, and certainly never culturally situated in the way that I propose. See, for example, such surveys as Walter Blair's books: *The Mirth of a Nation* (Minneapolis: University of Minnesota Press, 1983), *America's Humor: From Poor Richard to Doonesbury*, written with Hamlin Hill (New York: Oxford University Press, 1978), and *Horse Sense in American Humor* (Chicago: University of Chicago Press, 1942).

3. I am once again referring to the divisions created between "low" and "high" theater and culture, especially from midcentury on, including the emergence of "respectable" theaters, the expulsion from them of burlesque and variety, and the proliferation of minstrel halls and music halls; the disciplining in "legitimate" theaters of boisterousness and its flourishing in "low" venues; and the consolidation of associated contrasts in taste and spectatorship. These are developments especially of the 1850s and 1860s, and therefore form a crucial background for Twain's and Jefferson's performances. See especially Levine, *Highbrow/Lowbrow*, but also the other sources listed in my Introduction, notes 6 and 7. More than thirty years ago, Raymond Williams, writing about English entertainment, described the configuration of cultural developments I want to explore: the burgeoning of music halls in the 1840s, the related expansion of "serious" and "respectable" theater and audiences, especially between 1860 and 1900, and the consolidation of sentimental comedy, with its mixture of comedy and pathos, as the beloved form of the newer middle-class audiences. See Williams's essay, "The Social History of Dramatic Forms," in *The Long Revolution* (New York: Columbia University Press, 1961), 246–73.

4. My sense of the deadpan style as a popular form that is contradictory, open to multiple readings, resonant with both vernacular traditions and bourgeois values, and generally an acting-out of cultural tensions is influenced by work in "cultural studies"—for example, Stuart Hall's well-known essay, "Notes on Deconstructing the Popular," in *People's History and Socialist Theory*, ed. Raphael Samuel (London: Routledge and Kegan Paul, 1981), 227–41, which characterizes popular culture as always composed of "antagonistic and unstable elements," and as a "ground" for a "double movement" of popular resistance and the superimposition of dominant cultural forms to contain that resistance. Also see, for example, Tony Bennett's "The Politics of 'the Popular' and Popular Culture," in *Popular Culture and Social Relations*, ed. Tony Bennett, Colin Mercer, and Janet Woollacott (London: Open Uni-

versity Press, 1986), 6–21, which pertinently argues that "the very organisation of cultural forms" is shaped by the intermingling within them of antagonistic cultural values and ideologies. Helpful, too, is John Clarke's essay, "Pessimism Versus Populism: The Problematic Politics of Popular Culture," in *For Fun and Profit*, ed. Butsch, 28–44, because it underscores the instability and variability of meaning in any popular cultural text, but also insists on the ways in which culture limits the range of possible meanings, and on the ways in which bourgeois forms and meanings work to incorporate and dominate the pleasures and practices of subordinate groups. For a similar account of popular culture that focuses on nineteenth-century American theater—that stresses multiple audiences and various possible audience responses and identifications, but that also puts a somewhat greater stress than I do on the power of containment and hegemony—see Bruce A. McConachie, "Using the Concept of Cultural Hegemony to Write Theatre History," in *Interpreting the Theatrical Past: Essays in the Historiography of Performance*, ed. Thomas Postlewait and Bruce A. McConachie (Iowa City: University of Iowa Press, 1989), 37–58.

5. Stuart Hall's "Notes on Deconstructing the Popular" is pertinent on this point as well; Hall stresses that languages, cultural practices, and cultural forms (and the deadpan style is a good example) never simply belong to a particular class, but are used variously by different class cultures (238).

6. Despite the unpredictability of individual response to popular forms, and despite the many variations in response shaped by people's differences in gender, race, class, ethnicity, nationality, age, sexual orientation, and so on, there do seem to be persistent configurations in popular culture and its reception that signal widespread preoccupations, anxieties, desires, conflicts. My aim here is to identify one such configuration, in which an extensive range of deadpan performances, and the existing responses to them, continually suggest and rehearse a prevalent concern over a separation between class cultures and gender ideals. These conflicts, I suggest, work to constitute a "horizon" of reading—or to set a group of canonical procedures for reading—that clearly shaped (even if it could never fully determine) what particular audiences saw in particular performances. Relevant to this conception is the work of Tony Bennett, who has argued that extratextual "codes," "discourses," "cultures," and protocols or conventions of interpretation can converge as "reading formations" that shape, organize, regulate, and activate readings and popular texts (or, I might add, viewings and performances); the effect is that readings are structured (though, often, very indirectly or unevenly) by larger social, cultural, and ideological relationships, and do not, therefore, dissolve into infinite idiosyncratic interpretations. See Bennett's essays, "Texts, Readers, Reading Formations," *Bulletin of the Midwest Modern Language Association* 16, no. 1 (1983): 3–17; "Marxism and Popular Fiction," *Literature and History* 7 (1981): 138–65; and "Texts in History: The Determinations of Readings and Their Texts," in *Poststructuralism and the Question of History*, ed. Derek Attridge, Geoff Bennington, and Robert Young (Cambridge: Cambridge University Press,

208   Notes to Pages 59–61

1987), 63–81. Also see Michael Denning's *Mechanic Accents: Dime Novels and Working-Class Culture in America* (New York: Verso, 1987), 69–71, which argues against totalizing ideas of "the public" but nonetheless argues for discernible regularities and tendencies in readings, some of them tied to class cultures and their worries and interests.

7. On the practical anxiety among men, in the new urban situations of crowds of strangers, to avoid exposing themselves—partly by adopting an impassive visage—and the concomitant middle-class anxiety that the public world was filled with manipulating con men whose intentions could hardly be read from their faces, see Karen Halttunen, *Confidence Men and Painted Women: A Study of Middle-Class Culture in America, 1830–1870* (New Haven: Yale University Press, 1982), especially chaps. 1 and 2, "The Era of the Confidence Man" and "Hypocrisy and Sincerity in the World of Strangers." The deadpan style obviously crystallized anxiety about self-exposure and about not being able to detect the masking of another.

8. Mark Twain's comment on Fred Franks appears in *Early Tales and Sketches, Volume 2,* 11; also see his remark on seeing Franks in San Francisco, in *Clemens of the "Call,"* 40; and on Franks's performances in Virginia City in 1863, see *Early Tales and Sketches, Volume 2,* 521–22, and Watson, *Silver Theatre,* 133, 186, 192. On Billy O'Neil's deadpan performance, see *Mark Twain of the "Enterprise,"* 132; on O'Neil's performances in Virginia City, see Watson, *Silver Theatre,* 186, 240–41. Twain's notice of Stephen Massett's performance appears in *Clemens of the "Call,"* 96; also see Watson, *Silver Theatre,* 317. For Twain's comment on Billy Birch, see *Early Tales and Sketches, Volume 1,* 316; for remarks on Birch's acting style, see Toll, *Blacking Up,* 150–51, and *Minstrelsy,* vol. 13 of *The San Francisco Theatre Research Monographs,* ed. Estavan, 64. Finally, for Twain on Setchell, see *Early Tales and Sketches, Volume 2,* 169–73. Setchell later starred in *Artemus Ward, Showman*—which further ties Twain, Ward, and Setchell together as kindred humorists and theatrical performers.

9. Richard Moody, *America Takes the Stage: Romanticism in American Drama and Theatre, 1750–1900* (Bloomington: Indiana University Press, 1955), 110, and Rourke, *American Humor,* 87.

10. *Early Tales and Sketches, Volume 2,* 49–56.

11. Twain's comment on Billy O'Neil is in *Mark Twain of the "Enterprise,"* 132.

12. On *Toodles* at Ben de Bar's Theatre in St. Louis, see Mark Twain's Notebook, #46, typescript p. 10, in the Mark Twain Papers, Bancroft Library, University of California at Berkeley (hereafter Mark Twain Papers).

13. William Evans Burton, *The Toodles: A Domestic Drama in Two Acts* (New York: Samuel French, [1853?]).

14. See Garff B. Wilson's report on the reception of Burton's Toodles in *A History of American Acting,* 158–60. To cite a possible influence on Twain, I also note that Burton and John Brougham played the Siamese twins, Chang as the drinker and Eng as helplessly and unintentionally drunk; see Laurence Hutton, *Plays and Players* (New York: Hurd and Houghton, 1875), 243.

15. Burton and other deadpan performers, that is, represent a kind of continuous self that has moved somewhat beyond the sureties of "character" that such historians as Joseph Kett, Warren Susman, and Karen Halttunen have placed earlier in the century. Kett has observed that, between 1840 and 1880, "character" as "a configuration of moral qualities molded in each person" dominated American conceptions of the self (*Rites of Passage: Adolescence in America 1790 to the Present* [New York: Basic Books, 1977], 105–8, 112–14). Halttunen has elaborated this conception of character as a matter of "fixed principles" and "stable character"—something antebellum Americans opposed to indulgence and pleasure (*Confidence Men and Painted Women*, especially chap. 2). Susman, compatibly, has argued that such a concept of character as a developing structure began to erode in mainstream thinking after 1880, culminating in twentieth-century versions of the self as shaped by ephemeral determinants (" 'Personality' and the Making of Twentieth-Century Culture," in *Culture as History: The Transformation of American Society in the Twentieth Century* [New York: Pantheon, 1984], 274, 280). The "unified" self of the drunken or befuddled deadpan obviously is not that of character "structure," which was becoming obsolete and untenable, but it *is* that of interior integrity, of a unity and continuity of consciousness, of a psychologistic consciousness of ongoing free associations which could accommodate drunkenness and pleasure and yet keep a coherent, private identity intact. It is a reassurance of continuity and flow rather than of structural solidity.

16. "Jim Smiley and His Jumping Frog," *Early Tales and Sketches, Volume 2*, 282–88.

17. On the Marsh troupe in Carson City, see *Mark Twain of the "Enterprise*," 129–31. Hutton is quoted in Rella, *A History of Burlesque*, 53. Also see Watson, *Silver Theatre*, 240.

18. For accounts of Burton's Captain Cuttle, see Donald Mullin, ed., *Victorian Actors and Actresses in Review* (Westport, Conn.: Greenwood Press, 1983), 96–97, and William C. Young, *Famous Actors and Actresses on the American Stage*, 2 vols. (New York: Bowker, 1975), I, 139–42. Twain's fondness for Captain Cuttle was long-standing; from 1862 through 1903 he made a variety of references to Cuttle in his notebooks (to Cuttle's catch phrases, to his movements and mannerisms) and seems generally to have thought, as he wrote in 1885, that "Captain Cuttle is good anywhere," whether on the stage or in a novel (see the entry for *Dombey and Son* in Gribben, *Mark Twain's Library*, I, 189).

19. The praise for Setchell appears in "A Voice for Setchell," *Early Tales and Sketches, Volume 2*, 169–73.

20. Edgar M. Branch, " 'My Voice Is Still for Setchell': A Background Study of 'Jim Smiley and His Jumping Frog,' " *PMLA* 82 (1967): 598.

21. Cox, *Mark Twain: The Fate of Humor*, 28–30. For the opposing point of view, see, for example, Kenneth Lynn, *Mark Twain and Southwestern Humor* (Boston: Little, Brown, 1959), 145–47, and Paul Schmidt, "The Deadpan on Simon Wheeler," *Southwest Review* 51 (1956): 270–77.

22. Michael Fried, *Absorption and Theatricality: Painting and Beholder in the Age of Diderot* (Berkeley and Los Angeles: University of California Press, 1980).

23. Quoted in the editors' note to the "Jumping Frog" story, *Early Tales and Sketches, Volume 2,* 272.

24. Rourke, *American Humor,* 169.

25. On the history of lecturing in the United States, see Paul Fatout, *Mark Twain on the Lecture Circuit* (Bloomington: Indiana University Press, 1960), 97–98; and Fatout's Introduction to *Mark Twain Speaking,* xv. On Twain's quickly growing popularity, see Fred W. Lorch, *The Trouble Begins at Eight: Mark Twain's Lecture Tours* (Ames: Iowa State University Press, 1968), 224. Also see Donald M. Scott, "The Popular Lecture and the Creation of a Public in Mid-Nineteenth-Century America," *Journal of American History* 66 (March 1980): 791–809. On Redpath and lecturing see Justin Kaplan, *Mr. Clemens and Mark Twain: A Biography* (New York: Simon and Schuster, 1966), 84–86.

26. See, for example, Fatout, *Lecture Circuit,* 142.

27. On Holland, see ibid., but also Lorch, *Trouble Begins,* 232, and Kaplan, *Mr. Clemens and Mark Twain,* 146 and, for Twain's response, 147.

28. Lorch, *Trouble Begins,* 230, and Fatout, *Lecture Circuit,* 112. Both Lorch and Fatout refer to responses to a January 1869 lecture in Decatur, Illinois, reported in the Decatur *Herald* and *Republican.*

29. Fatout, *Lecture Circuit,* 136, 127, 73, 59.

30. Lorch, *Trouble Begins,* 44, 114, 128.

31. Cox, *Mark Twain: The Fate of Humor,* 59.

32. See Twain's remarks about pauses in *Mark Twain in Eruption,* 225–27, and in a letter to his wife, Livy, in *The Love Letters of Mark Twain,* ed. Dixon Wecter (New York: Harper and Brothers, 1949), 162.

33. See Fatout's remarks in *Mark Twain Speaking,* xviii, and in Fatout, *Lecture Circuit,* 134–35.

34. Quoted in Lorch, *Trouble Begins,* 219.

35. For example, ibid., 71, 200, 227, and Fatout, *Lecture Circuit,* 42, 70, 75–76, 86, 107, 182.

36. See especially Fatout's quotation, from the January 28, 1896, Bombay *Gazette,* in *Lecture Circuit,* 260.

37. In a letter to Livy Clemens, from Bennington, Vermont, November 27, 1871, in *Love Letters,* 165.

38. *Mark Twain Speaking,* 247–49; also see 230, 450.

39. Hutton, *Plays and Players,* 46–47; Mark Twain's comment appears in Autobiographical Dictation, April 28, 1908, in the Mark Twain Papers. Quoted with permission.*

40. Mullin, *Victorian Actors,* 416–17, and Moses J. Montrose, *Famous Actor-Families in America* (1906; rpt. New York: Johnson Reprint Corp., 1968), 98.

41. Henry Austin Clapp, *Reminiscences of a Dramatic Critic* (Boston: Houghton Mifflin, 1902), 99–100.

42. Jefferson began playing the role of Rip Van Winkle in 1865 (for a run of 170 nights), and by 1881 he had performed the part 2,500 times. On Jeffer-

son's popularity, see Richard Moody, "American Actors and Acting before 1900: The Making of a Tradition," in *American Theatre: A Sum of Its Parts,* ed. Henry B. Williams (New York: Samuel French, 1971), 59.

43. L. Clarke Davis, "Among the Comedians," *Atlantic Monthly* 19 (June 1867): 751, and Joseph Jefferson, *Rip Van Winkle,* in *Nineteenth-Century American Plays,* ed. Myron Matlaw (New York: Applause, 1967), 166–67, 179, 183.

44. "Editor's Study," *Harper's Monthly* 82 (March 1891): 643.

45. Mullin, *Victorian Actors,* 273, and "Jefferson in 'Rip Van Winkle,' " *The Nation* 9 (23 September 1869): 248.

46. Mullin, *Victorian Actors,* 272–74.

47. Jefferson's remark is quoted in Young, *Famous Actors,* I, 585. Jefferson, *Rip Van Winkle,* 153, 155, 162, 175.

48. Mullin, *Victorian Actors,* 274.

49. Davis, "Among the Comedians," 752.

50. Young, *Famous Actors,* I, 586.

51. Mullin, *Victorian Actors,* 273, and Young, *Famous Actors,* I, 583.

52. Jerry Wayne Thomason has helpfully made the play available, and has fully recounted its history, in his dissertation, "Colonel Sellers: The Story of His Play" (Ph.D. diss., University of Missouri—Columbia, 1991). For more succinct and accessible accounts of the play, which Twain took originally from a copyright violator's dramatization of the novel, see *Mark Twain–Howells Letters,* II, 861–62; Phillip Walker, "Mark Twain, Playwright," *Educational Theatre Journal* 8 (1956): 185; Gilder, "Mark Twain Detested the Theatre," 111; and Schirer, *Mark Twain and the Theatre,* 41–48. Brenda Murphy discusses the trend of plays focused on one comic character in *American Realism and American Drama, 1880–1940,* 4, 48.

53. September 20, 1874, *Mark Twain–Howells Letters,* I, 26; July 15 or 25, 1874, ibid., I, 20.

54. Twain's comment on *Rip Van Winkle* and *Solon Shingle* appears in his letter to Mr. Watt, January 26, 1875, quoted in Gribben, *Mark Twain's Library,* I, 359.

55. William Dean Howells, "Drama," *Atlantic Monthly* 35 (1875): 749–51.

56. Brander Matthews and Laurence Hutton, *Actors and Actresses of Great Britain and the United States,* 5 vols. (Boston: L. C. Page, 1900), V, 235, 231.

57. Brander Matthews, "The American on the Stage," *Scribner's Monthly* 18 (1879): 329.

58. *New York Times,* September 17, 1874, p. 6.

59. Ibid., August 17, 1875, p. 4, and September 17, 1874, p. 6.

60. See Matthews and Hutton, *Actors and Actresses,* V, 236, 240–41, and Mullin, *Victorian Actors,* 374.

61. Matthews and Hutton, *Actors and Actresses,* V, 234. "The Gilded Age," *Rochester Evening Express,* September 1, 1874, p. 2, col. 2, quoted in Thomason, "Colonel Sellers," 332. Thomason has brought together in his dissertation a host of otherwise difficult to acquire reviews of the play.

62. *Mark Twain Speaking,* 88.

63. *The Autobiography of Mark Twain,* ed. Charles Neider (New York: Harper and Row, 1959), 21.

64. Matthews, "The American on the Stage," 328.

3. "ABSORB THE CHARACTER"

1. *Mark Twain in Eruption,* 214–17.

2. Paine, *Mark Twain: A Biography,* II, 786.

3. *Mark Twain's Letters, Volume 1,* 16.

4. See Twain's defenses of Forrest quoted in Pat M. Ryan, Jr., "Mark Twain: Frontier Theatre Critic," *Arizona Quarterly* 16 (1960): 201; also see Twain's piece praising Forrest in *The Washoe Giant in San Francisco,* 101–2. Twain revised his estimation of Forrest—linking his acting to an "adolescent taste" that America had outgrown—in one of the originally unpublished passages of *Life on the Mississippi* (1883). See *Life on the Mississippi, Illustrated by Thomas Hart Benton, with an Introduction by Edward Wagenknecht and a Number of Previously Suppressed Passages, Now Printed for the First Time, and Edited with a Note by Willis Wager* (New York: Heritage Press, 1944), 393.

5. As Jerry Wayne Thomason reports in his dissertation, "Colonel Sellers," there exist four versions of the play (none in Twain's hand): two in the Mark Twain Papers (one of which Thomason reproduces in his thesis); a copyrighted script in the Library of Congress; and a typescript in the Stanford University Theatre Collection.

6. On the playwriting, see Schirer, *Mark Twain and the Theatre.*

7. *Mark Twain–Howells Letters,* I, 81.

8. William Dean Howells, "Drama," *Atlantic Monthly* 35 (1875): 749–51. Howells's opinion was in accord with some other, early, reviewers of the play. The *New York Times* (September 17, 1874) said Raymond "assumed this *role* with an earnestness which insured his success" and an "absence of self-consciousness" that made the "personation as artistic as it was striking." The Rochester, New York, *Union and Advertiser* (September 1, 1874) said Raymond "appears to have caught the very inspiration of the author's meaning"; and the Rochester *Democrat and Chronicle* (September 1, 1874) said that Twain and Charles Dudley Warner "have found in Mr. Raymond the faithful interpreter of their conception" (quoted in Thomason, "Colonel Sellers," 333).

9. *Mark Twain–Howells Letters,* I, 82. It seems indeed to have become a commonplace in criticism of *Colonel Sellers* that the play was weak, but Raymond's fleshing out of Sellers was superb. George H. Jessop, for example, asserted that "the author had only created a shell into which Raymond infused his vigorous and glowing individuality, animating it into bustling, scheming life" (in Matthews and Hutton, *Actors and Actresses,* V, 234). And reviewer after reviewer wrote that the role of Sellers was "admirably adapted," "suited," or "fitted" to Raymond's "talent," "style," or "personality"—implying that the success of the play lay largely in the self that Raymond brought to his part. (See the reviews of the play quoted by Thomason, "Colonel Sellers," 26, 307, 309.)

10. *Mark Twain–Howells Letters*, I, 82–83. Also see the slightly tongue-in-cheek curtain speech Twain gave on opening night, in which he complains that Raymond transforms all the pathos and "tragedy" in Sellers into laughs (*Mark Twain Speaking*, 88).

11. *Mark Twain's Autobiography*, ed. Paine, I, 89–90.

12. As a member of the Players Club, Twain attended dinners in the late 1880s with Boucicault, Coquelin, and Irving (see *Mark Twain Speaking*, 240–41, 338–39). Twain's connection with Irving deepened in the 1890s, when Twain not only dined with Irving but also enlisted the actor as a financial backer for the Paige typesetting machine (see *Love Letters*, 278, and Kaplan, *Mr. Clemens and Mark Twain*, 305).

13. Diderot's text, with Irving's introduction, is bound together with Archer's in *The Paradox of Acting by Denis Diderot and Masks or Faces? by William Archer*, intro. Lee Strasberg (New York: Hill and Wang, 1957). Coquelin's essay, with an 1887 review of it by Henry James, was reprinted as part of the series "Papers on Acting," published by the Dramatic Museum: Constant Coquelin, *Art and the Actor*, trans. Abby Langdon Alger (New York: Dramatic Museum of Columbia University, 1915). The series also includes Joseph Talma, *Reflexions on the Actor's Art*, intro. Sir Henry Irving (New York: Dramatic Museum of Columbia University, 1915), and *The Art of Acting: A Discussion by Constant Coquelin, Henry Irving and Dion Boucicault* (New York: Columbia University Press, 1926), which reprints the 1887 discussions. For a helpful account of the influence of Diderot and Coquelin in the late nineteenth century, with special reference to the writings of Henry James, see Steven H. Jobe, "Henry James and the Philosophic Actor," *American Literature* 62 (1990): 32–43; also see D. J. Gordon and John Stokes, "The Reference of *The Tragic Muse*," in *The Air of Reality: New Essays on Henry James*, ed. John Goode (London: Methuen, 1972), 127–32, for an account (again with special reference to James) of the dispute in the journals, and the assertion that "through the eighties no-one interested in acting or the theatre could forget the terms of reference of such discussions" (127). Finally, Benjamin McArthur, in *Actors and American Culture, 1880–1920* (Philadelphia: Temple University Press, 1984), writes of the resurgence in the 1880s of "the debate over head versus heart," precipitated partly by Diderot and Archer and given a new dimension by late-nineteenth-century interest in automatism, suggestion, and hypnotism (180–86).

14. See *Art of Acting*, 47, and Irving's introduction to Diderot's *Paradox*, 7.

15. On the general tendency in the nineteenth century for the language of physiology and the body to surface in discussions of actors' emotional expression, and for a discussion of the influence of Darwin on theories of acting (including William Archer's), see Joseph R. Roach, "Darwin's Passion: The Language of Expression on Nature's Stage," *Discourse* 13 (fall–winter 1990–91): 40–57.

16. *Adventures of Tom Sawyer*, 71–73.

17. *The Prince and the Pauper*, 54.

18. *Adventures of Huckleberry Finn,* ed. Walter Blair and Victor Fischer (Berkeley and Los Angeles: University of California Press, 1988), 254.

19. *A Connecticut Yankee in King Arthur's Court,* ed. Bernard L. Stein (Berkeley and Los Angeles: University of California Press, 1979), 320–25.

20. On both the longer history of "nature and art" in acting and Diderot's early versions of this opposition, see Joseph R. Roach, *The Player's Passion: Studies in the Science of Acting* (Newark: University of Delaware Press, 1985), 23–29, 148–49.

21. Many of the actors Archer surveyed for *Masks or Faces* voiced this cliché or some version of it; see, for example, 129.

22. *Pudd'nhead Wilson and Those Extraordinary Twins,* ed. Sidney E. Berger (New York: Norton, 1980).

23. See, for recent considerations of these matters, Susan Gillman and Forrest G. Robinson, eds., *Mark Twain's Pudd'nhead Wilson: Race, Conflict, and Culture* (Durham, N.C.: Duke University Press, 1990), especially the essays by Myra Jehlen, Michael Rogin, and Susan Gillman (Gillman's is a slightly different version of her chapter on *Pudd'nhead Wilson* in *Dark Twins*). Also see Brook Thomas, "Tragedies of Race, Training, Birth, and Communities of Competent Pudd'nheads," *American Literary History* 1 (1989): 754–85, and Lee Clark Mitchell, " 'De Nigger in You': Race or Training in *Pudd'nhead Wilson?" Nineteenth-Century Literature* 42 (1987): 295–312.

24. The idea that an actor could generate an emotion by duplicating its physical expression has a longer history—Archer associates it especially with Gotthold Ephraim Lessing (173). But late-nineteenth-century psychology put it on a different footing. William James, whose theory of the emotions made them epiphenomena of bodily responses, wrote similarly that "if our theory be true, a necessary corollary of it ought to be that any voluntary arousal of the so-called manifestations of a special emotion ought to give us the emotion itself" (*The Principles of Psychology,* vol. 2 [1890; rpt. New York: Dover, 1950], 462).

25. For a discussion related to my point that, for Twain, generating emotion or identity through mechanical manipulation of the body threatened the integrity of the self, see Walter Benn Michaels, "An American Tragedy, or the Promise of American Life," *Representations* 25 (winter 1989): 71–98. Michaels argues, particularly in reference to the writings of S. Weir Mitchell, that the belief that mechanical imitation of facial emotional expression could generate actual emotion posed a severe threat to ideas of individuality and originality (85–86).

26. *Mark Twain in Eruption,* 243.

27. Ibid., 198.

4. THE EXPRESSIVE BODY, GESTURE, AND WRITING

1. Quite relevant to my argument is Miles Orvell, *The Real Thing: Imitation and Authenticity in American Culture, 1880–1940* (Chapel Hill: University of North Carolina Press, 1989). Orvell argues that between 1880 and 1940 in

America a transformation took place from a "realist" culture that valued imitation and illusion to a "modernist" culture that valued "authenticity," rejecting the "sham" of mimesis and attempting to create works of art that, instead of being replications, would be "real things" themselves. I am arguing, differently, that a version of this tension is present in Mark Twain's work from a very early date. I am inclined, in fact, to agree with Mark Seltzer's argument in *Bodies and Machines* (New York: Routledge, 1992), that generally, in "the realist project," there existed a goal of "perfect referentiality: *bodies and matter writing themselves*" (108–9)—a kind of "real thing" tantamount to Orvell's modernist authenticity.

2. Charles Darwin, *The Expression of the Emotions in Man and Animals* (1955; rpt. New York: Greenwood, 1969), 364.

3. Howard Horwitz, in *By the Law of Nature: Form and Value in Nineteenth-Century America* (New York: Oxford University Press, 1991), 99–100, 117, argues quite differently that the "semiotics of the river" in *Life on the Mississippi* "amount to a critique of empiricism" because the signs on the water's surface seem unreliable. But they are radically unreliable only to the uninitiated cub, not to Bixby, his tutor. When Bixby stresses the shape of the river "that's *in your head*, and never mind the one that's before your eyes," and asserts that this is learned through "instinct," he is not articulating an epistemology of "romance," as Horwitz argues, that somehow bypasses the visible. Instead, in a process I shall make clearer in my next chapter, the pilot's way of knowing the river "unconsciously," "naturally," and instinctually by amassing observations of it is akin in its automatism not only to the machinery of a tear, but also to the mechanical, automatic registration of a bluff reef on the water's surface.

4. Linda Williams, in *Hard Core: Power, Pleasure, and the "Frenzy of the Visible"* (Berkeley and Los Angeles: University of California Press, 1989), discusses the way in which late-nineteenth-century scientific discourse on the mechanisms of the human body treated the female body, as "science" joined the drive for visibility and knowledge to prurience, and joined fetishism and voyeurism to "the positivist quest for the truth of visible phenomena" (46). Williams notes the centrality (as in Jean-Martin Charcot's research) of watching unconscious movements, involuntary spasms, and hysterical convulsions for such male glimpses into "hidden" truths of female bodies; see, especially, chaps. 1 and 2. Also germane, of course, and important for Williams's discussion, is Michel Foucault's attention to confession, exposure, the pursuit of truth, and the penetration and control of bodies, in *The History of Sexuality, Volume I: An Introduction*, trans. Robert Hurley (New York: Random House, 1978).

5. Charles S. Peirce, "Logic as Semiotic: The Theory of Signs," in *Philosophical Writings of Peirce*, ed. Justus Buchler (New York: Dover, 1955), 98–119.

6. Useful for my argument here was Rosalind Krauss's discussion of the pursuit in modernist art of indexical signs—traces, imprints, rubbings, "clues"—as "uncoded," more immediate, and therefore a security against

the loss of confidence in representation; see Krauss, "Notes on the Index: Part 1" and "Notes on the Index: Part 2," in *The Originality of the Avant-Garde and Other Modernist Myths* (Cambridge, Mass.: MIT Press, 1986), 196–219.

7. Clemens read George Sumner Weaver's *Lectures on Mental Science According to the Philosophy of Phrenology*. See *Mark Twain's Notebooks and Journals*, ed. Frederick Anderson, Michael B. Frank, and Kenneth M. Sanderson, 3 vols. (Berkeley and Los Angeles: University of California Press, 1975), I, 11–16. The fullest account of Mark Twain's lifelong interest in (and doubts about) phrenology is Alan Gribben, "Mark Twain, Phrenology, and the 'Temperaments': A Study of Pseudoscientific Influence," *American Quarterly* 24 (1972): 45–68. For a powerfully persuasive discussion of the interweaving of phrenology, physiognomy, and photography into a cluster of indexical signs useful for "assessing the character of strangers in the dangerous and congested spaces of the nineteenth-century city," providing "intelligence" about them, and documenting them, see Allan Sekula, "The Body and the Archive," *October* 39 (1986): 3–64. Phrenology and physiognomy, and Twain's interest generally in the legibility of character, are obviously related to an anxiety about and a desire to control seemingly troublesome "others"—in other words, to formations of discipline and surveillance.

8. *Mark Twain's Hannibal, Huck and Tom*, 152–242.

9. *Adventures of Huckleberry Finn*, 19.

10. Gillman, *Dark Twins*, 88–95; Michael Rogin, "Francis Galton and Mark Twain: The Natal Autograph in *Pudd'nhead Wilson*," in *Mark Twain's Pudd'nhead Wilson: Race, Conflict, and Culture*, ed. Gillman and Robinson, 78–81; and David R. Sewell, *Mark Twain's Languages: Discourse, Dialogue, and Linguistic Variety* (Berkeley and Los Angeles: University of California Press, 1987), 124–25.

11. Francis Galton, *Finger Prints* (1892; rpt. New York: Da Capo Press, 1965), 16–18.

12. See Graeme Tytler, *Physiognomy in the European Novel: Faces and Fortunes* (Princeton: Princeton University Press, 1982), which argues that Lavater's theory "permeated nineteenth-century literature" (xvii) and had a particularly strong hold on European and American culture through the 1860s. Also see Patrizia Magli, "The Face and the Soul," in *Fragments for a History of the Human Body, Part Two*, ed. Michel Feher, with Ramona Naddaff and Nadia Tazi (New York: Zone Books, 1989), 86–127. A broad-ranging history of physiognomy and of beliefs that the body registers the soul, Magli nonetheless helpfully provides a background for nineteenth-century physiognomy, discusses such crucial figures as Lavater and Charles le Brun, and suggests the social anxieties—about charting, classifying, and controlling "the other"—that provided such a powerful impetus for this "science."

13. *The Adventures of Tom Sawyer; Tom Sawyer Abroad; Tom Sawyer, Detective*, 412.

14. Darwin, *The Expression of the Emotions in Man and Animals*, 50. Alan Gribben, in *Mark Twain's Library*, notes that Twain made "numerous pencil

marks" on the pages of Darwin's book that dealt with habit and reflex action (I, 175).

15. Twain articulates his interest in and concern over this confusion explicitly in *What Is Man*, where the Old Man defines *instinct* as "inherited habit" and concludes that the term "confuses us; for as a rule it applies to habits and impulses which had a far-off origin in thought, and now and then breaks the rule and applies itself to habits which can hardly claim a thought-origin" (190).

16. James, *The Principles of Psychology*. On Mark Twain and James, see Gribben, *Mark Twain's Library*, I, 351, and Gillman, *Dark Twins*, 154.

17. *Cap'n Simon Wheeler, the Amateur Detective: A Light Tragedy*, in *Mark Twain's Satires and Burlesques*, 216–311.

18. The argument about deaf-mute sign language as natural or conventional had long occupied theorists of gesture and language. See James R. Knowlson, "The Idea of Gesture as a Universal Language in the XVIIth and XVIIIth Centuries," *Journal of the History of Ideas* 26 (October–December 1965): 496–97. Also see Jean-Christophe Agnew, *Worlds Apart: The Market and the Theater in Anglo-American Thought, 1550–1750* (Cambridge: Cambridge University Press, 1986), 88–91.

19. Forrest G. Robinson's *In Bad Faith*, 31, 37–39, attends to the control of "face" in *Tom Sawyer* in connection with the "dynamics of deception" Robinson is tracing—a concern quite different from mine.

20. *Mark Twain–Howells Letters*, I, 245, and II, 633.

21. Twain refers to the composite photograph in an 1895 interview, quoted in Blair and Fischer, "Explanatory Notes," *Adventures of Huckleberry Finn*, 371. Galton's practice of and ideas about composite photographs receive a full discussion in Sekula, "The Body and the Archive"; also see Orvell, *The Real Thing*, 89–94.

22. Quoted in Orvell, *The Real Thing*, 124.

23. Twain to Howells, November 17, 1879, *Mark Twain–Howells Letters*, I, 279.

24. Quoted in Kaplan, *Mr. Clemens and Mark Twain*, 226.

25. *Mark Twain's Letters*, ed. Paine, I, 371, 373.

26. *Mark Twain Speaking*, 167–68.

27. *Love Letters*, 116.

28. *Mark Twain–Howells Letters*, I, 279.

29. Roland Barthes's ideas in his essay "The Grain of the Voice" may help focus these nineteenth-century antecedents (*Image, Music, Text*, trans. Stephen Heath [New York: Hill and Wang, 1977]). Barthes writes: "The 'grain' is the body in the voice as it sings"—that is, the membranous fleshiness of the vocal cords, the throat, etc. The "grain" is also the body in "the hand as it writes, the limb as it performs" (188). Barthes echoes Twain not only in this connection between gesture and voice; he also similarly discovers a sexuality in the voice—derived from the body, and specifically from its metaphoric phalluses, "the tongue, the glottis, the teeth, the mucous membranes, the nose" (183).

30. Elaine Scarry, Introduction, *Literature and the Body: Essays on Popula-tions and Persons,* ed. Elaine Scarry (Baltimore: Johns Hopkins University Press, 1988), xxi.

5. MEDIUMSHIP, "MENTAL TELEGRAPHY," AND MASCULINITY

1. *Mark Twain's Hannibal, Huck and Tom,* 61–66.

2. Wecter reports on Hannibal mesmerists, spiritualists, and animal magnetists in *Sam Clemens of Hannibal,* 90, 196–97. See *The Washoe Giant in San Francisco,* 119–21, 125–36, for Twain's newspaper pieces on spiritualists. For a review of Twain's interest, see Howard Kerr, " 'Sperits Couldn't a Done Better': Mark Twain and Spiritualism," in *Mediums and Spirit Rappers and Roaring Radicals: Spiritualism in American Literature 1850–1900* (Urbana: University of Illinois Press, 1972), 155–89. Also Alan Gribben, " 'When Other Amusements Fail': Mark Twain and the Occult," in *The Haunted Dusk: American Supernatural Fiction, 1820–1920,* ed. Howard Kerr, John W. Crowley, and Charles L. Crow (Athens: University of Georgia Press, 1983), 171–89. Absolutely crucial for understanding Twain's attention to medi-umship is Susan Gillman's *Dark Twins,* chap. 5, especially because it shows the connections in his thinking between science and the occult, psychic re-search and spiritualism.

3. On the use of conceptions of femininity and domesticity to counter-act suspicions of fraud and imposture in mediumship, see, especially, Alex Owen, "The Other Voice: Women, Children, and Nineteenth-Century Spiri-tualism," in *Language, Gender, and Childhood,* ed. Carolyn Steedman, Cathy Urwin, and Valerie Walkerdine (London: Routledge and Kegan Paul, 1985), 34–73.

4. Robert Darnton, *Mesmerism and the End of the Enlightenment in France* (Cambridge, Mass.: Harvard University Press, 1968), provides a compelling account of mesmeric theorizing. On American versions of mesmerism see Robert C. Fuller, *Mesmerism and the American Cure of Souls* (Philadelphia: Uni-versity of Pennsylvania Press, 1982). Mesmer drew on eighteenth-century theories of electricity in formulating his idea of animal magnetism; see Henri Ellenberger, *The Discovery of the Unconscious: The History and Evolution of Dy-namic Psychiatry* (New York: Basic Books, 1970), 186–87.

5. On the amazingly versatile explanatory power of electricity, see Car-olyn Marvin, *When Old Technologies Were New: Thinking about Electric Com-munication in the Late Nineteenth Century* (New York: Oxford University Press, 1988), especially chap. 3, "Locating the Body in Electrical Space and Time." And on the tendency to attribute clairvoyance and thought transfer-ence to the powers of electricity, see R. Lawrence Moore, "Spiritualism and Science: Reflections on the First Decade of the Spirit Rappings," *American Quarterly* 29 (1972): 491–92.

6. The secondary literature on nineteenth-century mental physiology is extensive. But see, for example, Kurt Danziger, "Mid-Nineteenth-Century

British Psycho-Physiology: A Neglected Chapter in the History of Psychology," in *The Problematic Science: Psychology in Nineteenth-Century Thought,* ed. William R. Woodward and Mitchell G. Ash (New York: Praeger, 1982), 119–44. Also Bruce Haley, *The Healthy Body and Victorian Culture* (Cambridge, Mass.: Harvard University Press, 1978), especially his chapter "Victorian Psychophysiology," and most especially 35–45. Helpful, too, is Elaine Showalter's *The Female Malady: Women, Madness, and English Culture, 1830–1980* (New York: Pantheon, 1985), particularly her discussion of the psychophysiologist Henry Maudsley and his insistence on the physical basis of mental phenomena, mental illness, and hysteria (106–38).

7. "Mental Telegraphy," in *The American Claimant and Other Stories and Sketches by Mark Twain* (New York: Harper and Brothers, 1897), 374–96.

8. The letters on this between Twain and De Quille, and De Quille's comment on the "force," appear in Lawrence I. Berkove, " 'Nobody Writes to Anybody Except to Ask a Favor': New Correspondence between Mark Twain and Dan De Quille," *Mark Twain Journal* 26, no. 1 (spring 1988): 5, 7–8. For Twain's reference to odyle, see *Notebooks,* II, 172–75. For information about and a contemporary critique of odyle—a supposedly newly discovered natural force described by Karl, Baron von Reichenbach—see Thomas Laycock, "Odyle, Mesmerism, Electro-Biology, &c.," *The British and Foreign Medico-Chirurgical Review* 8 (1851): 378–431.

9. See George M. Beard, *The Study of Trance, Muscle-Reading and Allied Nervous Phenomena in Europe and America, with a Letter on the Moral Character of Trance Subjects and a Defence of Dr. Charcot* (New York: privately printed, 1882), and Beard's "Physiology of Mind-Reading," *Popular Science Monthly* 10 (1877): 459–73. Beard is concerned to debunk the claim that Brown could communicate by a wire, and to assert that other instances of Brown's mind-reading—done by placing his hands on a subject's head—were cases of "muscle-reading," accomplished by feeling involuntary and reflexive expressions of thought in the face. Also see Ricky Jay, "A Few Words about Death and Show Biz: Washington Irving Bishop, J. Randall Brown, and the Origins of Modern Mind Reading," in *Learned Pigs and Fireproof Women* (New York: Villard, 1986), 155–99; see 177 for an account of Brown's telegraphic demonstration.

10. In a letter to Howells, August 16, 1898 (*Mark Twain–Howells Letters,* II, 674), Twain claimed that in an unpublished version of "Simon Wheeler" "written in 1876 or '75," an execution was prevented by testimony transmitted by mental telegraph—systematized in a phrenophonic way through a contraption "like the old mesmerizer-button" which automatically translated thoughts into words. And in "Three Thousand Years among the Microbes" (1905) Twain imagined a "Recorder" into which one dictated thoughts, not words, that were retained in a state so "clear and limpid and superbly radiant in expression that they make all articulated speech—even the most brilliant and the most perfect— seem dull and lifeless and confused by comparison" (*Which Was the Dream,* 490).

11. See the collection of essays *The Correlation and Conservation of Forces,* ed. Edward Livingston Youmans (New York: D. Appleton, 1873), which includes essays by physicians, physicists, and physiologists, among them pieces by Hermann Ludwig Ferdinand von Helmholtz and Michael Faraday, and William Carpenter's essay "On the Correlation of the Physical and Vital Forces." Yehuda Elkana, *The Discovery of the Conservation of Energy* (Cambridge, Mass.: Harvard University Press, 1974), provides the larger history of these scientific advances, as does Thomas S. Kuhn, "Energy Conservation as an Example of Simultaneous Discovery," in his collection of essays, *The Essential Tension: Selected Studies in Scientific Tradition and Change* (Chicago: University of Chicago Press, 1977), 66–104.

12. William Carpenter, *Principles of Mental Physiology, with Their Application to the Training and Discipline of the Mind and the Study of Its Morbid Conditions,* 4th ed. (London: Henry S. King, 1876), 633. For examples of Carpenter's use of telegraphic metaphors to describe the nervous system, see 13, 35–38.

13. *The Autobiography of Mark Twain,* ed. Neider, 163–65.

14. Oliver Wendell Holmes, *Mechanism in Thought and Morals* (Boston: James R. Osgood, 1871).

15. For a discussion of hysteria as a reflexive "physiological and pathological action of the ovaria," see Thomas Laycock, *A Treatise on the Nervous Diseases of Women; Comprising an Inquiry into the Nature, Causes, and Treatment of Spinal and Hysterical Disorders* (London: Longman, Orme, Brown, Green, and Longmans, 1840). His investigations of hysteria led Laycock to extend the notion of reflex to other mental events; see "On the Reflex Functions of the Brain," *British and Foreign Medical Review* 19 (1845): 298–311.

16. Elin Diamond addresses this subject in "Realism and Hysteria: Toward a Feminist Mimesis," *Discourse* 13, no. 1 (fall–winter 1990–91): 59–91. However, inasmuch as Diamond broaches the issue of hysteria and mimetic immediacy, she characterizes hysteria as the figure of the breakdown of realism—the malady in which the symptoms seemingly have no referent. I am arguing, differently, that in the cases I cite, science thought it was able, after all, to root hysteria in the body—and hysteria therefore stood as the ideal model for realism, rather than the metaphor for its failure. Hysteria in these years raised the *question* of whether its symptoms were physiologically rooted; researchers had not come to the answer, yet, that they were not. Helpful on this point is Joan Copjec, "Flavit et Dissipati Sunt," *October* 18 (1981): 21–40, which discusses Jean-Martin Charcot's initial disposition to treat hysterical symptoms as indexical, physiological signs—as an instance of his more general "indexical neurology." See, too, Charcot's *Lectures on the Diseases of the Nervous System, Delivered at la Salpêtrière* (Philadelphia: Henry C. Lea, 1879), where, taking into account the criticisms made of the "ovarists" (220) and their diagnosis of hysteria, and acknowledging that hysterics may be "guilty of trickery" in their symptoms (205), he nonetheless insists on ailments of the ovaries as causes (if not *the* cause) of hysterical symptoms, promotes "compression" of the ovaries for relief of symptoms (222–33), and pur-

sues other physiological causes of hysteria. On Charcot's stress on the brain and ovaries (rather than the uterus) in his etiology, on his attention to male hysteria, and on the linkage he made between hysteria and hypnosis, see Martha Noel Evans, *Fits and Starts: A Genealogy of Hysteria in Modern France* (Ithaca: Cornell University Press, 1991), 28–29, 42.

17. Quoted in Gillman, *Dark Twins*, 139.

18. As far back as 1869, for example, Twain claimed that when he wanted to write a newspaper article he would simply "sit down & let it *write itself*" (letter to Mrs. Jervis Langdon, February 13, 1869, in *Love Letters*, 67). He similarly claimed in his autobiography that he completed *Tom Sawyer* only because "the book went on and finished itself" (*Mark Twain in Eruption*, 197). In 1893 he remarked to his wife that writing *Tom Sawyer, Detective* delighted him because "the story tells itself" (letter to Livy Clemens, November 10, 1893, *Love Letters*, 277). In his tale of how he wrote *Pudd'nhead Wilson*—in "Those Extraordinary Twins"—he explains that his writing "goes along telling itself" until "it spreads itself into a book" (119). Of *Joan of Arc*, he said, the novel seemed to write itself, "I merely have to hold the pen" (Twain to Rogers, September 2–3, 1894, in *Mark Twain's Correspondence with Henry Huttleston Rogers 1893–1909*, ed. Lewis Leary [Berkeley and Los Angeles: University of California Press, 1969], 72–73); later, in the autobiography, he remembered that Joan knew what she had to say without intervention from "Mark Twain" and "said it, without doubt or hesitation" (*Mark Twain in Eruption*, 199).

19. Letter to Emily G. Hutchings, November 14, 1902, in *Mark Twain the Letter Writer*, ed. Cyril Clemens (Boston: Meador, 1932), 25.

20. In relation to this, see Jan Goldstein, "The Uses of Male Hysteria: Medical and Literary Discourse in Nineteenth-Century France," *Representations* 34 (spring 1991): 134–65. Goldstein argues that nineteenth-century male writers, notably Flaubert, appropriated the concept of feminine hysteria, partly because the analogy between literary creation and biological procreation fostered a connection between hysteria and "the labors of male writing" (143). This resulted in a vacillation in such writers as Flaubert between embracing "feminine" passivity and giving rein to "the compensatory desire to exaggerate action beyond measure" (145). A similar vacillation and ambivalence, I argue, occurs in Mark Twain.

21. G. J. Barker-Benfield, "The Spermatic Economy: A Nineteenth-Century View of Sexuality," *Feminist Studies* 1 (1972): 46. Cynthia Eagle Russett and Charles E. Rosenberg also discuss conceptions of the body and psyche as a closed system of nervous energy or vital (or electrical) force depleted by discharge and strengthened by husbanding. See Cynthia Eagle Russett, *Sexual Science: The Victorian Construction of Womanhood* (Cambridge, Mass.: Harvard University Press, 1989), especially chap. 4, "The Machinery of the Body." And Charles E. Rosenberg, *No Other Gods: On Science and American Social Thought* (Baltimore: Johns Hopkins University Press, 1976), 4–7, and idem, "Sexuality, Class, and Role," *American Quarterly* 25 (May 1973): 151. Also, John L. Greenway recounts common conceptions of human physiol-

ogy (men's especially) as an electrical battery storing nervous energy, in " 'Nervous Disease' and Electric Medicine," in *Pseudo-Science and Society in Nineteenth-Century America,* ed. Arthur Wrobel (Lexington: University Press of Kentucky, 1987), 46–73.

22. Quite pertinent to Twain's self-sufficient electric system is the model of the bachelor machine that Michel Carrouges, in *Les machines célibataires* (Paris: Le Chêne, 1954), finds so common in the late nineteenth century—a solely masculine, often electric and masturbatory metaphor for the psychic economy and for artistic creation and mechanical reproduction. For further remarks on this "bachelor-machine logic" of male writers near the end of the nineteenth century, see Alice Jardine, "Of Bodies and Technologies," in *Discussions in Contemporary Culture, Number One,* ed. Hal Foster (Seattle: Bay Press, 1987), 151–58.

23. Mark Twain and William Dean Howells, *Colonel Sellers as a Scientist,* in *The Complete Plays of W. D. Howells,* ed. Walter J. Meserve (New York: New York University Press, 1960), 209–41.

24. Howells, *Literary Friends and Acquaintance,* 270.

25. See, for example, Clyde L. Grimm, *"The American Claimant:* Reclamation of a Farce," *American Quarterly* 19 (1967): 86–103. Also Berthoff, *The Ferment of Realism,* 69, and DeVoto, *Mark Twain's America,* 288.

26. Nicholas Royle, *Telepathy and Literature: Essays on the Reading Mind* (Oxford: Basil Blackwell, 1990), 5; on Bell and Watson, see Avital Ronell, *The Telephone Book: Technology—Schizophrenia—Electric Speech* (Lincoln: University of Nebraska Press, 1990), especially 240–50.

27. Mark Seltzer, in *Bodies and Machines,* argues that late-nineteenth-century technologies of representation (typewriters, telephones, telegraphs, typesetting machines, etc.) derailed a preexisting model of continuity from the spiritual and invisible mind, through the writing hand, to visible and physical inscription on paper by interposing their material systems of registration (9–10). I argue, differently, that for Mark Twain this distinction between bodies and machines was not so clearly drawn: the body and its expression looked analogous to telephones, telegraphs, phonographs, and so on, when Twain reduced them to a physical and mechanical plane (a move not incompatible with Seltzer's broader argument about the turn-of-the-century oppositions *and* correlations of bodies and machines). This mechanical model, moreover, could promise for Twain a continuity in certain forms of expression precisely because of its materiality—though, as we now see, that materiality could then turn around into an impediment to representation.

28. Quite relevant to this idea of Huck as an impeding medium is the history of perception that Jonathan Crary outlines in *Techniques of the Observer: On Vision and Modernity in the Nineteenth Century* (Cambridge, Mass.: MIT Press, 1992). Crary argues that conceptions of vision in the nineteenth century deposed the disembodied eye and its transparent seeing by locating vision "within the unstable physiology and temporality of the human body" (70). Discoveries of blind spots, afterimages, and less than instantaneous or reliable relays of impulses down nerve pathways showed the physiological

process of vision to be defective, prey to illusion, a basis for "subjective vision." Twain obviously was attuned to the same kind of science of perception, though he alternately took the corporeality of perception and expression as a promise of reliability *and* as an obstacle. Crary underplays the extent to which locating perception on the same material plane as the beheld object could be conceived as underwriting reliable perception and representation, and circumventing the distortions of interpretation and convention.

29. Ann D. Wood, "The 'Scribbling Women' and Fanny Fern: Why Women Wrote," *American Quarterly* 23 (1971): 7–9. Also see Mary Kelley, *Private Woman, Public Stage: Literary Domesticity in Nineteenth-Century America* (New York: Oxford University Press), 1984, especially chap. 5, which reports on identity-denying tendencies of these women—publishing anonymously, adopting pseudonyms, and so on.

30. Judith R. Walkowitz, "Science and the Séance: Transgressions of Gender and Genre in Late Victorian London," *Representations* 22 (spring 1988): 8–9; R. Lawrence Moore, "The Spiritualist Medium: A Study of Female Professionalism in Victorian America," *American Quarterly* 27 (1975): 201–7; Ann Braude, *Radical Spirits: Spiritualism and Women's Rights in Nineteenth-Century America* (Boston: Beacon, 1980), 82–83.

31. Alfred Habegger, *Gender, Fantasy, and Realism in American Literature* (New York: Columbia University Press, 1982), 56. Jay Martin has also suggested that Twain and his male peers learned from women writers, including lessons about the representation and workings of the unconscious gained from women who wrote and acted as mediums; see Martin, "Ghostly Rentals, Ghostly Purchases: Haunted Imaginations in James, Twain, and Bellamy," in *The Haunted Dusk*, ed. Kerr et al., 124.

32. Mary Poovey argues, with reference to English writers, that "literary men" such as Dickens conceived of their work in terms of the dominant representations of the domestic sphere and domestic labor as a means of attaining an aura of moral authority and nonalienated production; see Poovey, *Uneven Developments: The Ideological Work of Gender in Mid-Victorian England* (Chicago: University of Chicago Press, 1988), 125.

33. *Mark Twain's Autobiography*, ed. Paine, I, xv.

34. It appears, of course, that Twain, typically, was not consistently so sure of the "truth" of his autobiography; Howells observes that despite Twain's aim to tell only the truth, Twain announced one day that he had begun to lie, and "as to veracity [the autobiography] was a failure" (*Literary Friends and Acquaintance*, 316). But his excitement about this "truest of all books" (*Mark Twain–Howells Letters*, II, 782) and about the comparative truth of *his* autobiography was remarkably persistent (see the quotation in Gribben, *Mark Twain's Library*, II, 540, from "Mark Twain, the Greatest American Humorist, Returning Home, Talks at Length," *New York World*, October 14, 1900).

35. Ann Douglas notes that, because nineteenth-century Americans identified mourning as a private matter, opposed to the public world of mask, convention, and market, they saw it as one of their rare moments for sincere

and heartfelt emotion; see Douglas, "Heaven Our Home: Consolation Literature in the Northern United States, 1830–1880," *American Quarterly* 26 (1974): 496. Also see Halttunen, *Confidence Men and Painted Women,* particularly chap. 5, "Mourning the Dead: A Study in Sentimental Ritual."

36. Sandra M. Gilbert and Susan Gubar, *The Madwoman in the Attic: The Woman Writer and the Nineteenth-Century Literary Imagination* (New Haven: Yale University Press, 1979). The authors discuss trance writing and its relation to male impersonation most fully in reference to Charlotte Brontë, whose career they take as a paradigm for many nineteenth-century women writers (see 311–17).

37. Terry Lovell, *Consuming Fiction* (London: Verso, 1987), 9, 74, 145; Rachel Bowlby, *Just Looking: Consumer Culture in Dreiser, Gissing and Zola* (New York: Methuen, 1985), 11; Showalter, *Sexual Anarchy,* particularly chap. 5, "King Romance"; and Michael Davitt Bell, "The Sin of Art: William Dean Howells," in *The Problem of American Realism,* 17–38.

38. Mark Seltzer, in *Bodies and Machines,* argues similarly that the American male naturalists based creation on a seminal, abstract "force," which women could convert, in accord with the model of thermodynamics, but which nonetheless cancelled the power of female reproduction and made possible "an autonomous (and male) technique of creation" (31–35).

39. Paine, *Mark Twain: A Biography,* I, 476.

40. Howells makes this remark about Ulysses S. Grant's *Memoirs,* in *Criticism and Fiction and Other Essays* (New York: New York University Press, 1959), 26.

41. Howells to Twain, February 14, 1904, *Mark Twain–Howells Letters,* II, 780.

42. Doesticks is quoted in Kerr, *Mediums and Spirit Rappers,* 35.

6. "IT'S GOT TO BE THEATRICAL"

1. Philip Fisher, "Appearing and Disappearing in Public: Social Space in Late-Nineteenth-Century Literature and Culture," in *Reconstructing American Literary History,* ed. Sacvan Bercovitch (Cambridge, Mass.: Harvard University Press, 1986), 155–88.

2. See Max Horkheimer and Theodor Adorno, *Dialectic of Enlightenment,* trans. John Cumming (New York: Herder and Herder, 1972), 142–44.

3. "Queen Victoria's Jubilee," in *Europe and Elsewhere,* vol. 29 of *The Writings of Mark Twain,* Stormfield Edition (New York: Harper and Brothers, 1929), 193–94.

4. Michael Rogin, " 'Make My Day!': Spectacle as Amnesia in Imperial Politics," *Representations* 29 (1990): 99–123.

5. *Life on the Mississippi,* chap. 46.

6. Mark Twain, "About Play-Acting," in *The Man That Corrupted Hadleyburg and Other Essays and Stories,* vol. 23 of *The Writings of Mark Twain,* Stormfield Edition (New York: Harper and Brothers, 1929), 213–25.

7. Twain's remarks about the Children's Theatre are taken from speeches in *Mark Twain Speaking,* 546, 596, and 620, and from a typescript of

"The Great Alliance" (January 16, 1908), in the Mark Twain Papers. Quoted with permission.*

8. *Mark Twain in Eruption*, 110–15.

9. Macdonald, "Mark Twain: An Unsentimental Journey," 188. Howells's remark is in his letter to Twain, December 13, 1880, *Mark Twain–Howells Letters*, I, 338.

10. Mikhail Bakhtin, *Problems of Dostoevsky's Poetics*, trans. and ed. Caryl Emerson (Minneapolis: University of Minnesota Press, 1984), 124. On the crowning of fools, also see Bakhtin, *Rabelais and His World* (Bloomington: Indiana University Press, 1984), 79, 138, 217–19. These two books were initially helpful in framing the issues in Twain's fascination with spectacle and carnival. Ultimately, however, the Mark Twain of *The Prince and the Pauper* is more distressed than Bakhtin with the failures of official symbols, and less enamored of carnival licentiousness and "gay relativity."

11. Although Hank's discussion of "protection" and "free trade" certainly is related to the particular conflict in the 1880s between Republican party advocacy of tariffs and Democratic opposition to them, as Henry Nash Smith points out (in *Mark Twain's Fable of Progress: Political and Economic Ideas in "A Connecticut Yankee"* [New Brunswick, N.J.: Rutgers University Press, 1964], 57), focusing on this connection can obscure the larger tension raised here between fixed and circulating value.

12. Part of Mark Twain's grasp of Hank's performance business clearly draws on the tradition traced by Jean-Christophe Agnew in *Worlds Apart: The Market and the Theater in Anglo-American Thought, 1550–1750*, which argues that, in the years he studies, the abstractions of "the market," of money values, and of impersonal contracts raised fears of misrepresentation and ideas of temporary and artificial selves—matters reproduced and explored in the theater. The issues raised in Twain's clash between the sixth and the nineteenth centuries are much the same.

13. Twain here invokes a distinction akin to Roland Barthes's well-known contrast "between feudal society and bourgeois society, index and sign," the indexical sign in feudal society always fixed to an origin, the sign in bourgeois society released into the "limitless process of equivalences, representations that nothing will ever stop, orient, fix, sanction" (*S/Z*, trans. Richard Miller [New York: Hill and Wang, 1974], 39–40). Jean Baudrillard also writes of a pre-Renaissance security in signs and a post-Renaissance proliferation of signs (imitations, counterfeits, etc.) "emancipated" into a new culture of exchange that made their meanings quickly changeable (*Simulations*, trans. Paul Foss, Paul Patton, and Philip Beitchman [New York: Semiotext(e), 1983], 83–86). These are clearly among the contrasts Twain invokes between Arthur's England and Morgan's United States.

14. Georg Lukács, *History and Class Consciousness: Studies in Marxist Dialectics*, trans. Rodney Livingstone (Cambridge, Mass.: MIT Press, 1985), 83. Robert Shulman suggests that Hank Morgan introduces "the reifying process" and "commodity value" into sixth-century England; see his *Social Criticism and Nineteenth-Century Fictions* (Columbia: University of Missouri Press, 1987), 153.

15. The idea that capitalism annihilates not only referents but also signifieds is familiarly associated with Baudrillard, for example in *Simulations*, 43. A number of critics have situated a crisis in the sign, specifically the release of signifiers from signifieds, in the postmodern era, when, supposedly, capital finally fully penetrates the artistic sign and colonizes it with the forces of reification. See, for example, Fredric Jameson, "Postmodernism, or the Cultural Logic of Late Capitalism," *New Left Review*, no. 146 (1984): 56, and Hal Foster, "Wild Signs: The Breakup of the Sign in Seventies' Art," in *Universal Abandon? The Politics of Postmodernism*, ed. Andrew Ross (Minneapolis: University of Minnesota Press, 1988), 253. Since it is obvious, however, that the nineteenth century is a heyday of capitalist commodification of cultural production, I am arguing that Twain turns his astute attention to anatomizing a full-blown (not simply emergent) phenomenon. If postmodern spectacles are different from late-nineteenth-century ones (and certainly they are), the colonization by capital of the aesthetic realm must not be the decisive difference.

16. Note how the supposed magnificence of each of Hank's theatrical effects surpasses all precedents: he makes his threat of the eclipse "in as sublime and noble a way as ever I did such a thing in my life" (87–88); the miracle of the fountain is "the very showiest bit of magic in history" (282), and his theatrical chanting there was "one of the best effects I ever invented" (267); on his display of conspicuous consumption before Marco and friends, he says, "I don't know that I ever put a situation together better, or got happier spectacular effects out of the materials available" (365); but he soon surpasses that by producing a "fine effect" in arguing with them, "as fine as any I ever produced, with so little time to work it up in" (379); the rescue by the knights on bicycles was the "grandest sight that ever was seen" and "one of the gaudiest effects I ever instigated" (425–26). And so on.

17. James M. Cox, "*A Connecticut Yankee in King Arthur's Court*: The Machinery of Self-Preservation," in *A Connecticut Yankee in King Arthur's Court*, ed. Allison R. Ensor (New York: Norton, 1982), 392, and Michaels, "An American Tragedy, or the Promise of American Life," 73–78.

18. Francis Hodge, in his *Yankee Theatre: The Image of America on the Stage, 1825–1850*, gives the fullest account of the stage Yankees. Hank Morgan's predecessors, for example, appeared in David Humphrey's *The Yankey in England* (1815), Charles Mathews's *Jonathan in England* (1824), James Hackett's *Jonathan Doubikins* (1834), James Kirke Paulding's *The Bucktails; or, Americans in England* (1847), John Augustus Stone's *The Knight of the Golden Fleece* (1834) (which put Yankee Sy Saco in the world of Spanish medieval romance), Bayle Bernard's *Speculations, or Major Wheeler in Europe* (1838), and Charles Selby's *A Day in France* (1838).

19. *Burlesque Hamlet*, in *Mark Twain's Satires and Burlesques*, 49–87.

20. Bakhtin considers marketplace misrule and irreverence in *Rabelais and His World*; see especially chap. 2, "The Language of the Marketplace in Rabelais."

21. Ann Douglas's argument that Hank is a nineteenth-century manipulator of crowd psychology, freeing Arthurians from "the conformist mob-

mentality of serfs" only to instill "the conformist mob-mentality of consumers" strikes me as more persuasive than Forrest G. Robinson's argument that the Arthurians were the best audience for Hank, because his showmanship flourished best in a culture of aristocrats and slaves. See Douglas, *The Feminization of American Culture,* 189–90, and Robinson, *In Bad Faith,* 160, 235. Hank reconceives Arthurians in terms of nineteenth-century conceptions of crowds and mobs. For pertinent background, see Patrick Brantlinger, *Bread and Circuses: Theories of Mass Culture as Social Decay* (Ithaca: Cornell University Press, 1983), on the crowd psychologists of the turn of the century (e.g., Gustave Le Bon, Gabriel Tarde, William McDougall, William Trotter, Nietzsche, Freud) and the general, growing concern about "the masses"—their supposed barbarism, their irrationality, their surrender to animal instinct, etc. (19, 30–31, 109, 166–67). On late-nineteenth-century conceptions of crowds as primitive, irrational, instinctual, and credulous, also see Michael Schudson, *Discovering the News: A Social History of American Newspapers* (New York: Basic Books, 1978), 127, 131, and John F. Kasson, *Amusing the Million: Coney Island at the Turn of the Century* (New York: Hill and Wang, 1978), 97.

22. Forrest G. Robinson, in *In Bad Faith,* has relatedly traced depictions of "bad faith" in Twain's fiction—rationalizations, conscious dissimulations, self-deceptions, hypocrisies, distractions (sometimes in the form of amusements)—that serve to mask or deny racism, cruelty, and tragedy. Hank's spectacles suit this pattern, for they certainly divert his own attention from the ugliness of his acts at the same time that they invite his spectators and his readers to look at the astonishing rather than the repellent.

23. *Mark Twain Speaking,* 88.

7. MELODRAMA, TRANSVESTISM, PHANTASM

1. *Mark Twain's Correspondence with Henry Huttleston Rogers,* 125.
2. *Mark Twain–Howells Letters,* II, 698–99.
3. David B. Richards, in "Mesmerism in *Die Jungfrau von Orleans,*" *PMLA* 91 (1976): 856–70, argues that contemporaneous notions of mesmerism, hypnotism, clairvoyance, and somnambulism shaped Friedrich Schiller's story of Johanna. Twain, who appears to have read *Die Jungfrau,* probably was especially attentive to mesmeric overtones in nineteenth-century versions of Joan of Arc. (See Gribben, *Mark Twain's Library,* II, 606.)
4. Mark Twain, "Two Speeches," *New York Times,* July 7, 1900, p. 461.
5. Brooks, *The Melodramatic Imagination.* David Grimsted's analysis of "the melodramatic structure" in nineteenth-century American plays foregrounds the importance of feminine virtue, purity, and "perfect goodness" in a way that illustrates Brooks's characterization; see Grimsted, "The Melodramatic Structure," in *Melodrama Unveiled,* 172–83.
6. Christina Zwarg argues, valuably, that *Joan of Arc* is about the way masculine history and storytelling—including both the "authorities" that the "translator" supposedly draws on and the romanticizing narration of de Conte—obscure and imprison Joan, despite (or with the help of) their ap-

peals to privileged "proofs" and "personal recollections." But in "the few moments in which Joan is permitted to speak her own words" this male history is subverted, its grammar deconstructed, and a "feminist" Joan shines through. See Zwarg, "Woman as Force in Twain's *Joan of Arc:* The Unwordable Fascination," *Criticism* 27 (1985): 57–72. Zwarg obviously is registering the melodramatic structure of obscuring and unveiling, although in her effort to make Joan a saboteur of phallocentric discourse, she discounts too surely the sentimental womanhood that links *Joan of Arc* to nineteenth-century melodrama.

7. Mark Twain, *Personal Recollections of Joan of Arc* (New York: Harper and Brothers, 1896), vii–viii.

8. On the nineteenth-century popularity of Joan of Arc, see Marina Warner, *Joan of Arc: The Image of Female Heroism* (New York: Knopf, 1981), particularly chap. 12. Also see Ann Bleigh Powers, "The Joan of Arc Vogue in America, 1894–1929," *American Society Legion of Honor Magazine* 49 (1978): 177–92; Albert E. Stone, Jr., *The Innocent Eye: Childhood in Mark Twain's Imagination* (New Haven: Yale University Press, 1970), 206; and Showalter, *Sexual Anarchy*, 29. Among the main stage versions of Joan's story was Schiller's *Die Jungfrau von Orleans*, first performed in Weimar in 1801, and performed in the United States throughout the century (see the listings for the play in Odell, *Annals of the New York Stage*); John Brougham's *The Lily of France* (1840); George Henry Calvert's *The Maid of Orleans* (1873); and *Jeanne D'Arc*, by Jules Barbier, an English version of which—by William Young—was performed in New York in 1890 and 1891 (Odell, *Annals of the New York Stage*, XIV, 534, 575). Significantly, upon finishing *Joan of Arc* Twain turned quickly in 1896 to negotiations for its dramatization; though they were unsuccessful, a version of his *Joan* appeared on stage in 1926 to 1927, with his daughter Clara Clemens in the cast (see *Mark Twain's Correspondence with Henry Huttleston Rogers*, 221–22, 224, and Schirer, *Mark Twain and the Theatre*, 93). Pertinent for Twain's notions of femininity and performance, Adah Isaacs Menken played a version of Joan of Arc in New York, at least, in 1862—along with *Mazeppa* and *The French Spy*—just before taking her act out West, where Twain saw her and argued with his friends over her theatricality and expressiveness (Odell, *Annals of the New York Stage*, VII, 409).

9. Warner, *Joan of Arc*, 237, 260.

10. Jackson Lears, *No Place of Grace: Antimodernism and the Transformation of American Culture 1880–1920* (New York: Pantheon, 1981). Throughout this book Lears attends to the pursuit of "authentic experience" and a recoil from rationalized and commodified American culture, but see, especially, chap. 4, "The Morning of Belief: Medieval Mentalities in a Modern World."

11. This is the argument made throughout Marjorie Garber's *Vested Interests: Cross-Dressing and Cultural Anxiety* (New York: Routledge, 1992), but see, for example, 16.

12. Twain operates, in effect, with the version of the "public sphere" whose history Jürgen Habermas has traced—a conception of public interac-

tion grounded in privacy, private property, autonomy, and the intimate sphere of the nuclear family, with its ideals of equality, openness, mutual respect. See Habermas, *The Structural Transformation of the Public Sphere: An Inquiry into a Category of Bourgeois Society,* trans. Thomas Burger and Frederick Lawrence (Cambridge, Mass.: MIT Press, 1989), especially 27–29, 43–56. By denying the competition and economic interest endemic to this public sphere, and paradoxically constituting itself by excluding women, the conception posed the contradictions that Twain's obsession with sincerity and performance tried to grapple with. The urgency of this grappling became greater as the late nineteenth century brought fissures and erosions in the homosocial male public terrain.

13. Linda Williams's remarks in the first two chapters of *Hard Core* about the late-nineteenth-century melding of the will to truth and the male drive to expose the secrets of the female body are, again, highly pertinent. The larger relation between melodramatic unveilings of feminine virtue and scopophilic sexuality deserves further investigation. Catherine Clément, too, has made a number of connections among male displays of women that are relevant to Twain's Joan of Arc—e.g., the similarities between theater and the exhibition of female hysterics in the 1890s, between the hypnotized woman in Jean-Martin Charcot's lecture theater and scenes of public punishment, between the exposure of entranced women patients and the display of the delirium and the public burning of witches. See Clément, *The Weary Sons of Freud,* trans. Nicole Ball (New York: Verso, 1987), 51–59. And see Martha Noel Evans, *Fits and Starts: A Genealogy of Hysteria in Modern France,* on Charcot's amphitheater and theatrical performances of hysteria (21) and on the interplay of visibility, knowledge, desire, and gender in conceptions of hysteria (5).

14. On this nineteenth-century argument, see Warner, *Joan of Arc,* 246.

15. See, for example, Cox, *Mark Twain: The Fate of Humor,* 272–75; Cox puts irony, satire, showmanship, amorality, and bad-boy mischievousness on the side of Satan/44, and seriousness, morality, ideality, and piety with Joan. Also see Stone, *The Innocent Eye;* Stone objects to *Joan of Arc's* having "been dismissed as an aberration," but nonetheless contrasts it to "the hopeless pessimism" of *The Mysterious Stranger* (204).

16. *The Mysterious Stranger Manuscripts,* ed. with intro. by William M. Gibson (Berkeley and Los Angeles: University of California Press, 1969), 386.

17. For an account of Satan/44 as a showman, see Sargent Bush, Jr., "The Showman as Hero in Mark Twain's Fiction," in *American Humor: Essays Presented to John C. Gerber,* ed. O. M. Brack, Jr. (Scottsdale, Ariz.: Arete Publications, 1977), 79–98.

18. Sherwood Cummings, in *Mark Twain and Science: Adventures of a Mind* (Baton Rouge: Louisiana State University Press, 1988), sees a fundamental dichotomy in Twain's later writings between human organisms as machines and human beings as spirits. John S. Tuckey also discusses a similar split in "Mark Twain's Later Dialogue: The 'Me' and the Machine," *American Literature* 41 (1970): 532–42; the oppositions Tuckey identifies—between a psy-

chology of humans as mechanisms and a psychology of the unconscious and dreams, between automatism and spirituality (533)—put the matter in terms which, in light of my research and argument, show the connections of the pairs as much as their differences.

19. The connection William M. Gibson, in an undeveloped aside, sees between the materializations of Colonel Sellers as a scientist and the materializations of these duplicates is an important insight; see his Introduction to *The Mysterious Stranger Manuscripts,* 10.

20. On the mesmerists' ideas that somnambulists had an enhanced "sixth sense," that the body could be touched in order to correct the flow of magnetic fluid, and that mesmerists, through touching or the projection of fluid, could throw patients into somnambulistic trances, see Darnton, *Mesmerism and the End of the Enlightenment in France,* e.g., 3, 128, 153; also Maria Tatar, *Spellbound: Studies on Mesmerism and Literature* (Princeton: Princeton University Press, 1978), 13–15.

21. On the uncertainty in American phrenology between overt, atheistic materialism in explaining consciousness and religious attachment to ideas of spirit, see John D. Davies, *Phrenology, Fad and Science: A Nineteenth-Century American Crusade* (New Haven: Yale University Press, 1955), 156–57. Similar, enduring confusion in homeopathy and mesmerism over whether the "vital principle" pervading and animating the body is material or immaterial, physiological or spiritual, is discussed in Joseph F. Kett, *The Formation of the American Medical Profession: The Role of Institutions, 1780–1860* (New Haven: Yale University Press, 1968), 133–34, 141, 148.

22. R. Lawrence Moore recounts the tendency in spiritualism to speak of spirits, but to look to materialist science for conceptions of magnetic forces and imponderable fluids that could carry spirit communications; see Moore, "Spiritualism and Science," 474–500. Also see Owen, "The Other Voice: Women, Children, and Nineteenth-Century Spiritualism," 36.

23. Thomas Laycock, *Mind and Brain* (1860; rpt. New York: Arno Press, 1976), xv, 203, and Carpenter, *Principles of Mental Physiology,* xviii–xix, 2–3, 28, 691, 696–97, 701–2, 707–8. Also see L. S. Jacyna, "The Physiology of Mind, the Unity of Nature, and the Moral Order in Victorian Thought," *British Journal for the History of Science* 14 (1981): 109–32; Roger Smith, "The Human Significance of Biology: Carpenter, Darwin, and the *vera causa,*" in *Nature and the Victorian Imagination,* ed. U. C. Knoepflmacher and G. B. Tennyson (Berkeley and Los Angeles: University of California Press, 1977), 218–23; and Danziger, "Mid-Nineteenth-Century British Psycho-Physiology," 127. Even Oliver Wendell Holmes, in *Mechanism in Thought and Morals,* while promoting conceptions of humans, and their brains, as automatic mechanisms, ultimately rejected reducing morality or moral choice to mechanism (82, 87) or "materializing" human beings into "brute facts" (90).

24. Edmund Gurney, Frederic W. H. Myers, and Frank Podmore, *Phantasms of the Living,* 2 vols. (1886; rpt. Gainesville, Fla.: Scholars' Facsimiles and Reprints, 1970). On Twain's reading of this volume, see Gribben, *Mark Twain's Library,* I, 282.

25. On Myers, *Phantasms of the Living*, and Twain's relations with the Society for Psychical Research, see Gillman's *Dark Twins*, 136–80.

26. See Mary Baker Eddy, "Christian Science Versus Spiritualism," "Animal Magnetism Unmasked," and "Physiology," in *Science and Health with Key to the Scriptures* (Norwood, Mass.: Plimpton Press, 1934). Eddy, despite these attacks, and in a kind of uncertainty characteristic of nineteenth-century health "science," continued to believe in mesmeric and spiritualist phenomena. See Gail Parker's interesting discussion of Eddy in "Mary Baker Eddy and Sentimental Womanhood," *New England Quarterly* 43 (1970): 3–24, especially 13–14.

27. The relation between Quimby and Eddy is told in Stefan Zweig, *Mental Healers: Franz Anton Mesmer, Mary Baker Eddy, Sigmund Freud*, trans. Eden Paul and Cedar Paul (New York: Viking, 1932), 119–32, 154, 163, 190. Also see Frank Podmore, *Mesmerism and Christian Science: A Short History of Mental Healing* (London: Methuen, 1909), 251–67, 285.

28. Quoted in Gillman, *Dark Twins*, 139.

29. Ibid., 47.

30. On Twain and the ideas of Charcot and his followers, also see Gibson, Introduction, *The Mysterious Stranger Manuscripts*, 27; Tuckey, "Mark Twain's Later Dialogue," 535; and John S. Tuckey, *Mark Twain and Little Satan: The Writing of "The Mysterious Stranger"* (West Lafayette, Ind.: Purdue University Studies, 1963), 26–28. All of these scholars focus on the pertinence of the French research into somnambulism for Twain's notion of the autonomous dream self. But the research of Charcot and Janet into hysteria is also instructive and important for understanding Twain's work because it moved from a decidedly physiological and neurological focus, in Charcot's investigations in the 1880s, to a declaration, in Janet's work of the 1890s, that hysteria (and manifestations of it such as mediumship, trance writing, hypnotic states, and somnambulism) was caused by the mind, as an automatic bodily response to unconscious "ideés fixes" and "suggestion." Janet argued that responses of patients to magnetism and electricity were the function of suggestion, not physics or physiology. He reviewed his research and general position in lectures given at Harvard University in 1906, published as *The Major Symptoms of Hysteria* (New York: Macmillan, 1920), xi–xxiii; see also, in these lectures, his history of the study of hysteria, with attention especially to the Salpêtrière and Nancy schools and the move from physiological to psychological explanations (1–21). This movement must provide the background for Twain's declaration, in reference to a cure for Susy, that hypnotism as practiced by "Charcot's pupils & disciples" is "the same thing" as "mind-cure" (*Mark Twain–Howells Letters*, II, 659).

Index

Absorption, in the body, 67, 72. *See also* Identification

Acting. *See* Acting, theories of; Automatism; Expression; Gesture; Identification; Mimicry; Performance

Acting, theories of, 75; analogous emotion, use of, 84–85, 93; and automatisms, 77, 80; and multiple levels of consciousness, 85; and physiology, 7, 78, 85, 96, 213n. 15; self–dramatization or self-effacement, 75–80, 83, 88–89, 179. *See also* Expression; Identification

Adorno, Theodor, 141–42, 156

African Americans: and cakewalk, 43–44; "signifying," 45–46

Agnew, Jean-Christophe, 225n. 12

Amanuensis. *See* Mediums and mediumship; Writing

Archer, William, 77–80, 85, 88, 96

Armstrong, Nancy, 35

Arrah-na-Pogue, 40, 202n. 43

Arrah-no-Poke, 40, 202n. 43

Astor Place riot, 29

Atlantic Monthly, 69, 76

Auber, Daniel François, 40

Audience reception. *See* Spectatorship

Auerbach, Nina, 9

Automatism, 7, 91, 125, 134, 162–63, 175; in acting, 75, 77, 80, 82, 85, 88; and expression of emotion, 97–98, 105, 121; in writing, 126. *See also* Expression; Mediums and mediumship; Physiology, mental; Unconscious cerebration

Baender, Paul, 56

Baker, Houston A., Jr., 204n. 58

Bakhtin, Mikhail, 153, 225n. 10

Barnum, P. T., 13–14, 181

Barthes, Roland, 217n. 28, 225n. 13

Baudrillard, Jean, 156, 225n. 13, 226n. 15

Beard, George M., 219n. 9

Beecher, Henry Ward, 28

Bell, Michael Davitt, 139, 194n. 4

Bella Union Melodeon, 32, 51

Bennett, Tony, 206n. 4, 207n. 6

Berkhofer, Robert F., Jr., 196n. 21

Berthoff, Warner, 1, 23

Bhabha, Homi, 203n. 51

Birch, Billy, 46, 59

Bird, Robert Montgomery, 29

Blackness, uncertain boundaries of, 3, 93. *See also* Minstrelsy; Race; Racism

Blair, Walter, 201n. 43, 206n. 1

Body: absorption in, 67, 72; economy of energy in, 128; as means of emotional expression, 50–51, 78–79, 88, 96–98, 113, 174–75, 178; and mind, 10, 182, 184, 186; self-betrayal through, 112–13; and signs of identity, 81–83, 101–2, 104–5, 109–10; and voice, 115–18, 217n. 28; and writing, 115–16, 128. *See also* Expression

Bohemia: and burlesque, 202n. 43; fascination with outsiders and racial others, 23–24, 41–42, 53–54; and Adah Isaacs Menken, 49; middle class affronted by, 42; and middle-class identity formation, 53–54; as negotiation of middle-class ambivalences, 24, 32–34, 41

Booth, Edwin, 147

Booth, Junius Brutus, 41

The Bottle; or, The Drunkard's Doom, 36

Boucicault, Dion, 40, 77, 94, 202n. 43

Bowery Theater, 29

Bowlby, Rachel, 139

Branch, Edgar M., 1, 4, 62, 202n. 43

Brantlinger, Patrick, 227n. 21

Bree, Tommy, 37

British South Africa Company, 145

Brooks, Peter, 9, 108, 171–72

Brougham, John, 60, 61

Brown, Gillian, 197n. 2

Brown, Jacob Randall, 122–23, 219n. 9

Browne, Charles Farrar. *See* Ward, Artemus

tary reflex and, 79, 80–84, 88, 91,
96–98, 105–6, 117, 120–21, 132, 174–75.
See also Body; Gesture; Representation
*Expression of the Emotions in Man and
Animals, The,* 78, 88, 89, 97, 105–6,
108, 114

Fatout, Paul, 65
Femininity: and creation, literary, 118,
139; and creative body, 99, 190; culture, "feminization" of, 26; and domesticity, middle-class, 35; and emotion, 36, 49–50; and expression, 50–51,
114, 133, 174–75; masculinity, combined with, 176; and masculinity, definition of, 48–49; and mass culture,
36–37; and mediumship, 8, 120,
133–34, 138–40, 188–89; norms and
their violation, 52–53; and passivity, 8,
99, 120, 128, 133; and performance,
49–53; and privacy, 110, 133–34,
177–78; and realism, 128; and secrecy,
177–78; and self-exposure (unwitting),
110–12; and sincerity, 3, 49, 110,
133, 177
Fetishization: of commodities, 156,
159–60, 168; of "effects," 156, 159,
161–62, 168; and referents, obliteration
of, 141, 160–61; of signs, 156, 161–62,
226n. 15; in spectacles, 145–46. *See also*
Commodification; Spectacle
Finger Prints, 102
Fisher, Philip, 141
Fishkin, Shelley Fisher, 204n. 57
Forrest, Edwin, 29–30, 39, 41, 75,
152, 212n. 4
Foster, Hal, 226n. 15
Foucault, Michel, 215n. 4
Franks, Fred, 59
Fried, Michael, 62

Galton, Francis, 102, 115
Gates, Henry Louis, Jr., 45
Geertz, Clifford, 20
Gerber, John C., 1
Gesture: expression through, 107–9; as
indexical sign, 105; language of,
107–8, 112; and reflex or habit,
105–6; revelation of identity by,
104–5; writing as, 115, 117. *See also*
Body; Expression
Gibson, William M., 230n. 19, 231n. 30
Gilbert, Sandra M., 138–39
Gillman, Susan, 4, 90, 102, 126, 187
Gladiator, The, 29
Goldstein, Jan, 221n. 20

Goodman, Joe, 50–51
Gribben, Alan, 8
Grimsted, David, 227n. 5
Gubar, Susan, 138–39
Gurney, Edmund, 185

Habegger, Alfred, 134
Habermas, Jürgen, 228n. 12
Hall, Stuart, 206n. 4; 207n. 5
Halm, Friedrich, 39, 201n. 41
Halttunen, Karen, 89, 208n. 7; 209n. 15
Hannibal Journal, 15, 17, 21
Harper's Monthly, 77
Harper's Weekly, 77
Harry Hill's Saloon, 33
Harte, Bret, 46–47, 201n. 43
Hartford Courant, 55
"Heathen Chinee." *See* "Plain Language
from Truthful James"
Heenan, John C. (Benicia Boy), 49
Henry V (king of England), 144–45
Higham, John, 197n. 3
Hodge, Francis, 226n. 18
Holland, Josiah G., 63–64
Holmes, Oliver Wendell, 125, 127
Horkheimer, Max, 141–42
Horwitz, Howard, 215n. 3
Howells, William Dean, 2, 10, 41, 68, 71,
114, 134, 148, 150, 170; *Colonel Sellers
as a Scientist,* 129; reviews *Colonel
Sellers,* 69, 76–78
Huggins, Nathan, 43
Hutton, Laurence, 61, 67
Huyssen, Andreas, 201n. 37
Hysteria, 126, 178; of male writers, 128,
221n. 20; and realism, 220n. 16. *See
also* Physiology, mental

Identification: across gender, race, class,
species, 6–8, 81, 94; actors with roles,
61, 67–68, 70–71, 74–79, 90; and lecturing, 74; limits of, 80, 94; or mimicry, in
acting, 77–84; self-deception in, 79–80,
87–88; and unconscious expression,
84, 91. *See also* Acting, theories of
Identity: bodily revelation of, 81–83,
100–102, 104–5, 109–10; as commodity, 159–60; exposure (unconscious) of,
91, 100–101, 109–10; and gender, 110;
uncertainties of, 92–93, 95, 152. *See also*
Body; Self, conceptions of
Imperialism, 145–46
Ingersoll, Robert, 116
Ingomar the Barbarian, 39
Irving, Sir Henry, 10, 77–78, 213n. 12
Irving, Washington, 55